European Guide
to Social Science Information
and Documentation Services

Other Publications of the Vienna Centre

AMANN, A.
Open Care for the Elderly in Seven European Countries

BERTING, J., MILLS, S. C. & WINTERSBERGER, H.
The Socio-Economic Impact of Microelectronics

CAO-PINNA, V. & SHATALIN, S.
Consumption Patterns in Eastern and Western Europe

DURAND-DROUHIN, J-L. & SZWENGRUB, L-M.
Rural Community Studies in Europe, Volumes 1 & 2

FORSLIN, J., SARAPATA, A. & WHITEHILL, A.
Automation and Industrial Workers, Volume 1, Parts 1 & 2 and Volume 2

HERFURTH, M. & HOGEWEG-DE HAART, H.
Social Integration of Migrant Workers and Other Ethnic Minorities:
A Documentation of Current Research

MIHAILESCU, I. & MENDRAS, H.
Theory and Methodology in Rural Studies

NIESSEN, M. & PESCHAR, J.
International Comparative Research: Problems of Theory, Methodology and
Organisation in Eastern and Western Europe

PENOUIL, M. & PETRELLA, R.
The Location of Growing Industries in Europe

SZALAI, A. & PETRELLA, R.
Cross-National Comparative Survey Research: Theory and Practice

NOTICE TO READERS

Dear Reader

If your library is not already a standing/continuation order customer to this series, may we recommend
that you place a standing/continuation order to receive immediately upon publication all new volumes.
Should you find that these volumes no longer serve your needs, your order can be cancelled at any time
without notice.

ROBERT MAXWELL
Publisher at Pergamon Press

European Guide to Social Science Information and Documentation Services

Compiled by

SVOBODOZARYA GABROVSKA

for the European Cooperation in Social Science Information
and Documentation

Editors

SVOBODOZARYA GABROVSKA
MANFRED BISKUP
ANNA BOSSILKOVA

PERGAMON PRESS

OXFORD · NEW YORK · TORONTO · SYDNEY · PARIS · FRANKFURT

U.K.	Pergamon Press Ltd., Headington Hill Hall, Oxford OX3 0BW, England
U.S.A.	Pergamon Press Inc., Maxwell House, Fairview Park, Elmsford, New York 10523, U.S.A.
CANADA	Pergamon Press Canada Ltd., Suite 104, 150 Consumers Rd., Willowdale, Ontario M2J 1P9, Canada
AUSTRALIA	Pergamon Press (Aust.) Pty. Ltd., P.O. Box 544, Potts Point, N.S.W. 2011, Australia
FRANCE	Pergamon Press SARL, 24 rue des Ecoles, 75240 Paris, Cedex 05, France
FEDERAL REPUBLIC OF GERMANY	Pergamon Press GmbH, 6242 Kronberg-Taunus, Hammerweg 6, Federal Republic of Germany

First edition 1982

Library of Congress Cataloging in Publication Data

Gabrovska, S
European guide to social science information and documentation services.
Includes index.
1. Social sciences—Information services—Europe.
I. Biskup, Manfred. II. Bossilkova, Anna. III. European Cooperation in Social Science Information and Documentation (Organization) IV. Title.
H61.9.G3   1982   025'.063   81-23500
AACR2

British Library Cataloguing in Publication Data

Gabrovska, Svobodozarya
European guide to social science information and documentation services.
1. Social sciences—Information services—
Directories
I. Title II. Biskup, Manfred III. Bossilkova, Anna IV. European Cooperation in Social Science Information and Documentation V. European Coordination Centre for Research and Documentation in Social Sciences
025.5'2   H61
ISBN 0-08-028927-4

In order to make this volume available as economically and as rapidly as possible the authors' typescripts have been reproduced in their original forms. This method unfortunately has its typographical limitations but it is hoped that they in no way distract the reader.

This book is published on behalf of the European Cooperation in Social Science Information and Documentation (ECSSID) programme which is coordinated by the European Coordination Centre for Research and Documentation in Social Sciences (the Vienna Centre).

Printed in Great Britain by A. Wheaton & Co. Ltd., Exeter

Contents

v

Introduction

With the publication of EUROGUIDE the European Cooperation in Social
Science Information and Documentation (ECSSID) seeks to contribute
to the improvement of communication between SSID services in Europe.
EUROGUIDE should also help the user (as researcher, science policy-
maker, etc.) to find his way around these services, a matter of particular importance in view of the increasing international cooperation in social science.
Following a proposal by the Scientific Information Centre of the Bulgarian Academy of Sciences, the 1st ECSSID Conference (Moscow 1977)
adopted the continuous publication of EUROGUIDE in its programme.
To bring into being an all-European inventory of SSID services re-
quired both considerable effort and also an efficient division of
labour. The Scientific Information Centre of the Bulgarian Academy
of Sciences compiled and processed the questionnaires and took over
the task of making the copy ready for print. National ECSSID focal
points helped in the locating of SSID services in their countries
and the European Coordination Centre for Research and Documentation
in Social Sciences (Vienna Centre) coordinated this work.
The present first volume is the result of this joint effort. It includes 215 SSID services from 22 European countries (information
being updated in 1979). This is certainly an encouraging first step
towards gaining a satisfactory view of the European landscape in social science information and documentation.
The editors would like to draw attention to the fact that a certain
standardisation was made of the entries in the processing of the
questionnaires, especially concerning computer software. Further,
figures of library holdings are approximate and due to different concepts used by the SSID services to classify their holdings, a full
unification of these concepts could not be achieved. The questionnaires were originally designed also to gain information on the publications of the services. However, many of the services offer such
a broad range of publications that to include them all in a separate
chapter would have nearly doubled the present volume. On the other
hand, not all services had given information on their publications
and had to be addressed once again to complete this picture. For this
reason the material will be shortened to include only regular publication, in the form of an appendix to the Guide.

How to Use the Guide

SSID Services are grouped alphabetically under their English name in order of country. The services are numbered consecutively from 1 to 215 throughout the Guide. References in the subject index and in the chapter on automated information systems refer to these serial numbers.

The numbering of the items describing the services corresponds to the numbering of the questionnaire, a model of which is given on page 227-230.

Alphabetical List of Countries

```
 1   AUSTRIA
 2   BELGIUM
 3   BERLIN, WEST
 4   BULGARIA
 5   CZECHOSLOVAKIA
 6   DENMARK
 7   FINLAND
 8   FRANCE
 9   GERMAN DEMOCRATIC REPUBLIC
10   GERMANY, FEDERAL REPUBLIC OF
11   GREECE
12   HUNGARY
13   ITALY
14   NETHERLANDS
15   NORWAY
16   POLAND
17   ROMANIA
18   SPAIN
19   SWEDEN
20   SWITZERLAND
21   UNION OF THE SOVIET SOCIALIST REPUBLICS (USSR)
22   YUGOSLAVIA
```

INSTITUTIONS PROVIDING
SOCIAL SCIENCE INFORMATION

Austria

1   1. ADMINISTRATIVE LIBRARY OF THE FEDERAL MINISTRY OF EDUCATION
      AND ARTS AND THE FEDERAL MINISTRY OF SCIENCE AND RESEARCH

      AMSTBIBLIOTHEK DES BUNDESMINISTERIUMS FÜR UNTERRICHT UND
      KUNST UND d.BM. f.WISSENSCHAFT UND FORSCHUNG

    2. Subordinated to the central administration

    3. Minoritenplatz 5, A-1014 Wien, Postfach 65
       tel. 6621/4301
       telex: 5532

    4. 1849

    5. Director: Silvestri,Gerhard
       The staff numbers 7 professionals and 1 non-professional

    8. Major fields: education and related subjects
       Specific fields: research policy, research economy, futurolo-
       gy, etc.

    9. Foreign books and periodicals and national "gray" literature
       are processed

  11. Holdings: books
           periodicals   296 600 vols. in total
           abstract journals
       Alphabetical and keyword catalogues are used

  12. The library is open to the public

  13. Information services:
       Publications - abstract journals and bibliographies
       Lending service

  15. Photocopying machine

2   1. AUSTRIAN INSTITUTE OF EAST AND SOUTH-EAST EUROPEAN STUDIES.
        LIBRARY AND DOCUMENTATION DEPARTMENT

        ÖSTERREICHISCHES OST- UND SÜDOSTEUROPA INSTITUT.
        ABT.BIBLIOTHEK UND DOKUMENTATION

        OSI

     2. Subordinated to the Federal Ministry of Science and Research

     3. Josefsplatz 6, A-1010 Wien
        tel. 52 18 95 (Institute); 52 43 28 (Library)

     4. 1958

     5. Director: Lukan,Walter
        The staff numbers 5 professionals

     6. Regional Scientific Institute for East and South-East Euro-
        pean Studies

     8. Major fields: economics, geography, geographical denomination,
        history, sociology, sociology of science, politics, informa-
        tion and documentation

     9. National and foreign books and periodicals are processed

    11. Holdings: books   12 000 vols.
                  periodicals   1 500 titles
                  abstract journals   30 titles
        Numerus currens, authors' and keyword catalogues are used

    12. The library is open to the public

    13. Information services:
        Publications - abstract journals, directories and others
        Translation
        Bibliographical, literature and survey data searches
        Lending and reference services
        Provision of photocopies and/or microforms

    17. Information services free of charge

3   1. AUSTRIAN NATIONAL LIBRARY

        ÖSTERREICHISCHE NATIONALBIBLIOTHEK

        ÖNB

     2. Subordinated to the Federal Ministry of Science and Research

     3. Josefsplatz 1, A-1014 Wien
        tel. 52 16 84
        telex: 12624 ÖENB.A

     4. 15 c.

     5. General director: Kammel,Karl
        The staff numbers 116 professionals and 119 non-professionals

6. Library and information institution on national level

7. Departments or activities: Book; Special for manuscripts, and others

8. Major fields: DC-main classes - 0,1,2,3,4,7,8,9
   Specific fields: social sciences, philosophy, philology, theology, arts, geography, history

9. Foreign books, periodicals, "gray" literature and audio-visual materials are processed

11. Holdings: books   2 280 000 vols.
              current periodicals   15 100 vols.
              microcopies   21 000
              manuscripts   96 000
    Alphabetical and subject catalogues are used

12. The library is open to the public

13. Information services:
    Publications - Austrian bibliography
    Bibliographical, literature and survey data searches
    Lending service
    Provision of photocopies and/or microforms

15. Photogr., microfilm, printing machines, etc.

16. Relations with VÖB, IFLA and book exchange with all large libraries abroad.
    Participates in the Interlibrary lending system in the country

17. Information services free of charge

4   1. CHAMBER OF COMMERCE. DEPARTMENT OF SCIENCE AND EDUCATIONAL POLICY

        BUNDESKAMMER DER GEWERBLICHEN WIRTSCHAFT. WISSENSCHAFTLICHE UND BILDUNGSPOLITISCHE ABTEILUNG

     3. Stubenring 12, A-1010 Wien I
        cable address: Buhaka Wien
        tel. 52 15 11
        telex: 01/1871

     4. Documentation: 1945
        Archives: 1951

     5. Directors: Winkler,Gottfried (Documentation)
                   Steinbrecher,Hertha (Archives)
        The staff numbers 6 professionals and 7 non-professionals

     7. Departments or activities: Documentation; Archives

     8. Major fields: economic policy, national economy, economics of the enterprises, social policy and social legislation, economic law, social-political problems

Specific fields: contractor - workshop problems, social part-
nership - relations, economic unions, economic institutions

9. Foreign books, periodicals and newspapers are processed

10. The Department has a library

11. Holdings: books   150 000 vols. in total
             periodicals   450 titles
    Keyword and authors' catalogues are used

12. The library is open to the public

13. Information services:
    Publications - abstract journals, directories and others
    Bibliographical, literature and survey data searches
    Reference services
    Provision of photocopies and/or microforms

14. Automated information system in the field of periodical docu-
    mentation
    Hardware: IBM/370
    Software: PL/1 and ASSEMBLER and own keyword system

17. Information services free of charge

5   1. DOCUMENTATION CENTRE FOR URBAN STUDIES

     KOMMUNALWISSENSCHAFTLICHES DOKUMENTATIONSZENTRUM

     KDZ

     3. Linzerstrasse 452, A - 1140 Wien
        tel. 0222-941142

     4. 1969

     5. Director: Bauer,Helfried
        The staff numbers 5 professionals and 3 non-professionals

     7. Departments or activities: Documentation; Research; Statistics

     8. Major fields: urban management, environmental protection, ur-
        ban finances, communal economy, communal services, political
        sciences, regional and urban development, social undertakings,
        etc.

     9. Foreign books, periodicals and "gray" literature are processed

     10. The Centre has a library

     11. Holdings: books   6 600 vols. in total
                  periodicals   200 titles - 1600 vols. in total
                  abstract journals   9 titles -   72 vols. in total
         Kwic - index since 1977 and subject card document number file
         since 1978 are used

     12. The library is open to the public

13. Information services:
    Publications - abstract journals, bibliographies
    Bibliographical literature and survey data searches
    Lending service
    Provision of photocopies and/or microforms

15. Photocopying machines

16. Relations with the Documentation Union of Urban and Regional
    Planning, Austrian Institute of Urban and Regional Planning,
    ÖROK in the country and with ORLV-Berlin abroad

17. Information services free of charge

6   1. DOCUMENTATION OFFICE OF HIGHER EDUCATION AND SCIENCE POLICY

    HOCHSCHULDOKUMENTATION. DOKUMENTATIONSBÜRO FÜR HOCHSCHULWESEN
    UND WISSENSCHAFTSPOLITIK

    HDOK

    2. Subordinated to the Federal Ministry of Science and Research

    3. A-1010 Wien I, Universität
       Karl Lueger-Ring 1
       tel. 0222-427611/446,445

    4. 1965

    5. Director: Brechelmacher,Gertrud
       The staff numbers 3 professionals

    8. Major field: higher education in the country and abroad
       Specific fields: construction, planning, reforms, legislation,
       lecturers, students (social status), grants, students' organi-
       zations, studies, examinations, academic degrees, prospects
       for work, various profiles, etc. in higher educational insti-
       tutions, plans for the higher education in Austria

    9. Foreign books, periodicals and "gray" literature are processed

    10. The Office has no library

    11. Uses the collections of the University Library of Vienna and
        the Library of the Federal Ministry of Education and Arts

    13. Information services:
        Publications - abstract journals
        SDI

    15. Photocopying machine

    16. Relations with regional organizations in Germany, Federal Re-
        public of, and Switzerland

    17. Information services free of charge

7   1. INTERNATIONAL INFORMATION CENTRE FOR TERMINOLOGY
        INTERNATIONALES INFORMATIONSZENTRUM FÜR TERMINOLOGIE
        INFOTERM

     2. Parent institution: Austrian Standards Institute
        Subordinated to the Austrian Federal Economic Chamber as well
        as to UNESCO, General Information Programme

     3. Leopoldsgasse 4,   1020 Wien
        tel. 33 55 19/336,337,340,341
        telex: 7/5960

     4. 1971

     5. Director: Felber,Helmut
        The staff numbers 2 professionals and 2 non-professionals

     8. Major field: coordination of terminology work of all fields
        and all languages
        Specific fields: elaboration of bibliographies, of works of
        reference related to terminology, development of a network of
        terminology information and documentation

     9. Books, periodicals, partly "gray" literature, terminological
        standards, thesauri, etc. are processed

    10. The Centre has a library and uses
        also the Foreign Standards Archives of the Austrian Standards
        Institute

    11. Holdings: books, periodicals, microcopies and manuscripts

    12. The library is open to the public

    13. Information services:
        Publications - bibliographies, directories and others
        Translation (for own purposes)
        Bibliographical and literature searches
        Reference services
        Provision of photocopies

    14. EDP is used for the purposes of particular projects only in
        cooperation with computer centres of other countries.

    15. Photo-typesetting

    16. Relations with INTERCONCEPT (UNESCO)

    17. Information services free of charge

8   1. LIBRARY OF THE AUSTRIAN INSTITUTE FOR ECONOMIC RESEARCH
        BIBLIOTHEK ÖSTERREICHISCHES INSTITUT FÜR WIRTSCHAFTSFORSCHUNG

     2. Subordinated to the central administration

3. A-1103 Wien 3, Arsenal Obj.20 Postfach 91
   tel. 65 66 61

4. 1927

5. Director: Redl,Edeltraud
   The staff numbers 2 professionals

8. Major field: economics
   Specific field: empirical economics

9. Foreign books, periodicals and "gray" literature are processed

11. Holdings: books   30 000 vols. in total
              periodicals   500 vols. in total
    Card files and authors' index are used

12. The library is open to the public

13. Information services:
    Lending and interlibrary loan services

9   1. LIBRARY AND DOCUMENTATION OF THE AUSTRIAN INSTITUTE OF URBAN
           AND REGIONAL PLANNING

        BIBLIOTHEK UND DOKUMENTATION DES ÖSTERREICHISCHEN INSTITUTS
        FÜR RAUMPLANUNG

        ÖIK

     2. Parent institution: Austrian Institute of Urban and Regional
        Planning (a non-profit organization)

     3. Franz Josefs-Kai 27, A-1010 Wien
        tel. 638747/25,26,63

     4. 1957 (1951)

     5. Director: Schönbichler,Franz
        The staff numbers 2 professionals

     8. Major fields: urban and local planning, regional planning, na-
        tional planning, planning theories and methods, urban and re-
        gional research
        Specific fields: environmental planning, leisure, tourism, so-
        ciology, transport, economy, geography, etc.

     9. Foreign books, periodicals and "gray" literature are processed

    11. Holdings: books   approx. 20 000 vols. in total
                 periodicals   approx.   350 vols. in total
        Authors' file, union authors' file and punched cards are used

    12. The library is open to the public

    13. Information services:
        Publications - directories
        SDI

      Bibliographical and literature searches
      Compilation of documentary syntheses
      Lending service
      Provision of photocopies

16. Relations with national and foreign institutions

17. Information services free of charge and against payment

10 1. LIBRARY AND DOCUMENTATION OF THE INSTITUTE OF AGRICULTURAL ECONOMICS

    BIBLIOTHEK UND DOKUMENTATIONSSTELLE DES AGRARWIRTSCHAFTLICHEN INSTITUTS DES BUNDESMINISTERIUMS FÜR LAND- UND FORSTWIRTSCHAFT

2. Subordinated to the Federal Ministry of Agriculture and Forestry

3. Schwizertalstrasse 36, A-1133 Wien
   tel. 82 36 51

4. 1959

5. Director: Pevetz,Werner
   The staff numbers 1 professional and 1 non-professional

8. Major fields: agricultural economics, regional economics, rural sociology and related subjects

9. Foreign and national books, periodicals and "gray" literature are processed

11. Holdings: books   20 000 titles - 22 000 vols.
           periodicals   400 titles
           abstract journals   6 titles
    Alphabetical nominal, alphabetical analytical and systematical catalogues are used

12. The library is open to the public

13. Information services:
    Publications - abstract journals, bibliographies, directories
    Bibliographical, literature and survey data searches
    Lending service

15. Offset, Adressograph multigraph copier

17. Information services free of charge

11 1. LIBRARY OF THE FEDERAL MINISTRIES OF SOCIAL ADMINISTRATION AND HEALTH AND ENVIRONMENTAL PROTECTION

    MINISTERIALBIBLIOTHEK DER BUNDESMINISTERIEN FÜR SOZIALE VERWALTUNG UND FÜR GESUNDHEIT UND UMWELTSCHUTZ

2. Subordinated to the central administration

3. Stubenring 1, A-1010 Wien
   tel. 7500/6143
   telex: 011145 and 011780

4. 1918

5. Director: Wagner,Hans
   The staff numbers 3 professionals and 4 non-professionals

8. Major fields: social sciences, environmental protection, so-
   cial medicine, medical sociology, social policy, social security, social insurance, social aid, poverty labour, employment, women (social and professional position), vocational
   orientation, etc.

9. Foreign books, periodicals and "gray" literature are processed

11. Holdings: books   100 000 vols.
              periodicals   639 titles
    Author-title and subject catalogues are used

12. The library is open to the public

13. Information services:
    Lending service
    Provision of photocopies

12 1. MUSEUM FOR AUSTRIAN SOCIAL AND ECONOMIC AFFAIRS

    ÖSTERREICHISCHES GESELLSCHAFTS- UND WIRTSCHAFTSMUSEUM

    3. Vogelsanggasse 36, A-1050 Wien
       tel. 553105

    4. 1925

    5. Director: Docekal,Josef
       The staff numbers 7 professionals and 15 non-professionals

    8. Major field: Austrian history since 1900
       Specific fields: Austrian social and economic affairs since
       1900

    9. National books, periodicals and audio-visual materials are
       processed

    10. The Museum has a library

    11. Holdings: books   1700 vols. in total
                  periodicals   30 titles - 5000 vols. in total
        Austrian history and economic statistics since 1900

    12. The library is not open to the public

    13. Information services:
        Publications - statistics, maps of industry, charts, cata-
        logues for exhibitions

        SDI
        Survey data searches

16. Relations with other institutions in the country; with regio-
    nal and international organizations

17. Information services against payment

13   1. SOCIAL SCIENCES DOCUMENTATION

      SOZIALWISSENSCHAFTLICHE DOKUMENTATION D.KAMMER F.ARBEITER U.
      ANGESTELLTE F.WIEN

   2. Parent institution: Chamber of workers and employees from
     Vienna

   3. Prinz-Eugen-Strasse 20-22, A-1040 Wien
     tel. 0222-653765
     telex: 1690

   4. 1957

   5. Director: Biebl,Maria
     The staff numbers 9 professionals and 6 non-professionals

   8. Major fields: social sciences, economics, education, civil
     law, administration
     Specific fields: trade unions, politics, labour, organiza-
     tions, labour law, labour problems, social policy, social
     security, national economy, industrial relations, vocational
     training, adult education, environmental problems

   9. Foreign books and periodicals are processed

10. The Documentation has a library

11. Holdings: system.archives   2 200 000 sheets
    Card files are used

12. The library is open to the public

13. Information services:
    Publications - abstract journals
    SDI
    Literature searches
    Reference services
    Provision of photocopies

15. Photocopying machine

16. Information services against payment

14   1. SOCIAL SCIENCES LIBRARY

SOZIALWISSENSCHAFT STUDIENBIBLIOTHEK D.KAMMER F.ARBEITER U.
ANGESTELLTE F.WIEN

2. Parent institution: Chamber of workers and employees from
Vienna

3. Prinz-Eugen-Strasse 20-22, A-1040 Wien
tel. 0222-653765
telex:1690

4. 1921

5. Director: Vass,Josef
The staff numbers 14 professionals and 2 non-professionals

8. Major fields: social sciences, economics, education, civil
law, administration
Specific fields: trade unions, politics, labour organizations, labour law, labour problems, social policy, social
security, national economy, industrial relations, vocational
training, adult education, environmental problems

9. Foreign books and periodicals are processed

11. Holdings: books   180 000 vols. in total
periodicals   900 vols. in total
Card files are used

12. The library is open to the public

13. Information services:
Publications - bibliographies
Literature searches
Lending and interlibrary loan services
Provision of photocopies

15. Photocopying machine

17. Information services against payment

15   1. VIENNA INSTITUTE FOR COMPARATIVE ECONOMIC STUDIES. DOCUMEN-
TATION

WIENER INSTITUT FÜR INTERNATIONALE WIRTSCHAFTSVERGLEICHE,
DOKUMENTATION

WIIW

3. Arsenal Obj. 20, Postfach 87, A-1103 Wien
tel. 65 66 61/68

4. Institute - 1973, Documentation - 1974

5. Director: Levcik,Friedrich (Institute)
Pitrik,Rita (Documentation)
The staff numbers 1 professional and part-time non-professio-

nals

7. Departments or activities: Small reference library; Documentation

8. Major fields: comparative economic studies
   Specific fields: East-West relations, East-European economics, East-West comparisons in economics

9. Foreign books and periodicals are processed

10. The Institute has a library

11. Holdings: books   2 000 titles - 2 000 vols. in total
             periodicals   280 titles
    Authors' (for books) and subject catalogues; for books-classi-
    fication similar to "Index of Economic Journals", for articles
    - UDC are used

12. The library is not open to the public

13. Information services:
    Publications - bibliographies and others
    Bibliographical, literature and survey data searches
    Reference services

17. Information services free of charge and against payment

Belgium

16 1. CENTRAL LIBRARY OF THE STATE UNIVERSITY OF GHENT
    CENTRALE BIBLIOTHEEK VAN DE RIJKSUNIVERSITEIT - GENT

    2. Parent institution: State University of Ghent
    Subordinated to the Ministry of National Education and Culture

    3. Rozier 9, B-9000 Gent
    tel. 0-091-25.75.71; 0-091-25.76.11
    telex: 11793 ub gent b

    4. 1817

    5. Director: van Acker,K.
    The staff numbers 14 professionals (2 for social sciences
    and economics) and 82 non-professionals

    7. Departments or activities: Acquisitions; Lending, etc.

    8. Major fields: all fields of science

    9. National and foreign books and periodicals, and national
    "gray" literature are processed

    11. No figures for the social sciences holdings are available
    separately
    Authors' and systematical (UDC) catalogues and printed bib-
    liographies are used

    12. The library is open to the public

    13. Information services:
    Publications - acquisition-lists and printed catalogues of
    periodicals and special collections
    SDI
    Bibliographical and literature searches
    Lending and reference services
    Provision of photocopies and/or microforms

16. Photo-microform and offset techniques

17. Information services free of charge

17 1. LIBRARY OF ECONOMIC, SOCIAL AND POLITICAL SCIENCES

BIBLIOTHÈQUE DE LA FACULTÉ DES SCIENCES ECONOMIQUES, SOCIALES ET POLITIQUES - UNIVERSITÉ CATHOLIQUE DE LOUVAIN

2. Subordinated to the University of Louvain

3. Place Montesquièu, 1
1338 Louvain-la-neuve
tel. 010.41.81.81/4231

4. 1976

5. Director: d'Arras d'Haudrecy,Louis
The staff numbers 11 professionals

8. Major fields: economics, sociology, demography, history, politics, business, sociolinguistics, communications

9. National and foreign books and periodicals are processed

11. Holdings: books   40 000 titles - 50 000 vols.
           periodicals   10 000 titles - 60 000 vols.

12. The library is open to the public

13. Information services:
SDI
Bibliographical searches
Lending service
Provision of photocopies and/or microforms

14. Automated information system covering all bibliographical references
Hardware: IBM/370
Software: PL/1

15. Photocopying machine

17. Information services free of charge

18 1. LIBRARY OF HUMANITIES AND SOCIAL SCIENCES, FREE UNIVERSITY OF BRUSSELS

BIBLIOTHEEK HUMANE EN SOCIALE WETENSCHAPPEN, VRIJE UNIVERSITEIT - BRUSSEL

BIBLIOTHEEK HSW. VUB

2. Subordinated to the Free University of Brussels

3. Pleinlaan 2, 1050 Brussel

tel. 02/648.55.40
telex: 61051 VUBCO

4. 1970

5. Director: Namenwirth, Micha
   The staff numbers 10 professionals and 25 non-professionals

8. Major fields: all social sciences
   Specific fields: economics, management, sociology, politics,
   law, public administration, psychology, education

9. National and foreign books and periodicals are processed

11. Holdings: books   30 000 titles - 45 000 vols
             periodicals   1 000 titles

12. The library is open to the public

13. Information services:
    Publications - bibliographies
    Bibliographical and literature searches
    Lending and reference services
    Provision of photocopies and/or microforms

14. On-line interactive catalogue, public retrieval and catalogu-
    ing functions. A fully integrated system is in preparation
    Hardware: Minicomputer DIGITAL EQUIPMENT CORPORATION
    Software: MUMPS/VUBIS

15. Photocopying machines

16. Relation with the library of the Ministry of Economic Affairs

17. Information services against payment

Berlin, West

19 1. FEDERAL ENVIRONMENTAL AGENCY

UMWELTBUNDESAMT, FACHBEREICH I, GRUPPE INFORMATION UND DOKU-
MENTATION

UBA (UMPLIS)

2. Parent institution: Federal Ministry of Home Affairs

3. Bismarckplatz 1, 1000 Berlin (West) 33
   tel. 8903-1
   telex: 183756

4. 1974

5. Director: Seggelke,J.
   The staff numbers 40 professionals

6. A central position

8. Major field: environment
   Specific fields: water, air, solid waste, noise, etc.

9. Foreign books, periodicals, "gray" literature, audio-visual
   materials, magnetic tapes and directories (research projects,
   institutions) are processed

10. The Agency has a library

11. Holdings: books   21 000 vols.
             microcopies   24 000

12. The library is open to the public

13. Information services:
    Publications - abstract journals, bibliographies and direc-
    tories
    Literature searches
    Lending and reference services

Provision of photocopies or microforms

14. Hardware: SIEMENS
    Software: GOLEM, FIDAS, ADABAS

16. Relations with regional and international organizations - EG
    and UNEP and all other units of environmental approach

17. Information services free of charge

20   1. FREE UNIVERSITY OF BERLIN. CLEARING HOUSE FOR POLITICAL IN-
        FORMATION AND DOCUMENTATION

        FREIE UNIVERSITÄT BERLIN. LEITSTELLE POLITISCHE DOKUMENTATION

        LPD

     2. Parent institution: Free University of Berlin

     3. Paulinenstrasse 22, D-1000 Berlin (West) 45

     4. 1965

     5. Director: Krumholz,Walter
        The staff numbers 5 professionals and 5 non-professionals

     6. Clearing house in this field

     8. Major fields: politics, political sciences, peace research,
        international relations

     9. National periodicals and current research projects in politi-
        cal sciences are processed

    10. The Department has no library. Uses the Special Library for
        Political Sciences at the Free University of Berlin, Depart-
        ment 15 (Political Sciences)

    13. Information services:
        Publications - abstract journals
        Bibliographical, literature and survey data searches
        Provision of photocopies and/or microforms

    16. Relations with other information units in the country and
        abroad, regional and international organizations

    17. Information services free of charge and against payment

21   1. GERMAN CENTRAL INSTITUTION FOR SOCIAL PROBLEMS

        DEUTSCHES ZENTRALINSTITUT FÜR SOZIALE FRAGEN

        DZI

     3. Miquelstrasse 83, D-1000 Berlin (West) 33
        tel. 030/832 4041/2

4. 1893

5. Director: Bueren, Ilse
   The staff numbers 16 professionals and 6 non-professionals

7. Departments or activities: Library; Newspaper archives; Financial; Organizational archives; Information and documentation

8. Major fields: social problems and related subjects
   Specific field: social practice

9. Books, periodicals, documents in German, English, French and
   other, information about social organizations are processed

10. The Institution has a library

11. Holdings: books   80 000 vols.
              periodicals   1 200 vols. in total
              abstract journals   20 vols.
    Own systematical index and thesaurus, and a list of periodi-
    cals are used

12. The library is open to the public

13. Information services:
    Publications - bibliographies, directories and others
    SDI
    Bibliographical and literature searches
    Lending service
    Provision of photocopies

15. Photocopying machine

17. Information services against payment

22 1. INSTITUTE FOR FUTURE STUDIES
       INSTITUT FÜR ZUKUNFTSFORSCHUNG. GmbH
       IFZ

    2. Parent institution: Society of questions of the future

    3. Giesebrechtstrasse 15, D-1000 Berlin (West) 12
       tel. 030-881 9057
       telex: 184815

    4. 1968

    5. Directors: Buchholz,Hans, Flechtheim,Ossip, Kreibich,Rolf
       The staff numbers 28 professionals and 10 non-professionals

    7. Departments or activities: Public supported research pro-
       jects; Future research; Scenario-writing; Systems analysis

    8. Major fields: leisure research, documentation systems, infor-
       mation-technology telecommunications, technology assessment,

environmental research

9. National books/reports and foreign periodicals are processed

10. The Institute has a library

11. Holdings: books   5 000 titles
             periodicals   150 titles
             abstract journals   20 titles

12. The library is not open to the public

13. Information services:
    Publications
    Lending (not regular) and reference services

17. Information services free of charge and against payment

23   1. MAX-PLANCK-INSTITUTE OF EDUCATIONAL RESEARCH
         MAX-PLANCK-INSTITUT FÜR BILDUNGSFORSCHUNG

      2. Parent institution: Max-Planck-society for promotion of
         science

      3. Lentzeallee 94, D-1000 Berlin (West) 33
         cable address: Bilfo Berlin
         tel. 8295-1

      4. 1963

      5. Director: Becker,Hellmut
         The staff numbers 68 professionals and 73 non-professionals

      8. Major fields: educational research, psychology, sociology,
         economics

     10. The Institute has a library

     11. Holdings: books   160 000 vols. in total
                  periodicals   20 000 vols. in total

     12. The library is not open to the public

     13. Information services:
         Publications - lists of acquisitions
         Reference services

Bulgaria

24 1. CENTRAL LIBRARY AT THE BULGARIAN ACADEMY OF SCIENCES
   CENTRALNA BIBLIOTEKA PRI BĂLGARSKA AKADEMIJA NA NAUKITE

2. Parent institution: Scientific Information Centre with Central Library and Scientific Archives - BAS
   Subordinated to the Bulgarian Academy of Sciences

3. 1, "7 Noemvri" St., Sofia-1084
   tel. 8-41-41/251

4. 1869

5. Director: Savova,Elena
   The staff numbers 56 professionals and 8 non-professionals

6. Sub-system

7. Departments or activities: Acquisitions and exchange of books and periodicals; Processing of scientific literature; Reference-bibliographical, methodical and branch libraries; Services and book stocks

8. Major fields: natural, mathematical and social sciences

9. National and foreign books, periodicals and audio-visual materials are processed

11. Holdings: books   685 152 vols.
    periodicals   563 002 vols.
    abstract journals   553 titles
    microcopies   8 954
    manuscripts   5 617
    Alphabetical and systematical catalogues, catalogue of periodicals are used

12. The library is open to the public

13. Information services:

Publications - bibliographies and others
Bibliographical and literature searches
Lending and reference services
Provision of photocopies and/or microforms

14. Publication of machine-readable catalogues and lists of periodicals
Hardware: EC-1040 of the Institute of Mathematics - BAS
Software: "BISES", worked out at the Institute of Mathematics - BAS

15. Uses the mechanical means of the Scientific Information Centre - BAS

16. Relations with the "Cyril and Methodius" National Library;
the Sofia University Library, the Central Medical Library,
the Scientific and Technical Library and other large libraries in the country; 3319 various institutions abroad

17. Information services free of charge and against payment

25   1. CENTRE OF PEDAGOGIC DOCUMENTATION AND INFORMATION
CENTĂR ZA PEDAGOGIČESKA DOKUMENTACIJA I INFORMACIJA

2. Subordinated to the Scientific Centre of Education, Ministry
of Public Education

3. 125, boul.Lenin, block 5, Sofia-1113
tel. 72-07-01/51

4. 1965

5. Director: Todorova,Rajna
The staff numbers 11 professionals and 3 non-professionals

6. Branch information unit

8. Major fields: pedagogics, education, staff training

9. National and foreign books and periodicals are processed

10. The Centre has a library

11. Holdings: books   22 494 titles - 40 000 vols.
            periodicals   170 titles - 5 000 vols.
            abstract journals   33 titles -   70 vols.
            manuscripts   3 341
Alphabetical, systematical, topographical catalogues and the
special classification table for science libraries in Bulgaria are used

12. The library is open to the public

13. Information services:
Publications - abstract journals, bibliographies and directories

SDI
Translation
Bibliographical, literature and survey data searches
Lending and reference services

15. Photographic camera, offset, cyclostyle, reproduction camera

16. Relations with the national, branch and local information
    units in the country and in the socialist countries, and the
    Documentation Office at the International Education Service

17. Information services free of charge

26 1. CYRIL AND METHODIUS NATIONAL LIBRARY

    NARODNA BIBLIOTEKA "KIRIL I METODIJ"

    NBKM

   2. Subordinated to the Committee of Culture

   3. 11,boul.Tolbuhin,   Sofia-1504
      tel. 88-28-11
      telex: 22432 natlib

   4. 1878

   5. Director: Kalajdzieva,Konstantinka
      The staff numbers 217 professionals and 176 non-professionals

   6. National Library of Bulgaria and a national information in-
      stitution

   7. Departments or activities: Acquisitions; Cataloguing; Reader;
      Special (music, cartographic, oriental, etc.); Information
      centre; Bibliographical centre; MSS & Documentation centre;
      Methodical centre for library science; Administrative & eco-
      nomic (printing office, bindery, etc.)

   8. Major fields: all fields of science
      Specific fields: library & information science, foreign pub-
      lications dealing with Bulgarian and foreign translations of
      Bulgarian materials, foreign official publications of inter-
      national organizations

   9. National and foreign books, periodicals, "gray" literature,
      audio-visual materials, magnetic tapes, microfilms, maps,
      portraits, graphic arts and music are processed

  11. Holdings: books   946 806 vols.
               periodicals   405 734 vols.
               abstract journals   1 322 vols
               microcopies   20 102 single units
      Alphabetical and subject catalogues; special classification
      table for science libraries in Bulgaria are used

  12. The library is open to the public

13. Information services:
    Publications - bibliographies, directories and others
    Bibliographical and literature searches
    Lending service
    Provision of photocopies and/or microforms

14. An automated information system for the processing of perio-
    dicals is in preparation
    A subject rubricator is used as information language and ISIS

15. Photocopying machine, offset, reader-printer, microfilm sys-
    tem, relief-printing

16. Relations with the Central Institute for Scientific & Tech-
    nical Information (CINTI) in Sofia, the Scientific Informa-
    tion Centre at the BAS, etc.; with the International Centre
    for Scientific & Technical Information in Moscow

17. Information services against payment

27   1. DEPARTMENT OF SCIENTIFIC INFORMATION AND DOCUMENTATION AT
        THE INSTITUTE OF SOCIOLOGY. BULGARIAN ACADEMY OF SCIENCES

        OTDEL ZA NAUČNA INFORMACIJA I DOKUMENTACIJA PRI INSTITUTA PO
        SOCIOLOGIJA. BĂLGARSKA AKADEMIJA NA NAUKITE

     2. Parent institution: Institute of Sociology at the BAS

     3. 39, boul.Vitosha, Sofia-1000
        tel. 88-45-62; 88-13-91

     4. 1968

     5. The staff numbers 8 professionals

     6. Branch information unit

     8. Major fields: sociology, social psychology, demography, his-
        tory of sociology, subject matter, methodology of sociologi-
        cal research, social structure of society, social dimensions,
        sociology of human reproduction, sociology of science, so-
        ciology of economics, sociology of mass media

     9. National and foreign books, periodicals and "gray" litera-
        ture are processed

    10. The Department has a library

    11. Holdings: books   4 219 titles
                  periodicals   157 titles
                  abstract journals   11 titles
        Alphabetical, subject, topographical and card indices are
        used

    12. The library is open to the public

    13. Information services:

    Publications - bibliographies, directories and others
    SDI
    Translation
    Bibliographical, literature and data survey searches
    Lending and reference services
    Provision of photocopies

14. Participates in the AIS-OBNA in the field of social sciences
    (sociology) at the Scientific Information Centre - BAS
    Hardware: IBM 370/135
    Software: STAIRS

16. Relations with the Central Institute for Scientific and Tech-
    nical Information (CINTI) and the Scientific Information Cen-
    tre at the BAS

17. Information services free of charge and against payment

28   1. INFORMATION CENTRE OF THE INSTITUTE FOR INTERNATIONAL RELA-
        TIONS AND SOCIALIST INTEGRATION. BULGARIAN ACADEMY OF SCIENCES

        INFORMACIONEN CENTÀR NA INSTITUTA ZA MEZDUNARODNI OTNOŠENIJA
        I SOCIALISTIČESKA INTEGRACIJA. BÀLGARSKA AKADEMIJA NA NAUKITE

     2. Parent institution: Institute for International Relations
        and Socialist Integration at the BAS

     3. 8, Kalojan St., Sofia
        tel. 87-42-75
        telex: 22271

     4. 1976

     5. Director: Vassilev,Robert
        The staff numbers 39 professionals and 40 non-professionals

     6. Branch information centre

     7. Departments or activities: Foreign economic information;
        Marketing; Commodity and price information; International
        political and cultural information; Library and documenta-
        tion; Information issues

     8. Major fields: economics, foreign trade, political and cul-
        tural international relations

     9. National and foreign books and periodicals are processed

    10. The Centre has a library

    11. Holdings: books, periodicals and abstract journals
        Alphabetical and subject catalogues, thesaurus are used

    12. The library is open to the public

    13. Information services:
        Publications are for office use only

SDI
Translation
Compilation of documentary syntheses
Lending and reference services
Provision of photocopies

15. Photocopying machine, rotaprint, offset

16. Relations with other information units in the country and
abroad, regional and international organizations

17. Information services free of charge

29   1. INTERNATIONAL INFORMATION CENTRE OF BALKAN STUDIES

CENTRE INTERNATIONALE D'INFORMATION SUR LES SOURCES D'HIS-
TOIRE BALKANIQUE

MEŽDUNARODEN INFORMACIONEN CENTĂR PO BALKANISTIKA

CIBAL

2. Subordinated to the International Association of South-East
European Studies

3. 45, Moskovska St., Sofia
tel. 88-51-97

4. 1966

5. The staff numbers 8 professionals and 5 non-professionals

6. Specialized information centre

7. Departments or activities: Analytical - synthetical processing; Retrospective information; Specialized library

8. Major fields: history, economics, law, sociology, religion,
ethnography, folklore, literature, art, languages of the
Balkan peoples
Specific fields: political, economic and cultural history of
the Balkan peoples

9. Foreign and national books, periodicals and manuscripts are
processed

10. The Centre has a library

11. Holdings: books -   6 383 vols.
             periodicals   3 340 vols.
             abstract journals   7 vols.
Alphabetical and topographical catalogues are used

12. The library is open to the public

13. Information services:
Publications - bibliographies
SDI

    Bibliographical, literature and survey data searches
    Lending and reference services

14. Participates in AIS-OBNA in the field of social sciences
(history and cultural history of the Balkan peoples) at the
Scientific Information Centre - BAS
Hardware: IBM 370/135
Software: STAIRS

15. Offset

16. Relations with the Scientific Information Centre at the BAS
and SSID

17. Information services free of charge

30 1. LIBRARY OF SOFIA UNIVERSITY

UNIVERSITETSKA BIBLIOTEKA - SOFIA

2. Subordinated to the central administration of Sofia University "Kliment Ohridski"

3. 15, boul.Rouski, Sofia-1504
tel. 85-81
telex: 23296 SUKO R Bg

4. 1888

5. Director: Kǎncev,Stefan
The staff numbers 84 professionals and 21 non-professionals

6. Scientific and research library

7. Departments or activities: Information and bibliography; Acquisitions; Exchange; Periodicals; Processing; Branch libraries; Lending

8. Major fields: social and natural sciences
Specific fields: philosophy, history, philology, geography,
law, journalism, political economy

9. National and foreign books and periodicals are processed

11. Holdings: books   727 956 vols.
periodicals   420 102 vols.
cards   1 189 vols.
Authors', classified and topographical catalogues are used

12. The library is open to the public

13. Information services:
Publications - bibliographies and others
SDI
Bibliographical and literature searches
Compilation of documentary syntheses
Lending and reference services

Provision of photocopies

14. The library uses information on magnetic tapes of the fo-
    reign systems: INIS, INSPEC, COMPENDEX, BIOSIS, AGRIS

15. Photocopying machines, offset, minigraph

16. Relations with other information units and libraries in the
    country and abroad

17. Information services free of charge

31   1. NATIONAL SCIENTIFIC AND INFORMATION CENTRE OF CULTURE
         NACIONALEN NAUČNO-INFORMACIONEN CENTÁR PO KULTURA

      2. Subordinated to the Committee of Culture

      3. 39, boul.Dondukov,   Sofia-1000
         tel. 88-48-11

      4. 1977

      5. Director: Germanov,Milcho
         The staff numbers 90 professionals

      6. An information institution on national level

      7. Departments or activities: Sociological research; Content
         analyses; Information concerning cultural policy; Interna-
         tional cultural activities; Automated information system

      8. Major fields: culture, sociological research in the sphere
         of mass communications and arts, cultural policy, interna-
         tional cultural activities

      9. National and foreign books and periodicals are processed

     10. The Centre has a library

     11. Holdings: books, periodicals and manuscripts
         Alphabetical and systematical catalogues are used

     12. The library is not open to the public

     13. Information services:
         Publications in 4 series, for office use only
         Translation
         Bibliographical, literature and survey data searches
         Compilation of documentary syntheses
         Lending and reference services

     14. Automated information system in preparation
         Hardware: IBM 370/135, ES-1022
         Software: DOC-ES, OS-VS1, COBOL, FORTRAN, PL/1

     16. Relations with other information units in the country

17. Information services free of charge

32   1. OFFICE FOR SCIENTIFIC ECONOMIC INFORMATION AT THE INSTITUTE
        OF ECONOMICS. BULGARIAN ACADEMY OF SCIENCES
        SLUŽBA ZA NAUČNA IKONOMIČESKA INFORMACIJA PRI IKONOMIČESKIJA
        INSTITUT. BALGARSKA AKADEMIJA NA NAUKITE

     2. Parent institution: Institute of Economics at the BAS

     3. 3, Aksakov St., Sofia-1000
        tel. 8-41-21/812,813

     4. 1956

     5. The staff numbers 10 professionals and 2 non-professionals

     8. Major fields: political economy of capitalism, political
        economy of socialism

     9. National and foreign books, periodicals and "gray" literature
        are processed

    10. The Office has a library

    11. Holdings: books   27 599 vols.
                  periodicals   17 059 vols.
                  abstract journals   270 vols.
                  manuscripts   77
                  microcopies   79
        Alphabetical, systematical and topographical catalogues are
        used

    12. The library is open to the public

    13. Information services:
        Publications - bibliographies and others
        Translation
        Bibliographical, literature and survey data searches
        Lending and reference services

    14. Participates in AIS-OBNA in the field of social sciences
        (Political economy of socialism) at the Scientific Informa-
        tion Centre - BAS
        Hardware: IBM 370/135
        Software: STAIRS

    15. Photocopying machine

    16. Relations with the Central Institute for Scientific and Tech-
        nical Information (CINTI), Scientific Information Centre at
        the BAS

    17. Information services free of charge

33   1. OFFICE FOR SCIENTIFIC INFORMATION AND DOCUMENTATION. INSTI-
        TUTE OF THE STATE AND LAW. BULGARIAN ACADEMY OF SCIENCES

        SLUŽBA ZA NAUČNA INFORMACIJA I DOKUMENTACIJA. INSTITUT PO
        NAUKITE ZA DĂRŽAVATA I PRAVOTO. BĂLGARSKA AKADEMIJA NA NAU-
        KITE

     2. Parent institution: Institute of the State and Law at the BAS

     3. 3, Benkovski St.,   Sofia-1000
        tel. 8-41-21/884

     4. 1959

     5. The staff numbers 11 professionals

     6. Branch information unit

     8. Major fields: legal and political sciences

     9. National and foreign books and periodicals are processed

    10. The Office has a library

    11. Holdings: books   14 775 vols. in total
                  periodicals   168 titles - 6 776 vols.
                  microcopies   32
        Alphabetical, systematical and topographical catalogues are
        used

    12. The library is open to the public

    13. Information services:
        Publications - bibliographies and others
        Translation
        Bibliographical, literature and survey data searches
        Lending and reference services

    14. Participates in AIS - OBNA in the field of social sciences
        (law) at the Scientific Information Centre - BAS
        Hardware: IBM 370/135
        Software: STAIRS

    16. Relations with the Central Institute for Scientific and Tech-
        nical Information (CINTI), Scientific Information Centre at
        the BAS

    17. Information services free of charge

34   1. SCIENTIFIC INFORMATION CENTRE FOR NATURAL, MATHEMATICAL AND
        SOCIAL SCIENCES AT THE BULGARIAN ACADEMY OF SCIENCES

        CENTĂR ZA NAUČNA INFORMACIJA PO PRIRODNI, MATEMATIČESKI I
        OBSTESTVENI NAUKI PRI BĂLGARSKA AKADEMIJA NA NAUKITE

        CNI - BAN

     2. Parent institution: Scientific Information Centre with Cent-

ral Library and Scientific Archives - BAS
Subordinated to the Bulgarian Academy of Sciences

3. 1, "7 Noemvri" St.,   Sofia-1084
   tel. 8-41-41/336

4. 1959

5. Director: Gabrovska,Svobodozarya
   The staff numbers 65 professionals and non-professionals

6. National Centre in the national system for scientific and
   technical information
   National focal point for ECSSID

7. Departments or activities: Information on science abroad;
   Information on science in Bulgaria; Organization, coordina-
   tion, information systems and international cooperation;
   Production; Photolaboratory and microfilm information

8. Major fields: natural, mathematical and social sciences
   Specific fields: scientific information, science policy,
   science of science

9. National and foreign books, periodicals and national "gray"
   literature are processed

10. Uses the collections of the Central Library at the Bulgarian
    Academy of Sciences

13. Information services:
    Publications - abstract journals, bibliographies, directories
    and others
    SDI
    Translation
    Survey data searches
    Compilation of documentary syntheses
    Lending and reference services
    Provision of xerox-copies, photocopies and/or microforms

14. The Centre uses information on magnetic tapes of the foreign
    systems: INIS, INSPEC, AGRIS, COMPENDEX, BIOSIS, ASISTENT-
    USSR, ISIS - on-going research (ICSTI-Moscow). It also takes
    part in the Bulgarian automated systems for on-going research
    SIRENA and in the building up of AIS-MISON. Automated infor-
    mation system OBNA in the field of social sciences
    Hardware: IBM 370/135, TERMINALS-IBM, VIDEOTON. Computer com-
    munication leased-line terminal with INION data bases (Moscow)
    Software: STAIRS

15. Photocopying machines, offset, microfiche line and others

16. Relations with the Central Institute for Scientific and Tech-
    nical Information (CINTI) and other national, branch and lo-
    cal information units in social sciences in the country and
    abroad; international organizations: UNESCO, FID, the VIENNA
    CENTRE, ICSTI and others. Member of MISON

17. Information services free of charge and against payment

Czechoslovakia

35   1. CENTRAL LIBRARY OF THE SLOVAK ACADEMY OF SCIENCES
      ÚSTREDNÁ KNIŽNINA SLOVENSKEJ AKADÉMIE VIED
      ÚK SAV

     2. Parent institution: Slovak Academy of Sciences

     3. Klemensova 19, 886 19 Bratislava
       tel. 517 33, 336 285
       telex: 934 64 uk sav c

     4. 1953

     5. Director: Boldiš,Jozef
       The staff numbers 40 professionals and 5 non-professionals

     6. Specialized information institution, research library

     7. Departments or activities: Scientific information centre;
       Acquisition; Processing; Lending

     8. Major fields: social, natural and technical sciences
       Specific fields: methodological work for the network of
       scientific libraries and information services of the institu-
       tes of the Slovak Academy of Sciences

     9. National and foreign books and periodicals, publications of
       the academies of sciences, special papers, scientific and
       travel reports, and microfiches are processed

    11. Holdings: 1.5 mill. vols., including the holdings of libraries
       of the scientific institutes of the Slovak Academy of Scien-
       ces

books	610 000 vols.
periodicals	9 655 titles - 75 000 vols.
abstract journals	200 titles - 10 000 vols.
microcopies	5 000
manuscripts	15 000

Authors' and systematical catalogues are used

12. The library is open to the public

13. Information services:
    Publications - bibliographies, directories and others
    Translation
    Bibliographical and literature searches
    Lending service
    Provision of photocopies and/or microforms

14. Automated information system for new foreign books in the
    Slovak scientific libraries
    Hardware: TESLA/200;
    Software: ARDIS

15. Photocopying machine, microfiche line

16. Relations with 800 information units in the country, 3500 in-
    dividual organizations abroad, MISON, etc.

17. Information services free of charge or through exchange

36   1. MAIN LIBRARY - SCIENTIFIC INFORMATION CENTRE OF THE CZECHO-
        SLOVAK ACADEMY OF SCIENCES
        ZÁKLADNÍ KNIHOVNA - ÚSTŘEDÍ VĚDECKÝCH INFORMACÍ ČESKOSLOVEN-
        SKÉ AKADEMIE VĚD
        ZK-ÚVI ČSAV

     2. Parent institution: Czechoslovak Academy of Sciences

     3. Národní tř. 3, 115 22 Praha 1
        tel. 24-34-41

     4. 1952

     5. Director: Zahradil,Jiři
        The staff numbers 87 professionals and non-professionals

     6. Special information institution within the Czechoslovak sys-
        tem for scientific and technical information. Central Libra-
        ry of the library network CSAS (72 branch libraries) and in
        the library system of ČSSR

     7. Departments or activities: Methodology; Acquisition and ex-
        change; Processing; Reprographic; Lending and interlibrary
        loans; Retrospective bibliography

     8. Major fields: All fields of science
        Specific fields: social sciences, scientific information

     9. National and foreign books, periodicals and magnetic tapes
        are processed

    11. Holdings: books   824 000 vols. in total

periodicals and abstract journals 3 780 vols. in total
Alphabetical, subject and UDC catalogues are used

12. The library is open to the public

13. Information services:
    Publications - bibliographies and others
    Bibliographical and literature searches
    Lending service
    Provision of photocopies and/or microforms

14. Participates in the building up of AIS MISON
    Hardware: IBM 370, EC 1040

15. Reprographing machines, offset

16. Relations with national and foreign information services.
    Member of MISON

17. Information services free of charge

37   1. SLOVAK NATIONAL BIBLIOGRAPHY
        MATICA SLOVENSKÁ

       2. Subordinated to the Ministry of Culture of the Slovak Socia-
         list Republic

       3. 036 52 Martin, Hostihora
         tel. 313 46-9; 349 71-9
         telex: 075 331

       4. 1863

       5. Director: Krivuš, Štefan
         The staff numbers 202 professionals and 140 non-professionals

       6. National conservation library, national universal bibliogra-
         phy and special bibliographies of national cultural history,
         central library of library system in Slovakia

       7. Departments or activities: Holdings; Bibliographical; Theo-
         ry and research; Literary museum; Biographical; Slovaks ab-
         road; Mechanization and automation; Staff division; Econo-
         mics; Editorial

       8. Major fields: Slovak culture and libraries
         Specific fields: librarianship, bibliography, literary ar-
         chives, literary museum studies, biography

       9. National books, periodicals, "gray" literature, audio-visual
         materials, magnetic tapes and national iconic materials are
         processed

     11. Holdings: books   920 000 titles - 1 520 000 vols.
               periodicals   21 000 titles -   310 000 vols.
               microcopies   3 000

      Subject, systematical and authors' catalogues are used

12. The library is open to the public

13. Information services:
Publications - abstract journals, bibliographies and others
Bibliographical, literature and survey data searches
Compilation of documentary synthesis
Lending service
Provision of photocopies and/or microforms

14. Automated information system on current Slovak national bib-
liography
Hardware: HEWLETT-PACKARD 2100S
Software: ASSEMBLER, ALGOL, FORTRAN, ASTI

15. Duplication facilities

16. Relations with other members of the national system of scientific information, national libraries of the socialist countries; participates in MISON

17. Information services free of charge

38   1. STATE LIBRARY OF THE CZECH SOCIALIST REPUBLIC
STÁTNÍ KNIHOVNA ČSR
SK ČSR

2. Subordinated to the Ministry of Culture of the CSR

3. Klementinum 190, 110 01 Phaha 1 - Staré Město
tel. 266541-5
telex: 011609

4. 1348; 1958 - present name and status

5. Director: Kozelek, Karel
The staff numbers 470 professionals and 100 non-professionals

6. National Library of the CSR, central scientific library with
polythematical holdings (greatest in the ČSSR)
State information centre for culture and arts

7. Departments or activities: Directorate and administration;
Holdings; Services and special subdepartments; Bibliography
and information; Research and methodology of librarianship;
Technology and investment policy; Three special libraries:
Slavonic, French and Central economic

8. Major fields: all fields of science
Specific fields: social and natural sciences

9. National and foreign books, periodicals and audio-visual materials are processed

11. Holdings: books   4 805 000 **vols.**

```
           periodicals           9 400 titles a year
           microcopies          29 000
           manuscripts          17 000
     Authors', subject and systematical catalogues, specialized
     catalogues and union catalogue of foreign non-periodical li-
     terature are used
```

12. The library is open to the public

13. Information services:
    Publications - bibliographies, directories and others
    Literature and survey data searches
    Compilation of documentary syntheses
    Lending service
    Provision of photocopies and/or microforms

14. Technical project of automated information system covering
    the whole-state union catalogue of foreign non-periodical
    literature
    Hardware: EC 1040 (ROBOTRON R40);
    Advanced pre-project stage of computer processing of the
    Czech national bibliography
    Hardware: EC 1040 + DIGISET 40 Tl;
    Computerized cataloguing line for the State Library
    Hardware: SIEMENS 7755
    (The State Library does not possess any of these devices)
    Software: for EC 1040 should be used the USS (Universal
    Software System) with data format compatible in all CMEA
    countries

15. Offset, monitor camera

16. Relations with other information institutions in the country;
    participates in MISON

17. Information services free of charge

Denmark

39   1. DANISH DATA ARCHIVES
     DANSK DATA ARKIV
     DDA

     2. Parent institution: University of Odense (Formerly the Danish
        Social Science Research Council)

     3. Niels Bohrs Allé 25, DK-5230 Odense M
        cable address: Denarchives [OK!]
        tel. (nat'l) 09-158600   or 09-157920
             (int'l) 45.1.15.8600 or 45.1.15.7920

     4. 1973

     5. Director: Nielsen,Per
        The staff numbers 4 professionals and 7 non-professionals

     6. University social science data bank of national coverage

     7. Departments or activities: Clearing house and acquisition;
        Processing; Servicing; Software development and maintenance

     8. Major fields: all social sciences, computer science
        Specific fields: political sciences, sociology, demography,
        economics, psychology, law, social medicine, and related
        subject fields

     9. National magnetic tapes are processed

    10. The Archives have no library

    13. Information services:
        Publications - abstract journals, directories and others
        SDI
        Survey data
        Provision of photocopies

14. Retrieval of text information consisting of machine-readable
    survey data documentation
    Hardware: IBM 3033 MVS
    Software: ASSEMBLER, PL/1, APL

15. Photodocumentation system for automatic photosetting of ma-
    chine-readable texts

16. Participates in CESSDA, IFDO, IASSIST

17. Information services free of charge and against payment

40   1. DENMARKS STATISTICS

     DANMARKS STATISTIK

     2. Subordinated to the Ministry of Economics

     3. Sejrøgade 11, DK-2100 København Ø, Postbox 2550
        tel. 01-298222
        telex: 16236

     4. 1966

     5. Director: Skak-Nielsen,N.
        The staff numbers 114 professionals and 591 non-professionals

     7. Departments or activities: Population; Foreign trade; Agri-
        culture; Labour market; Public finance and credit market; Na-
        tional accounts; Secretariat; Industry; Data processing; Edu-
        cation social services; Denmark's statistics and external
        services; Business accounts; Price indices, commerce and
        transport; Central register of enterprises and establishments

     8. Major field: descriptive statistics

     9. National books and periodicals are processed

    10. The Institution has a library

    11. Holdings: books, periodicals, abstract journals 122 000 vols.
                                                              in total
                  periodicals   2 800 titles
        Card-files are used

    12. The library is open to the public

    13. Information services:
        Publications
        SDI
        Bibliographical, literature and survey data searches
        Compilation of documentary syntheses
        Lending service
        Provision of photocopies and/or microforms

    15. Printing machines

17. Information services free of charge and against payment

41   1. INSTITUTE OF POLITICAL SCIENCE, UNIVERSITY OF ÅARHUS
        INSTITUT FOR STATSKUNDSKAB, ÅARHUS UNIVERSITY

     2. Subordinated to the Ministry of Education

     3. Universitet sparken DK-8000 Åarhus C
        tel. 06.1301 11

     5. Director: Siune,Karen
        The staff numbers 34 professionals and 14 non-professionals

     7. Departments or activities: Comparative politics; Sociology;
        International politics; Political issues; Public administra-
        tion

     8. Major fields: political sciences, international politics,
        public administration, political sociology

     9. Foreign books and periodicals and national "gray" literature
        are processed

    10. The Institute has a library

    11. Holdings: books   10 000 vols. in total
                  periodicals   250 titles - 4 500 vols.
                  manuscripts   250
        SSCI index is used

    12. The library is partly open to the public

    13. Information services:
        Publications - abstract journals, bibliographies, directories
        and others
        SDI (through the State Library)
        Bibliographical and literature searches
        Lending service
        Provision of photocopies and/or microforms

    15. Offset

    16. Relations with other units in the country and regional and
        international organizations

42   1. LIBRARY OF THE ÅARHUS SCHOOL OF BUSINESS AND ECONOMICS
        HANDELSHØJSKOLENS BIBLIOTEK - ÅARHUS

     2. Subordinated to the Ministry of Education

     3. Fuglesangsalle 4,   8210 Åarhus V
        tel. 06-15 55 88

4. 1952

5. Director: Frandsen,Arne
   The staff numbers 7 professionals and 12 non-professionals

6. A special library and a member of the national union of special libraries

7. Departments or activities: Information and documentation,
   and others
   The library is an EEC documentation centre

8. Major fields: business administration, economics, European
   Community questions

9. Foreign books, periodicals and "gray" literature are processed

11. Holdings: books   62 000 vols.
              periodicals   3 000 titles - 23 000 vols.
              abstract journals   30 titles -   200 vols.
    Card catalogues for books and catalogues for journals are
    used

12. The library is open to the public

13. Information services:
    Publications - bibliographies, directories and others
    Bibliographical, literature and survey data searches
    Lending service
    Provision of photocopies and/or microforms

16. Relations: in the country - DANDOK; abroad - SCANP, SCIMP;
    regional organization - NORDINFO

17. Information services free of charge

43   1. ODENSE UNIVERSITY LIBRARY

        ODENSE UNIVERSITETSBIBLIOTEK

     2. Subordinated to the central administration

     3. Campusvei 55,   5230 Odense M
        tel. (09) 158600
        telex: 599 18 oubibl dk

     4. 1965

     5. Director: Olsen,Torkil
        The staff numbers 30 professionals and 83 non-professionals

     8. Major fields: linguistics, literature, philosophy, history,
        social sciences, music, natural sciences, etc.

     9. Foreign books, periodicals and maps are processed

11. Holdings: books   430 000 vols. in total
             periodicals   7 173 titles
             microcopies   6 100
    Alphabetical and systematically arranged subject catalogues
    are used

12. The library is open to the public

13. Information services:
    Bibliographical and literature searches
    Lending service
    Provision of photocopies

15. Offset and photocopying machine

16. Participates in interlibrary loans in the country and abroad

17. Information services free of charge

44   1. ROYAL LIBRARY

     DET KONGELIGE BIBLIOTEK

     KB

     2. Subordinated to the Ministry of Cultural Affairs

     3. Christians Brygge 8,   DK-1219 København K
        tel. 01 150111
        telex: 15009

     4. 1673

     5. Director: Birkelund,Palle
        The staff numbers 112 professionals and 214 non-professionals

     6. National Library, University Library, Copenhagen and princi-
        pal research library for theology, humanities and social
        sciences

     7. Departments or activities: Cataloguing; Classification; Da-
        nish; Foreign; Judaica and Hebraica; Lending; Maps and print-
        ing; Public relations; National bibliography; Oriental; Se-
        rials; Western manuscripts; Accounting; Rare books; Photo-
        graphic studio; Printing; Binding; Technical; Music

     8. Major fields: theology, humanities, social sciences

     9. Foreign books, periodicals, "gray" literature and audio-vi-
        sual materials are processed

    11. Holdings: books   2 300 000 vols.
                  periodicals   13 531 titles

    12. The library is open to the public

13. Information services:
    Publications - abstract journals, bibliographies, directories
    and others
    Bibliographical and literature searches
    Lending service
    Provision of photocopies and/or microforms

14. Information retrieval in social sciences and humanities using
    Dialogsystem (Polo Alte)
    Hardware: TTY terminal

15. Photocopying machine, offset

17. Information services free of charge and against payment

45   1. STATE AND UNIVERSITY LIBRARY

     STATSBIBLIOTEKET

     3. Universitetsparken,   DK-8000 Åarhus C
        tel. (06) 122022
        telex: 64515

     4. 1902

     5. Director: Thomsen,Karl
        The staff numbers 100 professionals and 163 non-professionals

     6. University library of the university of Åarhus and central
        lending library of the public libraries of Denmark

     8. Major fields: all fields of science
        Specific fields: Christian missionary literature, mass in-
        formation media, Frisian literature and culture

     9. Foreign books and periodicals, national "gray" literature
        and foreign audio-visual materials microformats only, are
        processed as well as microprints of the USA government
        (Publ. 1953/56) and Canadian Government Publ.

    11. Holdings: books   approx. 1 400 000 vols. in total
                  periodicals   12 000 titles
                  microcopies   approx.   600 000
        Card-catalogue and a special classification system are used

    12. The library is open to the public

    13. Information services:
        Publications - abstract journals, bibliographies
        Bibliographical and literature searches
        Lending service
        Provision of photocopies and/or microforms

    14. On-line searches in sciences represented in the library co-
        vered by data bases
        Hardware: 3 on-line terminals

16. Relations with regional and international organizations: Depository Library for the United Nations, UNESCO, ILO, WHO, IMCO, IBRD, IMF, IDA and EEC

17. Information services free of charge

Finland

46 1. CENTRAL UNION FOR SOCIAL SECURITY
    SOSIAALITURVAN KESKUSLIITTO
    STKL

    3. Vironkatu 6 A 11, 00170 Helsinki 17
       tel. 90-170455

    4. 1917

    5. Director: Ruohonen,Markku
       The staff numbers 9 professionals

    7. Departments or activities: Education; Research; Information;
       International affairs

    8. Major field: social welfare

    9. National and foreign books, periodicals and "gray" literature
       are processed

   10. The Institution has a library

   11. Holdings: books   approx. 1 400 vols.

   12. The library is not open to the public

   13. Information services:
       Publications - bibliographies and directories
       Bibliographical and literature searches
       Lending service
       Provision of photocopies

   16. Relation with the Finnish Committee of the International
       Council on Social Welfare, cooperation with the Ministry of
       Social Affairs and Health, the National Board of Social Wel-
       fare, universities, etc.

17. Information services free of charge and against payment

47   1. FINNISH INSTITUTE OF INTERNATIONAL AFFAIRS
      ULKOPOLIITTINEN INSTITUUTTI - UTRIKESPOLITISKA INSTITUTET

   3. Dagmarinkatu 8 c 40,   SF-00100, Helsinki 10
     tel. 90/40 11 88

   4. 1960

   5. Director: Möttölä,Kari
     The staff numbers 5 professionals (2 of them part time)

   7. Departments or activities: Research; Information and publica-
     tions; Documentation; Library; Exchange

   8. Major fields: Finnish foreign policy and international af-
     fairs
     Specific fields: Finnish foreign policy, international af-
     fairs concerning Finland, European security and cooperation,
     East-West relations, disarmament, economic integration

   9. National books, national and foreign periodicals and foreign
     mimeographic publications are processed

  10. The Institute has a library

  11. Holdings: books   4 200 vols
           periodicals   100 titles
     Alphabetical and subject catalogues are used

  12. The library is open to the public

  13. Information services:
     Publications - bibliographies
     SDI
     Bibliographical, literature and survey data searches
     Lending service
     Provision of photocopies and/or microforms

  15. Photocopying machine

  16. Relations with approx. 20 other institutions in the country
     and 80 institutions abroad

  17. Information services free of charge and against payment

48   1. HELSINKI SCHOOL OF ECONOMICS LIBRARY
      HELSINGIN KAUPPAKORKEAKOULUN KIRJASTO

   2. Parent institution: Helsinki School of Economics
     Subordinated to the central administration

3. Runeberginkatu 22-24,   00100 Helsinki 10
   tel. 90-44-12 91
   telex: 122220 econ sf

4. 1911

5. Director: Broms, Henri
   The staff numbers 13 professionals and 17 non-professionals

6. Central library in the field of economics and business sciences

7. Departments or activities: Main library; Textbook library;
   Eight Departmental libraries

8. Major fields: economics and business sciences, applied psychology, economy, economic geography, economic history, sociology, statistics, languages, etc.

9. National and foreign books, periodicals, "gray" literature,
   audio-visual materials and magnetic tapes are processed

11. Holdings: books   170 000 vols.
             periodicals   1 200 titles
             abstract journals   80 titles
             microforms (fiches) 30 000
    Card and printed catalogues are used

12. The library is open to the public

13. Information services:
    Publications - abstract journals, bibliographies, directories
    and others
    SDI
    Bibliographical and literature searches
    Lending service
    Provision of photocopies and/or microforms

14. Automated union catalogue of periodicals, service of Finnish
    economic periodical articles, service of Scandinavian perio-
    dical articles
    Hardware: HEWLETT-PACKARD 3000
    Software: FORTRAN

15. Photocopying machine, offset

16. Relations with the International Committee for Social Science
    Information, European business librarians' group

17. Information services free of charge

49   1. INSTITUTE FOR EDUCATIONAL RESEARCH
        KASVATUSTIETEIDEN TUTKIMUSLAITOS
        KTL

     2. Parent institution: University of Jyväskylä

3. Seminaarinkatu 15,   SF-40100 Jyväskylä 10
   tel. 941-291211

4. 1957 - on private initiative; officially established and at-
   tached to the University of Jyväskylä in 1968

5. Director: Marin,Maryatta
   The staff numbers 30 researchers, 5 information professionals
   and 20 non-professionals

6. Disseminates information about educational research in Finland and abroad. Together with the library of the University
   of Jyväskylä, the Institute constitutes the coordinating
   centre responsible for information and documentation services in the field of behavioural sciences

7. Departments or activities: Applied research; School research;
   Evaluation; Higher education research; Educational research
   methodology; Information and documentation

8. Major field: educational research
   Specific fields: general education, higher education

9. National books, periodicals and "gray" literature are processed

10. The Institute has a library

11. Holdings: books and research report series   5 200 titles
              periodicals   150 vols.
              abstract journals   2 vols.
    Alphabetical card index is used

12. The library is open to the public

13. Information services:
    Publications - bibliographies and directories
    Translation
    Compilation of documentary syntheses
    Lending service

15. Offset

16. Cooperation with the University of Jyväskylä library in the
    country and relations with the CCC: the EUDISED-project and
    UNESCO/IBE: CEAS-Abstracting Service

17. Information services free of charge

50 1. JYVASKYLA UNIVERSITY LIBRARY

       JYVÄSKYLÄN YLIOPISTON KIRJASTO

       JYK

    2. Parent institution: Jyvaskyla University
       Subordinated to the Ministry of Education

3. Seminaarinkatu 15,   40100 Jyväskylä 10
   tel. 941-291/211
   telex: 28219 jyk sf

4. 1912

5. Director: Tammekann,Eeva-Maija
   The staff numbers 28 professionals and 27 non-professionals

6. National central library for education, psychology and physical education

7. Departments or activities: Acquisition (exchanges); Finnish
   collections; Information service; Lending; Foreign collections

8. Major fields: humanities, social and fundamental sciences,
   collection of Finnish deposit copies
   Specific fields: education, psychology, physical education

9. Foreign books, periodicals, "gray" literature and audio-visual materials are processed

11. Holdings: books, abstract journals and periodicals
                approx. 570 000 vols. in the main library and
                        130 000 vols. in the institute libraries
            microcopies 6 500
            manuscripts 2 900

12. The library is open to the public

13. Information services:
    Publications - bibliographies and directories
    SDI
    Bibliographical and literature searches
    Lending and reference services
    Provision of photocopies and/or microforms

14. On-line literature searches in the special fields of the lib-
    rary
    Hardware: NOKIA NOP 30 terminals
    Software: (no input of information)

15. Photocopying machine, addresses on Multiline, offset

16. Relations with the Institute for Educational Research,
    Jyväskylä (which participates in EUDISED and IBE activities)
    and with LOCKHEED, Systems Development Corporation abroad

17. Information services free of charge and against payment

51 1. LIBRARY OF ABO ACADEMY
       ÅBO AKADEMIS BIBLIOTEK
       ÅAB

    2. Parent institution: Åbo Academy

3. Domkyrkogatan 2-4,   20500 Åbo 50
tel. 335133
telex: 62301 aabib sf.

4. 1918

5. Director: Mustelin, Olof
The staff numbers 21 professionals and 26 non-professionals
(12 of them part time)

6. General research library, law depository library

7. Departments or activities: Fennica; Gifts and exchanges;
Lending; Manuscripts; Cataloguing; Undergraduate library;
Departmental libraries

8. Major fields: subjects taught at the Åbo Academy, Scandinavica

9. Foreign books, periodicals, audio-visual materials and national "gray" literature are processed

11. Holdings: books, abstract journals,
                periodicals   1 050 000 vols.
                microcopies   8 535
                manuscripts   11 000
Card catalogues and printed bibliographies are used

12. The library is open to the public

13. Information services:
Publications - directories and others
Bibliographical searches
Lending service
Provision of photocopies and/or microforms

15. Duplicating and photocopying machines, including microfilm
reader-printer

16. Participates in the national information service

17. Information services free of charge and against payment

52   1. LIBRARY OF THE DEPARTMENT OF INTERNATIONAL DEVELOPMENT COOPE-
        RATION, MINISTRY OF FOREIGN AFFAIRS

        ULKOASIAINMINISTERIÖN KEHITYSYHTEISTYÖOSASTON KIRJASTO/
        BIBLIOTEKET VID UTRIKESMINISTERIETS AVDELNING FÖR INTERNA-
        TIONELLT UTVECKLINGSSAMARBETE

     2. Subordinated to the Ministry of Foreign Affairs

     3. Tehtaankatu la,   SF-00140 Helsinki 14
        cable address: Ulkoasiat Helsinki
        tel. 1602398, 1602399

     4. 1970

5. Librarian: Virtanen,Kari
   The staff numbers 2 professionals

6. Specialized library for developing countries related with
   Finland through development cooperation

7. Departments or activities: Information section

8. Major fields: development cooperation, developing countries,
   references about development aid, statistics, etc., Ethiopia,
   Kenya, Mozambique, Tanzania, Zambia, Cuba, Namibia, Peru,
   Bangladesh, Vietnam

9. Foreign books and periodicals, national "gray" literature
   and audio-visual materials are processed

11. Holdings: books   8 500 vols. in total
             periodicals   274 titles in total

12. The library is open to the public

13. Information services:
    Publications - bibliographies
    Bibliographical searches
    Lending service
    Provision of photocopies and/or microforms

16. Information services free of charge

53 1. LIBRARY OF PARLIAMENT
       EDUSKUNNAN KIRJASTO RIKSDAGSBIBLIOTEKET

    2. Parent institution: Finnish Parliament

    3. SF-00102 Helsinki 10
       tel. 90-4321
       telex: 121464 sf

    4. 1872

    5. Director: Schauman,Henrik
       The staff numbers 17 professionals and 13 non-professionals

    6. Central library of law, political science and international
       politics, depository library (mainly of Finnish materials),
       exchange-centre of official publications, depository library
       of publications of international organizations, compilation
       of bibliography of official publications

    7. Departments or activities: Cataloguing; Collections and ser-
       vices

    8. Specific fields: law, international politics, political
       sciences, international organizations, parliamentary docu-
       ments, governmental publications

9. National and foreign books, periodicals, "gray" literature, micropublications and archives of the Finnish Parliament are processed

10. Holdings: books and periodicals   400 000 vols.
                periodicals   1 100 vols. a year
                micropublications   4 400 vols.
    Main alphabetical and subject catalogues are used

12. The library is open to the public

13. Information services:
    Publications - bibliographies and directories
    Bibliographical, literature and survey data searches
    Lending service
    Provision of photocopies and/or microforms

15. Printing and duplicating machines, microfilming

16. Interlibrary loans, exchange of parliamentary papers and governmental publications in the country and abroad. Depository library for the publications of several organizations. Cooperation with other Nordic parliamentary libraries within Scandiaplan.
    Participates in Nordic union catalogues

17. Information services free of charge

54 1. NORDIC DOCUMENTATION CENTRE FOR MASS COMMUNICATIONS RESEARCH
       POHJOISMAINEN TIEDOTUSTUTKIMUKSEN PALVELUKESKUS, NORDISK
       DOKUMENTATIONSCENTRAL FÖR MASSKOMMUNIKATIONS-FORSKNING
       NORDICOM

    2. Parent institution: University of Tampere
       Affilliated to the Nordic network of documentation centres
       (an international organization)

    3. University of Tampere, (Kalevanti), P.O.B. 607
       SF-33101 Tampere 10
       tel. 931-156 324

    4. 1972

    5. Director: Nordenstreng, Kaarle
       The staff numbers 1 professional

    6. Autonomous part of a decentralized system

    8. Major field: Mass communications research

    9. National books, periodicals and "gray" literature are processed

    10. The Centre has a library

11. Holdings: books   1 500 titles
             periodicals   80 vols.
             manuscripts   1 000
    Card index is used

12. The library is open to the public

13. Information services:
    Publications - bibliographies, directories and others
    SDI
    Bibliographical and literature searches
    Lending service
    Provision of photocopies

15. Photostat, offset

16. Relations with other information units in the country and
    regional and international organizations - COMNET

17. Information services free of charge

55 1. OULU UNIVERSITY LIBRARY

    OULUN YLIOPISTON KIRJASTO

    UNIVERSITETSBIBLIOTEKET IN ULEÅBORG

    OYK

    2. Parent institution: Oulu University
       Subordinated to the central administration

    3. Kasarmintie 7, SF-90100 Oulu 10
       tel. 981-223455
       telex: 32256 oyk sf

    5. Director: Murhu,Rac
       The staff numbers 24 professionals and 39 non-professionals

    7. Departments or activities: in the main library: References;
       Lending; in the faculty, institute and clinical libraries:
       References; Information services in science, medicine and
       social sciences

    8. Major fields: humanities and social sciences, etc.
       Specific fields: materials concerning the nothern regions

    9. National periodicals and "gray" literature are processed

   10. Holdings: periodicals   approx. 5 000 titles
                abstract journals   120 titles
                manuscripts   700 000
       Card catalogue, international and national indices and ab-
       stracts are used

   11. The library is open to the public

   13. Information services:

Publications - directories and others
SDI
Bibliographical, literature and survey data searches
Lending service
Provision of photocopies and/or microforms

15. Photocopying machine

16. Relations with the Jyväskylä university library in the counry

17. Information services against payment

56   1. SOCIAL INSURANCE INSTITUTION LIBRARY
        KANSANELÄKELAITOKSEN KIRJASTO
        FOLKPENSIONSANSTALTENS BIBLIOTEK

     2. Subordinated to the Social Insurance Institution

     3. P.O.B. 450, 00101 Helsinki 10
        tel. (90) 413011
        telex: 122375 kela sf

     4. 1963

     5. Director: Lehtinen,Mirja
        The staff numbers 5 professionals

     7. Departments or activities: Acquisition and direction; Cata-
        loguing; Interlibrary loans; Lending; Circulation of periodi-
        cals

     8. Major fields: social insurance, social security

     9. Catalogue of recent acquisition files in microform is pro-
        cessed

    11. Holdings: books   35 000 vols. in total
                  periodicals   681 vols. in total
                  abstract journals   10 vols. in total
        Alphabetical and classified catalogues in microform are used

    12. The library is open to the public

    13. Information services:
        Publications - bibliographies and copies of catalogues in
        microform
        Bibliographical, literature and survey data searches
        Lending service
        Provision of photocopies and/or microforms

    14. Automated cataloguing
        Hardware: IBM 370/168
        Software - ASSEMBLER, own system

    15. Photocopying machine, copies of microfiches, offset

17. Information services free of charge and against payment

57   1. SOCIAL SCIENCES LIBRARY OF HELSINKI UNIVERSITY
        HELSINGIN YLIOPISTON VALTIOTIETEELLISEN TIEDEKUNNAN KIRJASTO

     2. Parent institution: Faculty of Social Sciences of Helsinki
        University

     3. Hallituskatu 11-13,   00100 Helsinki 10
        tel. 90-191 2546

     4. 1950

     5. Director: Lamminen,Hilkka-Sisko
        The staff numbers 5 professionals and 5 non-professionals

     8. Major field: social sciences

     9. Foreign books and periodicals, national "gray" literature,
        collections of unpublished master and doctoral theses are
        processed

    11. Holdings: books   40 000 vols. in total
                  periodicals   500 titles ⎫
                  abstract journals 20 titles ⎬ 12 500 vols. in total
                  manuscripts   5 100   ⎭
        Alphabetical and systematical (UDC and subject headings) ca-
        talogues are used

    12. The library is not open to the public

    13. Information services:
        Bibliographical and literature searches
        Lending and reference services
        Provision of photocopies

    17. Information services free of charge

58   1. STATISTICS LIBRARY
        TILASTOKIRJASTO/STATISTIKBIBLIOTEKET

     2. Parent institution: Central Statistical Office of Finland
        Subordinated to the Ministry of Finance

     3. Annankatu 44,   SF-00100 Helsinki 10
        tel. 17341
        telex: 12-2656

     4. 1865

     5. Director: Yrjölä,Hellevi
        The staff numbers 6 professionals and 4 non-professionals

     6. Central statistics and statistical information library (in-

EGSSI - C

formal)

8. Major fields: social and economic statistics
   Specific fields: Finnish government statistics

9. National and foreign books, periodicals and "gray" literature
   are processed

11. Holdings: books   120 000 vols.
                periodicals   750 titles
                abstract journals   25 titles
    Manual card catalogues are used

12. The library is open to the public

13. Information services:
    Publications - bibliographical and directories
    Literature and survey data searches
    Lending and reference services
    Provision of photocopies and/or microforms

17. Information services free of charge or against payment

59   1. TURKU UNIVERSITY LIBRARY
        TURUN YLIOPISTON KIRJASTO

     2. Subordinated to the central administration of Turku Univer-
        sity

     3. SF-20500 Turku 50
        tel. 921-645 111
        telex: 62123 tyk sf

     4. 1920

     5. Director: Eskelinen,Heikki
        The staff numbers 40 professionals and 40 non-professionals

     6. University library

     7. Departments or activities: Main library; six Faculty libra-
        ries

     8. Major fields: Finnish literature, humanities, natural scien-
        ces, social sciences, law, educational sciences, etc.

     9. Foreign books and periodicals are processed

     11. Holdings: books, periodicals and
                   abstract journals   1 000 000 vols. in total
                   microcopies   1 500 in total
                   manuscripts   4 700 in total
        Card catalogues are used

     12. The library is open to the public

13. Information services:
    Publications - different indexes
    Bibliographical and literature searches
    Lending service
    Provision of photocopies and/or microforms

15. Offset

17. Information services free of charge

60 1. UNIVERSITY OF TAMPERE. LIBRARY

    TAMPEREEN YLIOPISTON KIRJASTO

    TaYK

 2. Parent institution - University of Tampere
    Subordinated to the Ministry of Education

 3. Tammelan puistokatu 38, Box 617, SF-33101 Tampere 10
    tel. 931-156111
    telex: 22263 tayk sf

 4. 1925 - Helsinki, moved to Tampere in 1960

 5. Director: Soini,Hannele
    The staff numbers 33 professionals and 11 non-professionals

 7. Departments or activities: Main Library; Education; Textbooks;
    Medicine

 8. Major fields: humanities, education, economics and adminis-
    tration, social sciences, etc.
    Specific fields: library and information science, journalism
    and mass communications, social sciences

11. Holdings: books   443 431 vols. in total
             periodicals   2 605 vols. in total
             abstract journals   59 vols. in total
             microcopies   7 812 in total
    Adapted Dewey Classification and National Library of Medicine-
    Classification (Department of Medicine) are used

12. The library is open to the public

13. Information services:
    Publications
    Bibliographical and literature searches
    Lending service
    Provision of photocopies and/or microforms

15. Photocopying machine, offset, reader-printer

16. Relations with the University of Jyväskylä Library and the
    Central Medical library, Helsinki

17. Information services against payment

France

61 1. CENTRE OF RESEARCH AND DOCUMENTATION ON CONTEMPORARY CHINA

   CENTRE DE RECHERCHES ET DE DOCUMENTATION SUR LA CHINE CON-
   TEMPORAINE

   2. Parent institution: Higher School of Social Sciences
      Subordinated to the Ministry of Universities

   3. 54 Bd.Raspail, 75006 Paris
      tel. 544 06 55

   5. Director: Bianco,Lucien
      The staff numbers 1 professional and 4 non-professionals

   6. Central information service concerning the corresponding
      field

   8. Major fields: China since 1840 (history, social sciences)

   9. Foreign books, periodicals, audio-visual materials and ar-
      chives are processed

  10. The Centre has a library

  11. Holdings: books (Chinese)   4 800 titles⎫ 11 700 titles in total
                       (Western)   6 900 titles⎭
               periodicals and abstract journals
                       (Chinese)   600 titles⎫ 1 100 titles in total
                       (Western)   500 titles⎭
               microcopies   800
               manuscripts   10
      Authors' and systematical catalogues and title catalogue of
      Chinese collections are used

  12. The library is open to the public

  13. Information services:
      Publishing through the parent institution

Reference services
Provision of photocopies and/or microforms

15. Offset

17. Information services free of charge

62   1. CENTRE FOR SCIENTIFIC AND TECHNICAL DOCUMENTATION
        CENTRE DE DOCUMENTATION SCIENTIFIQUE ET TECHNIQUE
        CDST

     2. Parent institution: National Centre of Scientific Research
        (CNRS)
        Subordinated to the Ministry of Universities

     3. 26 Rue Boyer, 75971 Paris Cedex 20
        tel. 797 35 59
        telex: cnrsdoc 220880 f

     4. 1939

     5. Director: d'Olier,J.
        The staff numbers 400 professionals

     8. Major fields: exact sciences, life sciences, etc.

     9. Foreign periodicals, books, "gray" literature and theses,
        congress reports, etc. are processed

    10. The Centre has a library

    11. Holdings: books   50 000 titles
                  periodicals   16 000 titles
                  congress reports   17 000 titles
                  theses   55 000 titles
                  reports   5 000 titles
        Authors', title, geographical, subject and UDC (for periodi-
        cals) catalogues are used

    12. The library is open to the public

    13. Information services:
        Publications - abstract journals and others
        SDI
        Translation
        Bibliographical searches
        Provision of photocopies and/or microforms

    14. Multidisciplinary automated information system
        Hardware: IBM 370/168 and 135
        LINOTRON, SFENA lourd terminal
        Software: ASSEMBLER, PL/1, System PASCAL/3

    15. Duplicating facilities

    16. Relations with AFNOR, for social sciences: DICA, ENSB, the

National Library, SEI, CDSH PASCAL and SPLEEN in the country
and abroad with CNR and VINITI; participates in UNISIST, ISO,
ICSU-AB, CDIST

17. Information services against payment

63   1. CENTRE FOR USSR AND EAST EUROPEAN STUDIES
          CENTRE D'ETUDES SUR L'URSS ET L'EUROPE ORIENTALE

       2. Parent institution: Higher School of Social Sciences
          Subordinated to the Ministry of Universities

       3. 54, Bd.Raspail, 75270 Paris Cedex 06
          tel. 544 39 79

       4. 1960

       5. Directors' Council: Bennigsen,A., Besançon,A., Confino,M.,
          Dagron,G., Ferro,M., Kerblay,B., Paris,R., Portal,R.,
          Reberioux,M., Scherrer,J., Veinstein,G.
          The staff numbers 8 professionals and 2 non-professionals

       7. Departments or activities: Research group on Mediaeval His-
          tory of East Europe and the Ottoman Empire

       8. Major fields: history of Russia and the Soviet Union, poli-
          tical, economic and social conditions and policies of the
          Soviet Union, Balkan countries and Turkey
          Specific fields: ethnic and nationality problems, research
          on the Ottoman Empire 15-18 c., Russian-Ottoman relations,
          history of socialism

       9. Foreign books, periodicals and visual materials are processed

      10. The Centre has a library

      11. Holdings: books   16 000 vols. in total
                    periodicals and abstract journals   210 vols. in total
                    microfilms   1 500
          Alphabetical, authors' and subject catalogues are used

      12. The library is not open to the public

      13. Information services:
          Publications - bibliographies, directories and others
          Lending service

      15. Reader-printer of microfilms

      16. Relations with the National Institute of Slavic Studies in
          Paris, the Paris Institute of Turkish Studies - Aix-en-Pro-
          vence, Strasbourg in the country, and with the Centre for
          Russian and East-European Studies, University of Birmingham,
          the Historical Institute N.Iorga, Bucarest, the Institute of
          History and Slavic Studies, University of Chicago

64   1. DEPARTMENT OF FRENCH DOCUMENTATION
     DIRECTION DE LA DOCUMENTATION FRANÇAISE

     2. Parent institution: General Governmental Secretariat
        Subordinated to the Office of the Prime Minister

     3. 29,31 quai Voltaire, 75 340 Paris, Cedex 07
        cable address: Docfran - Paris
        tel. 261-50-10
        telex: 204826 Docfran-Paris

     4. 1945

     5. Director: Cremieux-Brilhac,Jean Louis
        The staff numbers 100 professionals and 250 non-professionals

     6. Official editorial and documentation centre of the French Go-
        vernment

     7. Departments or activities: Documentation and publications;
        Administration; Editorial and dissemination

     8. Major fields: economics, political and social problems in
        France and abroad

     9. National and foreign books, periodicals and national audio-
        visual materials are processed

     10. The Department has a library

     11. Holdings: books   150 000 titles in total
                    periodicals   2 500 titles in total
                    abstract journals   40 titles in total

         Alphabetical, subject, authors', titles catalogues are used

     12. The library is open to the public

     13. Information services:
         Publications - bibliographies, directories and others
         Translation
         Bibliographical and survey data searches
         Compilation of documentary syntheses
         Reference services
         Provision of photocopies and/or microforms

     14. Data base on politics
         Hardware: IRIS 80
         Software: MISTRAL

     15. Offset, photocomposition

     16. Relations with the Commission for coordination of administra-
         tive documentation, CNRS, the National Library, with UNO,
         UNESCO, OECD, CEE

     17. Information services free of charge

65   1. DOCUMENTATION CENTRE. COOPERATION AND AUTOMATION DEPARTMENT
         DIVISION DE LA COOPERATION ET DE L'AUTOMATISATION, CENTRE DE
         DOCUMENTATION
         DICA - CEDICA

      2. Subordinated to the Ministry of Universities - library service

      3. 61 rue de Richelieu,   75084 Paris, Cedex 02
         tel. 2974815, 2974934

      4. 1972

      5. Director: Pouderoux,Andrée
         The staff numbers 1 professional and 1 non-professional

      6. Links with the National bureau of scientific and technical
         information BNIST

      7. Departments or activities: Selecting; Collecting; Processing

      8. Major fields: information science, library science
         Specific fields: library services, interlibrary loans, in-
         formation network, automation in libraries, automatic docu-
         mentation

      9. National and foreign books, periodicals, "gray" literature
         and audio-visual materials are processed

     10. The Department has a library

     11. Holdings: books   3 500 vols. in total
                    periodicals   135 titles
                    abstract journals   1 title
                    microcopies   50
         Authors'-titles, subject and geographical catalogues are used

     12. The library is open to the public

     13. Information services:
         Publications - abstract journal
         SDI
         Bibliographical and literature searches
         Lending service
         Provision of microforms and/or photocopies

     14. Participates in the PASCAL system - CNRS

     15. Offset

     16. Relations with other information units in the country

     17. Information services free of charge

66   1. DOCUMENTATION CENTRE. INSTITUTE OF POLITICAL SCIENCES - UNI-
        VERSITY OF SOCIAL SCIENCES, GRENOBLE II

        CENTRE,DE DOCUMENTATION - INSTITUT D'ETUDES POLITIQUES - UNI-
        VERSITÉ DES SCIENCES SOCIALES DE GRENOBLE II

        CD-IEPG

     2. Parent institution: Institute of political sciences
        Subordinated to the University of Social Sciences, Grenoble II

     3. Domaine Universitaire de Grenoble
        BP 34-38401 Saint Martin d'Heres
        tel. (76)54-13-54

     4. IEPG - 1948, IEPG Documentation centre - 1955

     5. Director: Verdiel,Andrée
        The staff numbers 7 professionals and 9 non-professionals

     6. The Documentation centre coordinates documentary activities
        of the various research centres: Land use planning, Economic
        and social planning (CEPES), Gerontology (CPDG), Latin Ame-
        rica (GRESAL)

     7. Departments or activities: Books; Serials; Contemporary in-
        formation

     8. Major fields: political economy and social sciences, admi-
        nistration, land use planning, law, history since 1789, geo-
        graphy, press, management
        Specific fields: economic and social planning, gerontology,
        documents from European communities, on Italian politics,
        from OECD, GATT, Latin America, etc.

     9. Books, periodicals and "gray" literature are processed

    10. The Centre has a library

    11. Holdings: books   38 500 vols.
                  periodicals and daily newspapers   600 titles
                  microcopies   29
        Alphabetical, authors', title, geographical, analytical sub-
        ject, special and cooperation catalogues are used

    12. The library is open to the public

    13. Information services:
        Publications
        SDI
        Bibliographical searches
        Lending service
        Provision of photocopies and/or microforms

    15. Offset, etc.

    16. Relations with the Inter-University Library and other docu-
        mentation centres in the Rhône-Alpes region; member of the
        Association of documentalists and specialized librarians

(ADBS) and of the Association of librarians in France (ABF)
and of the economic bibliographical files of INSEE

67   1. DOCUMENTATION CENTRE FOR SOCIAL SCIENCES AND HUMANITIES
        CENTRE DE DOCUMENTATION SCIENCES HUMAINES
        CDSH

     2. Parent institution: National Centre of Scientific Research

     3. 54, bd Raspail, B.P. 140, 75260 Paris Cedex 06
        tel. 544 38 49

     4. 1970

     5. Director: Brunet,Roger
        The staff numbers 85 professionals

     6. Multidisciplinary documentation centre in social sciences and
        humanities; leading position in several information networks

     7. Departments or activities: Several editorial teams; Some de-
        centralized units in several towns; Several cooperative net-
        works coordinated by the centre; Service of "Selective Dis-
        semination of Information"; Computer processing team; Repro-
        graphic laboratory; Information service on research in pro-
        gress

     8. Major fields: all humanities and social sciences (FRANCIS
        Files)
        Specific fields: history of France, transportation economics
        (non automated bibliographies), etc. Humanities and Social
        Sciences yearbook (automated), theses (automated)

     9. Foreign books, periodicals (4000 subscriptions), national
        "gray" literature, foreign magnetic tapes are processed

    10. The Centre has no library. Uses the MSH library

    13. Information services:
        Publications - abstract journals, bibliographies, directories,
        syntheses and others
        SDI and on-line searches (FRANCIS)
        Bibliographical and literature searches
        Compilation of documentary syntheses
        Provision of photocopies and/or microforms

    14. Almost all the activities of the Centre are automated
        Hardware: IBM 370/168
        Software: PL/1, ASSEMBLER, SPLEEN, MISTRAL, SEGUR, CARAT, In-
        terfaces with ISIS, STAIRS, etc.

    15. Photocopying machines, offset AB-Dick 1600, microfiche camera
        "Schlumberger" and Micle

    16. Relations mainly with French information centres, various bi-

lateral agreements with individual organizations abroad, and with EEC, UNESCO, ECSSID, ILD, LOCKHEED (California), etc.

17. Information services free of charge and against payment

68   1. DOCUMENTATION ON "NORD-PICARDIE" MANAGEMENT

     DOCUMENTATION A MENAGEMENT NORD-PICARDIE

     DOCAMENOR

     3. 2, rue de Brixelles,   59046 Lille Cedex
        tel. (20) 52 20 22
        telex: cetelil 110570 f

     4. 1970

     5. Director: Griffon,Michel
        The staff numbers 9 professionals and 2 non-professionals

     8. Major fields: administrative sciences, demography, economics,
        geography, law, social and cultural anthropology, sociology,
        statistics
        Specific fields: town and country planning, regional plann-
        ing, etc.

     9. National and foreign books, periodicals, "gray" literature,
        national audio-visual and magnetic tapes are processed

     10. The Institution has a library

     11. Holdings: books   12 000 vols. in total
                   periodicals   400 vols. in total
                   abstract journals   50 vols. in total
                   microcopies   4 000 in total

     12. The library is open to the public

     13. Information services:
         Publications - abstract journals, bibliographies, directo-
         ries and others
         SDI
         Translation
         Bibliographical searches
         Lending service
         Provision of photocopies and/or microforms

     14. Automated information system
         Hardware: CII HB (IRIS 80)
         Software: MISTRAL V4

     15. Offset

     16. Relations with IAURIF, STU, etc. in the country

     17. Information services against payment

69   1. DOCUMENTATION AND RESEARCH CENTRE FOR MAINLAND AND INSULAR
        SOUTHEAST ASIA

        CENTRE DE DOCUMENTATION ET DE RECHERCHES SUR L'ASIE DU SUD-
        EST ET LE MONDE INSULINDIEN

        CEDRASEMI

     2. Parent institution: National Centre of Scientific Research
        and Higher School of Social Sciences
        Subordinated to the Ministry of National Education

     3. 6, rue de Tournon,   75006 Paris
        tel. Administration: 633 61 43
             Library: 326 64 49

     4. 1964

     5. Director: Condominas,Georges
        The staff numbers 96 professionals

     8. Major fields: sociology, anthropology, history, geography,
        linguistics
        Specific fields: French ethnography (ethno-linguistics,
        ethno-history, etc.)

     9. Books, periodicals, "gray" literature, audio-visual materi-
        als, maps and photographs are processed

    10. The Centre has a library

    11. Holdings: books and abstract journals   11 425 vols. in total
                  periodicals   159 titles in total
                  microfilms   66
        Authors', subject (in preparation), geographical and ethnic
        (in preparation) catalogues are used

    12. The library is open to the public

    13. Information services:
        Publications
        Lending and interlibrary services
        Provision of photocopies

70   1. DOCUMENTATION SERVICES OF THE NATIONAL FOUNDATION OF POLITI-
        CAL SCIENCES

        SERVICES DE DOCUMENTATION DE LA FOUNDATION NATIONALE DES
        SCIENCES POLITIQUES

     3. 27, rue Saint-Guillaume,   75341 Paris   Cedex 07
        tel. (1) 260-39-60

     4. 1873

     5. Director: Meyriat,Jean
        The staff numbers 46 professionals and 55 non-professionals

6. Cooperation with other libraries or documentation services,
   public or private

7. Departments or activities: Main library; Specialized library
   units (political sciences, economics, undergraduate studies);
   Serials; Contemporary documentation centre; Bibliographical
   bureau; Research and development bureau; Training bureau

8. Major field: social sciences
   Specific fields: economics, political science, administrative
   science, public law, international relations, contemporary
   history, economic geography, town and country planning, sociology, demography, contemporary culture

9. Foreign books, periodicals, "gray" literature, audio-visual
   materials, maps and newspapers are processed

10. The Services have a library

11. Holdings: books   450 000 vols.
            periodicals   6 350 current titles
            abstract journals   several dozen titles
            microcopies   several hundreds
    Authors' and subject catalogues are used

12. The library is ppen to authorized persons

13. Information services:
    Publications - abstract journals, bibliographies, bibliogra-
    phical reports and lists of unpublished dissertations
    Bibliographical and literature searches
    Lending service
    Provision of photocopies and/or microforms

14. Automated information system on cataloguing of periodicals
    Hardware: CII-HB (IRIS 55)
    Software: AGAPE

15. Photocopying machine, offset, typography

16. Relations with many information units in the country and
    abroad,with several international organizations

17. Information services free of charge and against payment

71 1. GEOGRAPHICAL INFORMATION AND DOCUMENTATION LABORATORY

       C N R S - LABORATOIRE D'INFORMATION ET DE DOCUMENTATION EN
       GEOGRAPHIE

       INTERGEO

    2. Parent institution: Ministry of Universities and CNRS

    3. 191, rue Saint Jacques, 75005 Paris
       tel. 633 74 31, 329 79 93

    4. 1976 (documentation service since 1947)

5. Director: Brunet,Roger
The staff numbers 18 professionals

6. Specialized documentation centre on national level

7. Departments or activities: Bibliographical data bases; International cartographical bibliography; Information; Photographic library; Map library; Research-Education; Translations from Russian into French

8. Major fields: human and economic geography, cartography

9. Foreign books, periodicals, audio-visual materials and magnetic tapes are processed

10. The Laboratory has a library

11. Holdings: books   630 vols.
             periodicals   100 titles
             abstract journals   5 titles
             microcopies   11
             manuscripts   325

12. The library is open to the public

13. Information services:
Publications - abstract journals, bibliographies, directories and others
SDI
Translation
Bibliographical research
Compilation of documentary syntheses
Lending service
Provision of photocopies and/or microforms

14. Automated information system on geographical bibliography and SDI
Hardware: IBM
Software: FORTRAN O.S.

15. Offset, etc.

16. Relations with CNRS (France) and the International Geographical Union (IGU)

17. Information services against payment

72   1. LIBRARY OF CONTEMPORARY INTERNATIONAL DOCUMENTS
     BIBLIOTHEQUE DE DOCUMENTATION INTERNATIONALE CONTEMPORAINE
     BDIC

   2. Subordinated to the Ministry of Universities

   3. Centre Universitaire, 92001 Nanterre
      tel. 721-40-22

4. 1914

5. Director: Blum,Véronique
   The staff numbers 45 professionals and 14 non-professionals

8. Major fields: the wars of 1914-1918 and 1939-1945, international relations in 20th c., political, economic and social
   history of European countries in 20th c., Russian revolution
   and the Soviet Union (as well as the pre-revolutionary pe-
   riod), East-European countries since 1945, Germany between
   the two World Wars and national-socialism in particular, etc.

9. National and foreign books, periodicals, "gray" literature,
   microfilms, posters and photographs are processed

11. Holdings: books   400 000 vols. in total
             periodicals   40 000 vols. in total
             microcopies   561
    Methodical catalogue with own classification is used

12. The library is open to the public

13. Information services:
    Publications - bibliographies and others
    Reference services

17. Information services free of charge and against payment

73 1. LIBRARY-DOCUMENTATION-ARCHIVES DEPARTMENT - LIBRARY OF THE
       NATIONAL INSTITUTE OF STATISTICS AND ECONOMICS

       DIVISION BIBLIOTHEQUE-DOCUMENTATION-ARCHIVES. BIBLIOTHEQUE DE
       L'INSTITUT NATIONAL DE LA STATISTIQUE ET DES ETUDES ECONO-
       MIQUES

       INSEE - Division BDA

    2. Parent institution: Ministry of Finance and Economy

    3. 18, bd.Pinard, 75675 Paris Cedex 14
       tel. 540-12-12
       telex: 204924 insee

    4. 1945

    5. Director: Chevalier,Bernard
       The staff numbers 3 professionals and 9 non-professionals

    6. Complementary unit to the regional economic network (22 cen-
       tres)

    7. Departments or activities: Library; Documentation; Archives
       (in preparation)

    8. Major fields: statistics, economic studies, economic theory

    9. Foreign books, periodicals and national "gray" literature
       are processed

11. Holdings: books   200 000 vols. in total
              periodicals   12 000 vols. in total

12. The library is open to the public

13. Information services:
    Publications - abstract journals and bibliographies
    Bibliographical searches
    Reference services
    Provision of photocopies and/or microforms

74   1. NATIONAL INSTITUTE FOR DEMOGRAPHIC RESEARCH

      INSTITUT NATIONAL D'ETUDES DEMOGRAPHIQUES

      INED

   2. Subordinated to the Ministry of Labour

   3. 27, rue de Commandeur, 75675 Paris Cedex 14
      cable address: Inedemo Paris
      tel. 336 44 45

   4. 1945

   5. Director: Calot,Gérard
      The staff numbers 130 professionals

   8. Major fields: social sciences, demography, geography, etc.

   9. Foreign books, periodicals and "gray" literature are process-
      ed

  10. The Institute has a library

  11. Holdings: books   25 000 vols. in total
              periodicals   1 000 titles
              microcopies   1 000

  12. The library is open to the public

  13. Information services:
      Publications - bibliographies and others
      SDI
      Bibliographical, literature and servey data searches
      Lending and interlibrary loans services

  17. Information services free of charge

75   1. SOCIOLOGICAL RESEARCH CENTRE. LIBRARY AND DOCUMENTATION SER-
         VICE

      CENTRE D'ETUDES SOCIOLOGIQUES. BIBLIOTHEQUE ET SERVICE DE DO-
      CUMENTATION

      CES

2. Parent institution: National Centre of Scientific Research

3. 82, rue de Cardinet, 75017 Paris
   tel. 267-07-60

4. 1945

5. The staff numbers 13 (library) and 3 (information services) professionals

7. Departments or activities: Processing of books; Processing of periodicals; Documentation

8. Major field: sociology

9. Foreign books, periodicals and national "gray" literature are processed

11. Holdings: books   30 000 vols. in total
            periodicals and abstract journals   556 titles

12. The library is open to the public

13. Information services:
    Publications - abstract journals, bibliographies and others
    SDI
    Lending service
    Provision of photocopies

14. Automated information system of retrospective and current bibliography; on-line regime
    Hardware: IBM
    Software: COBOL, ASSEMBLER, PL/1, SPLEEN 2, EPOS-VIRA and SPLEEN 3

15. Photocomposer

17. Information services free of charge and against payment

German Democratic Republic

76 1. CENTRAL INSTITUTE FOR ANCIENT HISTORY AND ARCHEOLOGY, DEPART-
MENT OF INFORMATION AND LIBRARY

ZENTRALINSTITUT FÜR ALTE GESCHICHTE UND ARCHAOLOGIE, ABTEI-
LUNG INFORMATION/BIBLIOTHEK

2. Parent institution: Academy of Sciences of the GDR

3. 108 Berlin, Leipziger Str. 3-4
telex: 114426 adw dd

4. 1969

5. Director: Rechenberg,Eberhard

6. Central institution for information in this field

8. Major fields: prehistory, history of Ancient Orient, Greek-
Roman history

9. Foreign books and periodicals are processed

11. Holdings: books, periodicals, abstract journals
and microcopies   -   approx. 81 000 vols.

12. The library is open to the public

13. Information services:
Publications - bibliographies and others
Lending service

16. Relations with other information units in this field in the
country.

17. Information services against payment

77   1. CENTRAL INSTITUTE OF HISTORY, DEPARTMENT OF INFORMATION AND
         DOCUMENTATION

         ZENTRALINSTITUT FÜR GESCHICHTE, ABTEILUNG INFORMATION/DOKU-
         MENTATION

      2. Parent institution: Academy of Sciences of the GDR

      3. 108 Berlin, Clara-Zetkin Str. 26
         tel. 207 1563/21
         telex: 114426 adw dd

      4. 1956

      5. Director: Wick,Peter

      6. Central institution for information in this field

      8. Major fields: German history, foreign history (esp. 20 c.),
         methodology

      9. National and foreign books and periodicals are processed

     10. The Department has a library

     11. Holdings: books   117 147 vols.
                   periodicals   1 100 titles - 30 000 vols.
                   abstract journals   10 titles -   120 vols.
         Alphabetical catalogue is used

     12. The library is open to the public

     13. Information services:
         Publications - abstract journals and bibliographies
         SDI
         Bibliographical and literature searches
         Lending service

     16. Relations with other information units in this field in the
         country

     17. Information services against payment

78   1. CENTRAL INSTITUTE FOR INFORMATION IN THE HISTORY OF THE
         WORKING-CLASS MOVEMENT AND RESEARCH ON MARX AND ENGELS

         ZENTRALSTELLE FÜR INFORMATION UND DOKUMENTATION DER GESCHICH-
         TE DER ARBEITERBEWEGUNG UND MARX-ENGELS-FORSCHUNG

      2. Parent institution: Institute of Marxism-Leninism at the
         Central Committee of the Socialist Unity Party

      3. 1054 Berlin, Wilhelm-Pieck Str. 1
         tel. 2024221

      5. Director: Grau,Roland

      6. Central institution for information in this field

8. Major fields: history of the working-class movement and re-
    search on Marx and Engels

9. National and foreign books and periodicals are processed

10. The Institute has no library

13. Information services:
    Publications - abstract journals

15. Offset

16. Relations with other information units in this field in the
    country

17. Information services against payment

79 1. CENTRAL INSTITUTE OF JUVENILE RESEARCH, DEPARTMENT OF INFOR-
        MATION AND DOCUMENTATION

        ZENTRALSTELLE FÜR JUGENDFORSCHUNG, ABTEILUNG INFORMATION UND
        DOKUMENTATION

    2. Parent institution: Central Institute of Juvenile Research

    3. 7022 Leipzig, Stallbaumstr. 9
        tel. 55226
        telex: 512548 zij

    4. 1970

    5. Director: Bruhm-Schlegel,Uta

    6. Central institution for information in this field

    8. Major field: juvenile research

    9. National and foreign books and periodicals are processed

    13. Information services:
        Publications - bibliographies, directories and others
        SDI
        Translation
        Bibliographical and literature searches
        Compilation of documentary syntheses

    15. Offset

    16. Relations with other information units in this field in the
        country

    17. Information services against payment

80 1. CENTRE FOR INFORMATION AND DOCUMENTATION IN LIBRARIANSHIP
        ZENTRALSTELLE FÜR INFORMATION UND DOKUMENTATION BIBLIOTHEK-
        SWESEN

2. Parent institution: Central Institute for Librarianship

3. 108 Berlin, Hermann-Matern-Strasse 57
   tel. 2362863
   telex: 113247

4. 1969

5. Director: Riedel,Hans

6. Central institution for information in this field

8. Major field: librarianship

9. Foreign books and periodicals are processed

10. The Centre has a library

11. Holdings: books   approx. 35 000 vols.
    Alphabetical, systematical (UDC) and geographical (UDC) ca-
    talogues are used

12. The library is open to the public

13. Information services:
    Publications - abstract journals and bibliographies
    SDI
    Translation
    Bibliographical, literature and survey data searches
    Compilation of documentary syntheses
    Lending service
    Provision of photocopies and/or microforms

15. Offset

16. Relations with other information units in this field in the
    country

17. Information services against payment

81   1. CENTRE FOR SCIENTIFIC INFORMATION IN PHYSICAL CULTURE AND
        SPORTS
        ZENTRUM FÜR WISSENSCHAFTSINFORMATION KÖRPERKULTUR UND SPORT
        SfW

     2. Subordinated to the International Association - IASI / CIEPS

     3. 701 Leipzig, Friedrich-Ludwig-Jahn-Allee 59
        tel. 4974 411

     4. 1973

     5. Director: Thilo,Werner

     6. Central institution for information in this field

8. Specific fields: fundamental research in physical culture and sports, its organization and planning theory and metho- dology of sports

9. National and foreign books and periodicals are processed

13. Information services:
Publications - bibliographies, directories and others
SDI
Translation
Bibliographical and literature searches
Lending and references services
Provision of photocopies and/or microforms

15. Microfilm duplicating equipment, offset, photocopying machine

16. Relations with other information units in this field in the country

17. Information services against payment

82   1. CENTRE FOR SOCIAL SCIENCE INFORMATION AND DOCUMENTATION AT THE ACADEMY OF SCIENCES OF THE GDR

ZENTRALE LEITUNG FÜR GESELLSCHAFTSWISSENSCHAFTLICHE INFORMA- TION UND DOKUMENTATION BEI DER AdW DER DDR

ZIGID

2. Parent institution: Academy of Sciences of the GDR

3. 108 Berlin, Universitatstrasse 8
tel. 2070 282
telex: 114 426 adw dd

4. 1965

5. Director: Wirkner,Ernst

6. National centre for coordination and development of the so- cial science information system of the GDR

7. Departments or activities: Methodology; Organization; Auto- mation; Publication; Education and training; International relations

11. The Centre has a library

13. Information services:
Publications

16. Relations with other information units in the country and abroad, international organizations: FID, UNESCO. Member of MISON

17. Information services against payment

83   1. CENTRE FOR SOCIOLOGICAL INFORMATION AND DOCUMENTATION
         ZENTRALSTELLE FÜR SOZIOLOGISCHE INFORMATION UND DOKUMENTATION
         Zentralstelle SID

      2. Parent institution: Academy of Social Sciences at the Central
         Committee of the Socialist Unity Party

      3. 108 Berlin, Johannes-Dieckmann-Str. 19-23
         tel. 2056/220,272
         telex: 115026

      4. 1965

      5. Director: Bronizkaja,Waltrand

      6. Central institution for information in this field

      8. Major fields: theory, methodology and methods of sociology,
         sociological problems of the socialist/communist society, so-
         ciological problems of the capitalist society
         Specific fields: development of the social structure of so-
         ciety, theoretical and methodological problems of the develop-
         ment of the personality, development of the way of life

      9. Foreign books and periodicals are processed

     10. The Centre has no library

     13. Information services:
         Publications - abstract journals and bibliographies
         SDI

     16. Relations with other information units in this field in the
         country

     17. Information services against payment

84   1. DEPARTMENT OF JOURNALISM, KARL MARX UNIVERSITY, LEIPZIG
         SEKTION JOURNALISTIK DER KARL-MARX-UNIVERSITÄT LEIPZIG

      2. Subordinated to the Ministry of Higher Education

      3. 701 Leipzig, Karl-Marx-Platz 9
         tel. 7192906

      4. 1954

      5. Director: Dusiska,Emil

      6. Central coordinating office of information and documentation
         in journalism

      7. Departments or activities: six scientific units for educa-
         tion and research, with information and documentation servi-
         ces; Archives and storage of information and documentation

8. Major fields: theory and practice of journalism (theoretical
   foundations, journalistic methodology, management, planning
   and organization of the journalistic working process, stylis-
   tics of language in journalism, specialized journalistic
   fields, media specific of the press, radio and television)

9. National and foreign books and periodicals, national audio-
   visual materials, magnetic tapes and scientific papers are
   processed

10. Uses the University Library
    Own catalogue covering all publications about journalism
    since 1950. Own list of keywords (based on the MISON Rubrica-
    tor)

13. Information services:
    Publications - card index and a scientific journal
    SDI
    Translation
    Bibliographical, literature and survey data searches
    Compilation of documentary syntheses
    Lending service
    Provision of photocopies and/or microforms

15. Photocopying machines

16. Relations with other information units in the country and ab-
    road, regional and international organizations

17. Information services against payment

85 1. DEPARTMENT FOR PHILOSOPHICAL INFORMATION AND DOCUMENTATION

       ZENTRALSTELLE FÜR PHILOSOPHISCHE INFORMATION UND DOKUMENTA-
       TION

       PHID

    2. Parent institution: Academy of Social Sciences at the Cen-
       tral Committee of the Socialist Unity Party. Institute for
       Marxist-Leninist Philosophy

    3. 108 Berlin, Johannes-Dieckmann-Strasse 19-23
       tel. 2056276
       telex: 115026

    4. 1965

    5. Director: Neumann,Christian
       The staff numbers 9 professionals and 5 non-professionals

    6. Central institution for information in this field

    8. Major field: philosophy

    9. Foreign books and periodicals are processed

    10. The Department has no library

13. Information services:
    Publications - abstract journals, bibliographies and others
    SDI
    Bibliographical searches
    Compilation of documentary syntheses

14. Automated information system on bibliography in philosophy
    SDI
    Hardware: ESSR 1040
    Software: SOPS AIDOS gen.var.

15. Printing equipment

16. Relations with other information units in the country, and
    regional and international organizations.

17. Information services against payment

86 1. INSTITUTE FOR THEORY, HISTORY AND ORGANIZATION OF SCIENCE,
           DEPARTMENT OF INFORMATION, DOCUMENTATION, LIBRARY

           INSTITUT FÜR THEORIE, GESCHICHTE UND ORGANIZATION DER WISSEN-
           SCHAFT, ABTEILUNG INFORMATION, DOKUMENTATION, BIBLIOTHEK

           IDB

     2. Parent institution: Academy of Sciences of the GDR

     3. 108 Berlin, Otto-Nuschke-Str. 22-23
        tel. 2070 520
        telex: 114426 adw dd

     4. 1970

     5. Director: Meyer,Siegmar

     8. Major fields: science of science, science policy
        Specific fields: theory of science, methodology and logic
        of science, sociology and psychology of science, history of
        science, science and society, research planning, research
        teams, science and production, scientific creativity, scien-
        tific manpower, scientific information, management of re-
        search, research development

     9. Foreign books, periodicals, microfilms, microfiches and doc-
        toral dissertations are processed

    10. The Department has a library

    11. Holdings: books   5 000 titles
                  periodicals   130 titles
                  abstract journals   20 titles
                  microcopies   30
                  manuscripts   100
        Alphabetical catalogue is used

    12. The library is open to the public

13. Information services:
    Publications - bibliographies and directories
    Bibliographical searches

16. Relations with other information units in this field in the
    country

17. Information services against payment

87   1. LINGUISTIC INFORMATION AND DOCUMENTATION CENTRE OF THE GDR

      ZENTRALSTELLE FÜR SPRACHWISSENSCHAFTLICHE INFORMATION UND
      DOKUMENTATION DER DDR

      2. Parent institution: Academy of Sciences of the GDR

      3. 108 Berlin, Otto-Nuschke-Strasse 22-23
         tel. 2070 513
         telex: 114426 adw dd

      4. 1968

      5. Director: Zigmund,Hans

      6. Central institution for information in this field

      8. Major fields: general linguistics, linguistic research me-
         thods
         Specific fields: German philology, Slavonic philology, An-
         glistics, Romanistics

      9. National and foreign books and periodicals are processed

     10. The Centre has a library

     11. Holdings: books   56 000 vols.
                   periodicals   290 titles
                   abstract journals   10 titles

     12. The library is open to the public

     13. Information services:
         Publications - abstract journals, directories and others
         SDI
         Lending service
         Provision of photocopies and/or microforms

     15. Offset

     16. Relations with other information units in this field in the
         country

     17. Information services against payment

Germany, Federal Republic of

88   1. CENTRAL ARCHIVES FOR EMPIRICAL SOCIAL RESEARCH, UNIVERSITY OF
       COLOGNE

       ZENTRALARCHIV FÜR EMPIRISCHE SOZIALFORSCHUNG DER UNIVERSITÄT
       ZU KÖLN

       ZA

    2. Parent institution: University of Cologne

    3. Bachemerst. 40, 5 Köln 41
       tel. 0221-44 40 86

    4. 1960

    5. Director: Scheuch,Erwin
       The staff numbers 25 professionals and 21 non-professionals

    6. National archives for Germany, Federal Republic of

    8. Major fields: all fields of empirical social research
       Specific fields: political behaviour, consumer behaviour,
       leisure, mass communications, occupation, mobility, family,
       sports, etc.

    9. National and foreign magnetic tapes, data from empirical so-
       cial research, survey research and research project documen-
       tation are processed

   10. The Archives have a library

   11. Holdings: books   7 000 titles
           periodicals   70 vols.
       Own classification is used

   12. The library is open to the public

   13. Information services:
       Publications

    Literature searches
    Reference services
    Provision of photocopies and/or microforms

14. Survey questions and study descriptions (Z.A.R.system)
    Hardware: IBM 370/158 OS VS2/MDS 2400, DELTA, ITT, Teleray
    CRT's
    Software: IBM-ASSEMBLER, PL/1, APL-GD

15. Photocopying machine

16. Relations with the Social Sciences Information Centre, Bonn,
    and the international organizations - IFDO, CESSDA, ECSSID,
    ICPSR, CIDSS, FID, ECPR

17. Information services against payment

89 1. COMMUNICATION CENTRE FOR FUTUROLOGY AND PEACE RESEARCH OF
       HANNOVER

       KOMMUNICATIONSZENTRUM FÜR ZUKUNFTS- UND FRIEDENSFORSCHUNG IN
       HANNOVER GmbH

       ZFF

    2. Parent institution: Society of Questions of the Future, Ber-
       lin, West

    3. Glockseestrasse 33, i.Hs.Gaswerk, D-3000 Hannover 1
       tel. 0511-324488

    4. 1976

    5. Director: Schulze,Lothar
       The staff numbers 3 non-professionals

    8. Major fields: peace research, futurology

    9. National periodicals, audio-visual materials and magnetic
       tapes are processed

   10. The Centre has a library

   11. Holdings: books   600 titles
                  periodicals   1 title - 8 vols.
                  abstract journals 2 titles - 22 vols.
                  manuscripts   3
       Alphabetical catalogue and authors' index are used

   12. The library is open to the public

   13. Information services:
       Publications - abstract journals and bibliographies
       Bibliographical and literature searches
       Compilation of documentary syntheses
       Lending service
       Provision of photocopies

   14. Information retrieval system

Hardware: CYBER 76-12, 73-16
Software: FORTRAN, SCOPE 2.1

16. Relations with the Canadian Peace Research Institute

17. Information services free of charge

90 1. DOCUMENTATION CENTRE OF THE GERMAN FOUNDATION FOR INTERNA-
    TIONAL DEVELOPMENT

    DEUTSCHE STIFTUNG FÜR INTERNATIONALE ENTWICKLUNG. ZENTRALE
    DOKUMENTATION

    DSE/ZD

  2. Parent institution: German Foundation for International De-
     velopment

  3. Endenicher Str.41,   5300 Bonn 1
     tel. 02221/63 18 81
     telex: 8 86710

  4. 1961

  5. Director: von Ledebur,Ernst Joachim
     The staff numbers 29 professionals and 4 non-professionals

  6. DSE/ZD belongs to the specialized information system for fo-
     reign area studies (FIS15)

  7. Departments or activities: Systematics and methodology; Li-
     terature documentation and information; Data documentation
     and information; National and international cooperation

  8. Major fields: development aid, development policy, developing
     countries
     Specific fields: socio-economic and socio-cultural changes in
     developing countries

  9. Foreign books, periodicals and "gray" literature are process-
     ed

 10. The Centre has a library

 11. Holdings: books   15 000 titles
              periodicals   700 titles
     Authors', union authors' catalogues and geographical, subject
     indices are used

 12. The library is open to the public

 13. Information services:
     Publications - bibliographies, directories and others
     SDI
     Bibliographical and literature searches
     Reference services
     Provision of photocopies and/or microforms

16. Relations with 4 regional documentation centres affiliated
to the German Overseas Institute, Hamburg

17. Information services free of charge and against payment

91   1. FEDERAL RESEARCH INSTITUTE FOR REGIONAL GEOGRAPHY AND REGIO-
NAL PLANNING. ABSTRACT LITERATURE INFORMATION

BUNDESFORSCHUNGSANSTALT FÜR LANDESKUNDE UND RAUMORDUNG. REFE-
RAT-LITERATURINFORMATION

BfLR

2. Subordinated to the Federal Ministry of Regional Planning,
Construction and Urban Development

3. Post Box 200 130,   D-5300 Bonn 2

4. 1950

5. Director: Weber,Jost
The staff numbers 8 professionals and 8 non-professionals

6. The BfLR functions within the specialized information system
8 "Regional planning, construction and urban studies", orga-
nized by the Federal Government

8. Major fields: regional science, regional planning, town and
country planning

9. Foreign books, periodicals and national "gray" literature
are processed

10. The Institute has a library

11. Holdings: books   100 000 titles
             periodicals   600 titles
             abstract journals   40 titles
Authors', titles, institutions, geographical names and subject catalogues are used. Subjects - according to a thesaurus

12. The library is open to the public

13. Information services:
Publications - abstract journals and bibliographies
Bibliographical searches
Reference services

17. Information services against payment

92   1. GERMAN SOCIETY FOR PEACE AND CONFLICT RESEARCH

DEUTSCHE GESELLSCHAFT FÜR FRIEDENS- UND KONFLIKTFORSCHUNG e.V.

DGFK

3. Theaterplatz 28,   D-5300 Bonn 2
tel. 02221/356032

4. 1970

5. Director: Koppe,Karlheinz
   The staff numbers 3 professionals and 6 non-professionals

6. DGFK is a research promoting and supporting organization in
   the field of peace and conflict research

8. Major fields: peace and strategies of transition in Europe,
   conflict and peaceful changes in the relations between West
   European industrial states and developing countries

9. National books, periodicals and "gray" literature are processed

10. The Society has a library

11. Holdings: books   1 700 titles
             periodicals   30 titles
             abstract journals   1 title
    Alphabetical list of authors' is used

13. Information services:
    Publications
    SDI
    Literature searches
    Reference services

15. Photocopying machine

17. Information services free of charge

93 1. HIGHER EDUCATION INFORMATION SYSTEM - LIBRARY AND DOCUMENTA-
       TION SERVICE

       HOCHSCHUL - INFORMATION - SYSTEM - BIBLIOTHEK UND DOKUMENTA-
       TION

       HIS

    2. Subordinated to the central administration

    3. Goseriede 9, 3000 Hannover
       tel. 0511/19201

    4. 1969

    5. Director: Rischowsky,Franziska
       The staff numbers 1 professional and 2 non-professionals

    7. Departments or activities: Special library for higher educa-
       tion; University courses documentation

    8. Major fields: higher education planning, data processing,
       economics, methods, law
       Specific field: university planning

    9. National and foreign books, periodicals and "gray" litera-
       ture are processed

11. Holdings: books   16 000 titles
              periodicals   200 titles
              manuscripts   4 000
    Authors' and management catalogues and keyword files are used

12. The library is open to the public

13. Information services:
    Publications - bibliographies
    Bibliographical and literature searches
    Lending and reference services
    Provision of photocopies and/or microforms

15. Photocopying machine

16. Relations with other information units in the country and
    abroad

17. Information services free of charge

94   1. INSTITUTE OF EMPLOYMENT RESEARCH

         INSTITUT FÜR ARBEITSMARKT- UND BERUFSFORSCHUNG DER BUNDES-
         ANSTALT FÜR ARBEIT

         IAB

      2. Parent institution: Federal Office of Labour

      3. Regensburger Strasse 104,   8500 Nürnberg
         tel. 0911/171
         telex: 06/22348

      4. 1967

      5. Director: Mertens,Dieter
         The staff numbers 37 professionals and 45 non-professionals

      7. Departments or activities: Medium and long-term forecasting;
         Labour market short-term analysis; Sociology; Occupational
         and qualification studies; Technology and economics of enter-
         prises; Analytical statistics, econometrics, international
         labour market; Documentation and information; Coordination
         and organization, regional studies

      8. Major fields: labour market studies (flexibility, relation-
         ship with technical development, modelling, forecasting),
         branch and regional structures of economic activity, inter-
         action between economic activity and growth, professional and
         qualification studies, etc.

      9. National and foreign books and periodicals and national
         "gray" literature are processed

     10. The Institute has a library

     11. Holdings: books   20 000 titles
                   periodicals   620 titles

    abstract journals   40 000 titles
Automated system and various kinds of registers are used

12. The library is open to the public

13. Information services:
Publications - abstract journals, bibliographies and direc-
tories
SDI
Bibliographical, literature and survey data searches
Compilation of documentary syntheses
Reference services
Provision of photocopies and/or microforms

14. Hardware: SIEMENS 4000/150
Software: GOLEM and own ASSEMBLER

17. Information services free of charge and against payment

95 1. INSTITUTE FOR FOREIGN CULTURAL RELATIONS, LIBRARY AND DOCU-
MENTATION DEPARTMENT

INSTITUT FÜR AUSLANDSBEZIEHUNGEN, BIBLIOTHEK UND DOKUMENTA-
TION

IFA

2. Subordinated to the Public Law Administration

3. Charlottenplatz 17, D 7000 Stuttgart 1
tel. 0711/221766/221760
telex: 07-23772

4. 1917

5. Director: Kuhn,Gertrud
The staff numbers 13 professionals and 3 non-professionals

6. The Library and Documentation Department serves as a special
library for foreign studies

7. Departments or activities: Library; Documentation

8. Major fields: Asian, African and Latin American studies, foreign cultural policy, foreign cultural relations, psychology of culture and of peoples, problems of development and
educational aid, history of emigration and Germans abroad,
demography and minorities' problems, German language abroad,
press issued abroad in German

9. Foreign books, periodicals, "gray" literature and audio-visual materials are processed

11. Holdings: books   265 000 vols.
             periodicals   4 900 titles
             microfilms   2 644
Alphabetical, systematical, personal data, union editors',

EGSSI - D

authors', etc. catalogues are used

12. The library is open to the public

13. Information services:
    Publications - bibliographies, directories and others
    Bibliographical and literature searches
    Lending service
    Provision of photocopies and/or microforms

15. Reader-printer, photocopying machine

16. Relations with organizations for foreign cultural policy,
    cultural institutions in Germany, Federal Republic of

17. Information services free of charge

96   1. LIBRARY OF THE FEDERAL WORKING SOCIETY FOR REHABILITATION
         BÜCHEREI DER BUNDESARBEITSGEMEINSCHAFT FÜR REHABILITATION

   3. Eysseneckstrasse 55,   6000 Frankfurt am Main 1
      tel. 0611/15221
      telex: 0412536

   4. 1969

   5. Directors: Berger,Rolf and Stroebel,Hubertus
      The staff numbers 17 professionals

   7. Abstracts and subject fields establishment

   8. Major fields: coordination of professional and social reha-
      bilitation, etc.

   9. Some national newspaper articles are processed

  11. Holdings: books   150 titles
               periodicals   50-60 titles

  12. The library is not open to the public

  13. Information services:
      Publications - directories and others
      Translation
      Compilation of documentary syntheses
      Reference services
      Provision of photocopies and/or microforms

  15. Printing and photocopying machines

  16. Relations with the National Association of the Handicapped,
      The Rehabilitation International, New York and the Interna-
      tional Union of Social Welfare, Geneva

  17. Information services free of charge

97   1. SOCIAL SCIENCES INFORMATION CENTRE

     INFORMATIONSZENTRUM SOZIALWISSENSCHAFTEN

     2. Parent institution: Association of Social Sciences Institutes

     3. Lennestrasse 30,   D-5300 Bonn 1
        tel. 02221 - 22 30 21

     4. 1969

     5. Director: Hagena,Jörg
        The staff numbers 53 professionals and non-professionals

     6. The Centre is a focal point of the specialized information
        system for social sciences

     7. Departments or activities: Management, marketing; Coordina-
        tion/infrastructure; Information acquisition; Information
        processing and indexing; Information service/public rela-
        tions; Electronic data processing

     8. Major fields: sociology, political sciences, mass communica-
        tions, psychology, social policy, industrial safety, labour
        problems
        Specific fields: leisure, social medicine, environment

     9. Literature, on-going research, numerical data, facts, compu-
        ter software in social sciences are processed

    10. The Centre has a library

    12. The library is not open to the public

    13. Information services:
        Publications - abstract journals, bibliographies and others
        SDI
        Bibliographical, literature and survey data searches
        Compilation of documentary syntheses
        Provision of photocopies and/or microforms

    14. On-line searches on social sciences in the broadest sense
        Hardware: SIEMENS 4004-151
        Software: GOLEM 2

    15. Magnetic tapes and photo-typing facilities

    16. Relations with the Working Group for Documentation in the
        Social Sciences

    17. Information services against payment

Greece

98 1. ATHENS CENTRE OF SETTLEMENT SYSTEMS
ATHENAIKO KENTRO OIKISTIKES. BIBLIOTHEKI
ACE

2. Parent institution: Athens Technological Organization

3. 24 Stratiotikou Syndesmou, P.O.Box 471
cable address: Atinst I
tel. 3623901/248

4. 1964

5. Director: Rooke, Rodney
The staff numbers 3 professionals

8. Major fields: sociology, statistics, economics, anthropology,
civil engineering, management, town and regional planning,
geography, history, etc.
Specific fields: anthropology, settlement systems, their future and impact on environment

9. Foreign books, periodicals, audio-visual materials, magnetic
tapes, maps are processed

10. The Centre has a library

11. Holdings: books   21 000 vols. in total
            periodicals   1 200 titles
            microcopies   490 in total
Dictionary catalogue is used

12. The library is open to the public

13. Information services:
Publications
SDI
Bibliographical searches

Compilation of documentary syntheses
Lending service
Provision of photocopies and/or microforms

17. Information services free of charge

99 1. LIBRARY AT THE NATIONAL CENTRE OF SOCIAL RESEARCH
       ETHNIKO KENTRO KOINONIKON EREYNON. BIBLIOTHEKI
       EKKE

    2. Parent institution: National Centre of Social Research

    3. 1 Sophocleous Str.
       Athens 22
       tel. 32.12.612

    4. 1959

    5. Director: Chryssanthopoulou,Zoe
       The staff numbers 4 professionals

    7. Departments or activities: Acquiring, processing, lending of
       materials; Assisting users (inquiries, literature and biblio-
       graphic searches); Preparing bibliographies and other library
       publications

    8. Major fields: social sciences, anthropology, history, psycho-
       logy, political sciences
       Specific fields: women, children, migration, social anthropo-
       logy, industrialization, social, economic, political condi-
       tions in Greece

    9. National and foreign books, periodicals, "gray" literature
       and national maps are processed

   11. Holdings: books   22 000 titles
                  periodicals   500 titles
                  abstract journals   6 titles
       Card catalogues are used

   12. The library is open to the public

   13. Information services:
       Publications - bibliographies and others
       Bibliographical and literature searches
       Lending service
       Provision of photocopies and/or microforms

   15. Mimeograph machine, offset

   16. Relations with other units in the country and abroad.

   17. Information services free of charge

100   1. LIBRARY AT THE PANHELLENIC CONFEDERATION OF UNIONS OF AGRI-
         CULTURAL COOPERATIVES

         PANELLENIOS SYNOMOSPONDIA ENOSEON GEORGIKON SYNETARISMON,
         BIBLIOTHEKI

         PASEGES

      2. Parent institution: Panhellenic Confederation of Unions of
         Agricultural Cooperatives

      3. 56 El.Venizelou Str., Athens 142
         Cable address: Paseges
         tel. 36.08.824 and 36.03.617
         telex: 21 4383 pase gr

      4. 1977

      5. Director: Moroni,Constance
         The staff numbers 1 professional

      7. Departments or activities: Documentation and international
         relations; Library

      8. Major fields: agricultural production, economic development,
         agricultural cooperatives, agricultural economics
         Specific fields: agricultural production development in
         Greece, EEC and worldwide, social and economic conditions of
         agricultural workers, agriculture and the state, education
         and training for better production management, laws and le-
         gislation, cooperation as an idea

      9. National and foreign books and periodicals are processed

     11. Holdings: books   3 800 titles
                   periodicals   160 titles
         Alphabetical card and subject catalogues, etc. are used

     12. The library is not open to the public

     13. Information services:
         Publications - bibliographies
         Lending and reference services
         Provision of photocopies and/or microforms

     15. Duplicating machines

     17. Information services free of charge

101   1. LIBRARY OF THE SCHOOL OF SOCIAL WORK - FOUNDATION FOR THE
         DEVELOPMENT OF SOCIAL WORK

         BIBLIOTHEKI ANOTERAS SXOLES KOINONIKES ERGASIAS - IDRUMA
         ANAPTUXEOS KOINONIKES ERGASIAS

         IAKE

      2. Parent institution: Foundation for the Development of Social
         Work

3. Xenofondos 15 A,   Athens
   tel. 32 36 407

4. 1965

5. Director: Hadjipoulou,Elga
   The staff numbers 1 professional

7. Departments or activities: Acquisition and processing of
   publications; Lending to students and staff of school; Pre-
   paring bibliographies for students and staff; Assisting users

8. Major fields: social work, sociology, psychology, literature,
   etc.
   Specific fields: social case work, social group work, social
   work with specific groups: mentally retarded, deaf and mute,
   physically handicapped, criminals, etc.

9. National and foreign books and periodicals are processed

11. Holdings: books   4 000 titles
              periodicals   5 titles
              abstract journals   1 title
    Dictionary card catalogue is used

12. The library is open to the public

13. Information services:
    Publications - bibliographies
    Bibliographical searches
    Lending service

16. Relations with EKKE, National Research Foundation of Greece,
    Athens College Library in the country and Demos Foundation -
    USA

17. Information services free of charge

102   1. NATIONAL STATISTICAL SERVICE OF GREECE - PUBLICATIONS AND
         INFORMATION DIVISION - LIBRARY

         ETHNIKI STATISTIKI IPIRESIA TIS ELLADOS - DIEFTHINSI DIMO-
         SIEFSEON KE PLIROFORION - BIBLIOTHEKI

      2. Parent institution: National Statistical Service of Greece

      3. 14-16, Lykourgou Str.,   Athens
         tel. 32 48 512/262
         telex: 6734 esye

      4. 1956

      5. Director: Ghevetsis,M.
         The staff numbers 4 professionals

      6. Official national information of statistics

7. Departments or activities: Statistical theses; Statistical publications from international institutions and foreign countries; Greek statistical publications; Statistical information

8. Major fields: statistical theory, statistical data

9. National and foreign books, periodicals and national magnetic tapes are processed

11. Holdings: books   23 000 titles
              periodicals   40 titles
              abstract journals   50 titles - 6 000 vols.
    OECD-catalogue is used

12. The library is open to the public

13. Information services:
    Publications - abstract journals and bibliographies
    Translation
    Lending and reference services
    Provision of photocopies and/or microforms

15. National printing house, offset

16. Relations with information units in the country, individual organizations abroad and international organizations, participates in SSID systems

17. Information services free of charge and against payment

Hungary

103   1. CENTRAL LIBRARY OF THE K.MARX UNIVERSITY OF ECONOMIC SCIEN-
       CES
       MARX KÁROLY KÖZGAZDASÁGTUDOMÁNYI EGYETEM KÖZPONTI KÖNYVTÁRA

      2. Parent institution: K.Marx University of Economic Sciences

      3. 1093 Budapest, Dimitrov tér 8, 1828 BP.5. Pf.489

      4. 1948

      5. Director: Walleshausen,Gyula
        The staff numbers 18 professionals and 46 non-professionals

      6. The library participates in the national information system
        on social sciences

      8. Major fields: social sciences, economics, research on the
        characteristics of the socialist enterprise

      9. Foreign books, periodicals and "gray" literature are pro-
        cessed

     11. Holdings: books   421 473 vols.
               periodicals   439 vols.
               "gray" literature   12 000 vols.

     12. The library is open to the public

     13. Information services:
        Publications - abstract journals, bibliographies and others
        SDI
        Compilation of documentary syntheses
        Provision of photocopies and/or microforms

     16. Information services free of charge and against payment

104   1. CENTRAL LIBRARY AND MUSEUM OF EDUCATION
         ORSZÁGOS PEDAGÓGIAI KÖNYVTÁR ÉS MUZEUM
         OPKM

      2. Parent institution: Ministry of Education

      3. 1363 Budapest, Honvéd u. 19 Pf 49
         tel. 126-862

      4. 1877, reorganized in 1958

      5. Director: Arató,Ferenc
         The staff numbers 51 professionals and 25 non-professionals

      6. National centre of educational information

      8. Major field: education
         Specific fields: educational psychology, educational socio-
         logy, educational statistics

      9. Foreign books, periodicals and "gray" literature are pro-
         cessed

     11. Holdings: books   280 316 vols.
                   periodicals   84 792 vols.
                   "gray" literature 5 100 copies
                   translations   41 965

     12. The library is open to the public

     13. Information services:
         Publications
         SDI
         Translation
         Bibliographical and survey data searches
         Compilation of documentary syntheses
         Lending service
         Provision of photocopies

     16. Relations with EDICO (designing educational information sys-
         tems), UNESCO

     17. Information services free of charge and against payment

105   1. ECONOMIC INFORMATION UNIT, HUNGARIAN ACADEMY OF SCIENCES
         MTA KÖZGAZDASÁGI INFORMÁCIOS CSOPORT
         MTA KICS

      2. Parent institution: Hungarian Academy of Sciences

      3. H-1112 Budapest, Budaörsi u.45
         tel. 850-878

      4. 1973

5. Director: Földi,Tamás
   The staff numbers 6 professionals and 6 non-professionals

8. Major fields: economics and international economic relations,
   economic and foreign economic policy of foreign countries
   Specific fields: world economy, economy of the socialist
   countries, East-West economic relations, economy of the de-
   veloped capitalist countries

11. Holdings: books, periodicals, reports

13. Information services:
    Publications - bibliographies and others
    Translation
    Compilation of documentary syntheses

16. Relations with the Institute of Economics of the Hungarian
    Academy of Sciences concerning professional, technical and
    management cooperation. Cooperation with the International
    Institute of Economic Problems of the Socialist System, Mos-
    cow

17. Information services free of charge

106   1. HUNGARIAN CENTRAL TECHNICAL LIBRARY AND DOCUMENTATION CENTRE
         ORSZÁGOS MÜSZAKI KÖNYVTÁR ÉS DOKUMENTÁCIOS KÖZPONT
         OMKDK

      3. H-1428 Budapest, P.O.B. 12   Reviczky u.6
         tel. 336-309
         telex: 22-4944 omkdk h

      4. 1883

      5. Director: Lázár,Péter
         The staff numbers 140 professionals and 284 non-professio-
         nals

      6. National information centre for science and technology

      8. Major fields: science and technology, applied economics

      9. Foreign books, periodicals, audio-visual materials and mag-
         netic tapes are processed

     11. Holdings: books   300 000 vols.
                   periodicals   5 900 titles - 223 000 vols.
                   abstract journals   850
                   microcopies   51 000
                   translations   527 000

     12. The library is open to the public

     13. Information services:
         Publications
         SDI

    Translation
    Bibliographical searches
    Compilation of documentary syntheses
    Lending service
    Provision of photocopies

14. SDI services in nuclear sciences (INIS); physics, electronics, etc. (INSPEC); engineering (COMPENDEX)
    Hardware: R 20
    Software: own

16. Relations with national social science information system and network of technical libraries, with information centres and libraries and the International Scientific and Technical Information Centre of the CMEA member-countries; UNIDO, IAEA, UNESCO/UNISIST, OECD Development Centre, etc., IDRC, SID, etc.

17. Information services against payment

107   1. INSTITUTE OF ECONOMICS AT THE HUNGARIAN ACADEMY OF SCIENCES, LIBRARY AND DOCUMENTATION
      MTA KÖZGAZDASÁGTUDOMÁNYI INTÉZETE, KÖNYVTÁR ÉS DOKUMENTÁCIÓ

2. Parent institution: Institute of Economics at the Hungarian Academy of Sciences

3. 1112 Budapest, Budaörsi u.43-45
    tel. 850-777

4. 1955

5. Director: Szalay,Sándor
    The staff numbers 10 professionals and 5 non-professionals

8. Major fields: economics, political economy, economic policy
    Specific fields: economic mechanism, control theory of economic growth, standard of living, economic integration, foreign trade, agricultural economics

9. Foreign books, periodicals and "gray" literature are processed

11. Holdings: books   15 000 vols.
          periodicals   12 000 vols.

12. The library is open to research workers

13. Information services:
    SDI
    Bibliographical searches
    Lending and reference services
    Provision of photocopies

17. Information services free of charge

108   1. LIBRARY AND DOCUMENTATION SERVICE OF THE CENTRAL STATISTICAL
         OFFICE
         KÖZPONTI STATISZTIKAI HIVATAL KÖNYVTÁR ÉS DOKUMENTÁCIÓS
         SZOLGÁLAT
         KSH KÖNYVTÁRA

      2. Parent institution: Central Statistical Office

      3. Budapest II, Keleti Károly u.5
         H-1525 Budapest Pf.10

      4. 1871

      5. Director: Dányi, Dozsö
         The staff numbers 18 professionals and 95 non-professionals

      8. Major field: statistics
         Specific fields: population, demography, sociology

      9. Foreign books, periodicals and "gray" literature are pro-
         cessed

     11. Holdings: books   377 765 vols.
                   periodicals   55 773 vols.
                   reports   4 852

     12. The library is open to the public

     13. Information services:
         Publications
         SDI
         Compilation of documentary syntheses
         Provision of photocopies and/or microforms

     17. Information services free of charge

109   1. LIBRARY OF THE ETHNOGRAPHICAL MUSEUM
         NÉPRAJZI MUZEUM KÖNYVTÁRA

      2. Parent institution: Ethnographical Museum

      3. 1055 Budapest, Kossuth Lajos tér 12
         tel. 326-340

      4. 1872

      5. Director: Lay,Anna
         The staff numbers 5 professionals and 1 non-professional

      8. Major field: ethnography

      9. Foreign books, periodicals and audio-visual materials are
         processed

     11. Holdings: books   48 743 vols.

                periodicals   62 782 vols.
                films and microfilms   1 115

    12. The library is open to research workers

    13. Information services:
        Lending service

    17. Information services free of charge

110. 1. LIBRARY OF THE HUNGARIAN ACADEMY OF SCIENCES
         MAGYAR TUDOMÁNYOS AKADÉMIA KÖNYVTÁRA
         MTAK

      2. Parent institution: Hungarian Academy of Sciences

      3. H-1361 Budapest, P.O.B. 7 V.Akadémia u.2
         tel. 112-400
         telex: 224132

      4. 1826

      5. Director: Rózsa,György
         The staff numbers 83 professionals and 60 non-professionals

      8. Major fields: humanities and social sciences
         Specific fields: linguistics, literary studies, classical
         studies, oriental studies, science policy and research orga-
         nization, publications of foreign academies, general prob-
         lems on social sciences, etc.

     11. Holdings: books   836 169 vols.
                   periodicals   221 051 vols.
                   manuscripts   411 632
                   microfilms   17 419

     12. The library is open to research workers

     13. Information services:
         Publications
         SDI
         Bibliographical searches
         Compilation of documentary syntheses
         Lending service
         Provision of xerocopies and photocopies

     14. Sciences, life sciences and overlapping social sciences -
         Science Citation Index machine readable data base
         Hardware: IBM/370 and 3031 computer
         Software: of the Institute for Scientific Information (Phi-
         ladelphia) ASCA

     16. Relations with National Centre of Scientific Research, Docu-
         mentation Centre for Humanities and Social Sciences, Paris
         (CNRS-CDSH). Member of MISON

     17. Information services free of charge and against payment

111   1. LIBRARY OF THE HUNGARIAN PARLIAMENT
          ORSZÁGGYÜLESI KÖNYVTÁR

       3. 1357 Budapest, V. Kossuth Lajos tér.1-3

          tel. 120-600

       4. 1849

       5. Director: Vályi,Gábor
          The staff numbers 42 professionals and 40 non-professionals

       6. National information centre for politics and legal and ad-
          ministrative sciences

       8. Major field: political sciences
          Specific fields: law, politics, contemporary history, inter-
          national relations

      11. Holdings: books   500 000 vols.
                    periodicals   450 000 vols.

      12. The library is open to the public

      13. Information services:
          Publications - bibliographies and others
          SDI
          Translation
          Bibliographical searches
          Compilation of documentary syntheses
          Reference services
          Provision of photocopies

      14. Card service and KWIC indices on world politics
          Hardware: R 20
          Software: own system

      16. Relations with UN and UNESCO (deposit)

      17. Information services free of charge and against payment

112   1. LIBRARY OF THE INSTITUTE OF INDUSTRIAL ECONOMICS AT THE
          HUNGARIAN ACADEMY OF SCIENCES
          MTA IPARGAZDASÁGTANI KUTATÓCSOPORT KÖNYVTÁRA

       2. Parent institution: Institute of Industrial Economics at
          the Hungarian Academy of Sciences

       3. 1112 Budapest, Budaörsi u.43-45
          tel. 850-777

       4. 1962

       5. Director: Vas,G.

       8. Major field: industrial economics

11. Holdings: books   3 500 vols.
             periodicals   120 titles

12. The library is open to research workers

113   1. LIBRARY OF THE INSTITUTE FOR LEGAL AND ADMINISTRATIVE SCIEN-
          CES
          MTA ÁLLAM - ÉS YOGTUDOMÁNYI INTÉZETÉNEK KÖNYVTÁRA

       2. Parent institution: Institute for Legal and Administative
          Sciences at the Hungarian Academy of Sciences

       3. H-1250 Budapest, P.O.B. 25, I.Országház u. 30

       4. 1950

       5. Director: Kürtös,Lelle
          The staff numbers 4 professionals and 2 non-professionals

       9. Foreign books and periodicals are processed

      13. Information services:
          Publications - bibliographies and others
          Compilation of documentary syntheses

      17. Information services free of charge

114   1. LIBRARY OF THE INSTITUTE FOR PSYCHOLOGY AT THE HUNGARIAN
          ACADEMY OF SCIENCES
          MTA PSZICHOLÓGIAI INTÉZETÉNEK KÖNYVTÁRA

       2. Parent institution: Institute for Psychology at the Hunga-
          rian Academy of Sciences

       3. 1051 Budapest V, Münnich F. u.7

       4. 1902

       5. Director: Gerö,Ágnes
          The staff numbers 1 professional and 1 non-professional

       6. The library is included in the system of libraries of the
          research institutes at the Hungarian Academy of Sciences

       8. Major field: psychology
          Specific fields: general and comparative psychology, psy-
          chology, development psychology, social psychology, educa-
          tional psychology, psychology of organizations

      11. Holdings: books   9 304 vols.
                  periodicals   1 150 vols.
                  translations, reprints and manuscripts

12. The library is open to research workers

13. Information services:
    Publications - bibliographies and others
    SDI
    Provision of photocopies and/or microforms

17. Information services free of charge

115   1. LIBRARY OF THE NATIONAL MANAGEMENT DEVELOPMENT CENTRE
          ORSZÁGOS VEZETÖKÉPZÖ KÖZPONT KÖNYVTÁRA

       2. Parent institution: Ministry of Labour

       3. Könyves Kálmán krt. 48-52, 1476 Budapest VIII
          tel. 344-500
          telex: 22-4221

       4. 1965

       5. Director: Majoros,Katalin
          The staff numbers 8 professionals and 6 non-professionals

       8. Major fields: management science, management development
          Specific fields: psychology, sociology, economics

      11. Holdings: books   15 376 vols.
                    periodicals   526 vols.
                    reports   512
                    translations   5 982
                    magnetic tapes

      13. Information services:
          Publications - bibliographies and others
          SDI
          Provision of photocopies and/or microforms

      14. Document processing is computerized
          Hardware: ICL 1905/E
          Software: own system

      17. Information services free of charge

116   1. MUNICIPAL LIBRARY ERVIN SZABÓ
          FÖVÁROSI SZABÓ ERVIN KÖNYVTÁR

          FSZEK

       3. H-1088 Budapest, Szabó E. tér 1
          1371 Budapest, Pf.487
          tel. 330-580

       4. 1904

5. Director: Révész,Ferenc
   The staff numbers 104 professionals and 146 non-professionals

6. The library is part of the Hungarian social sciences information system

8. Major field: sociology
   Specific fields: Budapestiniensa, musicology, literary cri-
   ticism, general problems of social sciences

11. Holdings: books   405 869 vols.
            periodicals   72 855 vols.
            films   166
            small printed materials   309 418

12. The library is open to the public

13. Information services:
    Publications - bibliographies and others
    SDI
    Compilation of documentary syntheses
    Provision of photocopies and/or microforms

17. Information services free of charge

117   1. REFERENCE LIBRARY OF THE NATIONAL BANK OF HUNGARY
          MAGYAR NEMZETI BANK SZAKKÖNYVTÁRA

       2. Parent institution: National Bank of Hungary

       3. H-1850 Budapest, Szabadság tér 5-6
          tel. 112-600, 323-320

       4. 1924

       5. Director: Romhányi,J.
          The staff numbers 3 professionals and 2 non-professionals

       8. Major fields: world economics, economics, finance
          Specific fields: money, banking, credit, monetary economics

       9. National and foreign books and periodicals are processed

      12. The library is open to the public

      13. Information services:
          Publications - bibliographies and others
          SDI
          Translation
          Bibliographical searches
          Lending service
          Provision of photocopies

      17. Information services free of charge

118   1. SCIENTIFIC INFORMATION SERVICE. INSTITUTE FOR WORLD ECONO-
          MICS AT THE HUNGARIAN ACADEMY OF SCIENCES
          MTA VILÁGGAZDASÁGI KUTATÓINTÉZETE, TUDOMÁNYOS TÁJÉKOZTATÓ
          SZOLGÁLAT

       2. Parent institution: Institute for World Economics at the
          Hungarian Academy of Sciences

       3. Budapest XII, Kálló esperes utca 15
          H-1531 Budapest, P.O.Box 35

       4. 1970

       5. Director: Felvinczi,Tamás
          The staff numbers 6 professionals and 9 non-professionals

       8. Major field: economics

       9. Books, periodicals and "gray" literature are processed

      10. The Service has a library

      11. Holdings: books   27 000 vols.
                    periodicals   800 vols.
                    reports, etc.   9 000

      12. The library is open to the public

      13. Information services:
          Publications - abstract journals and others
          SDI
          Compilation of documentary syntheses
          Provision of photocopies

      16. Relations with the network of the Library of the Hungarian
          Academy of Sciences

      17. Information services free of charge

Italy

119 1. DOCUMENTATION CENTRE ON INTERNATIONAL ORGANIZATIONS AND
        EUROPEAN COMMUNITIES

        CENTRO DI DOCUMENTAZIONE SULLE ORGANIZZAZIONI INTERNAZIONALI
        E LE COMUNITA'EUROPEE

        CEDOC

     2. Parent institution: Centre for Analysis on International Re-
        lations (CARI)

     3. Via della Scala, 87 - Palazzo degli Orti Oricellari
        50123 Firenze
        tel. 21-99-23
        telex: 572072 center I

     4. 1977

     5. Directors: Onori,Orio and Gori,Umberto
        The staff numbers 3 professionals and 4 non-professionals

     7. Departments or activities: European events; International
        commerce; International documents

     8. Major field: international relations
        Specific fields: data bank of European events, data bank of
        imports from Arab countries and Africa, data bank on inter-
        national organizations' documents

     9. Foreign books, periodicals and documents released by inter-
        national organizations are processed

    10. The Centre has a reference library only

    11. Computerized catalogue system is used

    12. The library is not open to the public

    13. Information services:

Bibliographical literature and survey data searches
Compilation of documentary syntheses
Reference services
Provision of photocopies and/or microforms

14. Data bank of international documents - import-export, Euro-
pean events
Hardware: IBM 370/145 and videodisplay unit
Software: DOS/VS, CICS, STAIRS

17. Information services against payment

120   1. GIANGIACOMO FELTRINELLI FOUNDATION

FONDAZIONE GIANGIACOMO FELTRINELLI

3. 20121 Milano, Via Romagnosi 3
tel. 02/874175, 02/803911

4. 1949

5. Director: Bo,Giuseppe del
The staff numbers 15 professionals

7. Departments or activities: Library archives; Current periodicals; Special collections; Research activities; Seminars;
Lectures

8. Major fields: history, economics, sociology, politics
Specific fields: history of labour movement and history of
socialism, communism

9. National and foreign books, periodicals, "gray" literature
and magnetic tapes are processed

10. The Foundation has a library

11. Holdings: books   400 000 vols. in total
periodicals   20 000 vols. in total
abstract jornals, microcopies and manuscripts
Alphabetical, topographical and systematical catalogues are
used

12. The library is open to the public

13. Information services:
Publications - bibliographies, directories and others
Bibliographical, literature and data survey searches
Compilation of documentation syntheses
Provision of photocopies and/or microforms

15. Photocopying machine

121   1. INSTITUTE OF SOCIOLOGY
ISTITUTO DI SOCIOLOGIA

2. Subordinated to the University of Bologna

3. Belle Arti 42, Bologna
   tel. 278839, 233380

4. 1964

5. Director: Guidicini,Paolo
   The staff numbers 60 professionals and 5 non-professionals

8. Major fields: sociology, anthropology, criminology, psychology

9. National and foreign books, periodicals and "gray" literature are processed

10. The Institute has a library

11. Holdings: books   11 500 vols. in total
             periodicals   120 vols. in total
             abstract journals   2 000 vols. in total
    Subject and authors' indices are used

12. The library is open to the public

13. Information services:
    Publications
    Translation
    Bibliographical searches
    Lending service

15. Cyclostyle and others

122   1. INSTITUTE OF STUDIES ON RESEARCH AND SCIENTIFIC DOCUMENTA-
         TION

         ISTITUTO DI STUDI SULLA RICERCA E DOCUMENTAZIONE SCIENTIFI-
         CA

         CNR

      2. Parent institution: National Council of Research. CNR
         Subordinated to the central administration

      3. Via Cesare de Lollis, 12 Roma
         tel. 06-4952351
         telex: 61076 coricerc

      4. 1968

      5. Director: Bisogno,Paolo
         The staff numbers 27 professionals and 11 non-professionals

      8. Major fields: scientific policy, studies on documentation
         and informatics
         Specific fields: science sociology, science philosophy,
         science statistics, science planning, science instruction,

science documentation, techniques and methodology

9. National and foreign books, periodicals and "gray" literature are processed

10. The Institute has a library

11. Holdings: books   5 000 vols. in total
              periodicals   300 vols. in total
              manuscripts and "gray" literature 700 in total
    Automated catalogues are used

12. The library is open to the public

13. Information services:
    Bibliographical searches
    Lending service
    Provision of photocopies

14. Automated catalogues
    Hardware: IBM 370/158
    Software: COBOL/OS

15. Photocopying machine

17. Information services free of charge

123   1. ITALIAN COUNCIL FOR SOCIAL SCIENCES
         CONSIGLIO ITALIANO PER LE SCIENZE SOCIALI
         CSS

      3. Viale Mazzini, 88,   00192 Roma 00195
         tel. 312951

      4. 1974

      5. Director: Coddetta,Romano
         The staff numbers 2 professionals and 2 non-professionals

      8. Major fields: education, information, scientific research
         policy, policy of professional orientation

     10. The Council has a library

     11. Holdings: books   3 100 vols.
                   periodicals   200 vols.
                   abstract journals   5 vols.
         Authors' and subject indices (own classification) are used

     13. Information services:
         Publications
         SDI
         Translation
         Bibliographical searches
         Reference service

Provision of photocopies and/or microforms

15. Photocopying machine

17. Information services free of charge and against payment

Netherlands

124 1. DOCUMENTATION CENTRE OF THE ECONOMIC INFORMATION SERVICE
CENTRALE DOCUMENTATIE VAN DE ECONOMISCHE VOORLICHTINGSDIENST

2. Parent institution: Economic Information Service
Subordinated to the Ministry of Economic Affairs

3. Bezuidenhoutseweg 151, 2509 LK The Hague
cable address: Econinf
tel. 070-814111
telex: 310099

4. 1907

5. Director: Schultz,J.
The staff numbers 26 professionals and 25 non-professionals

6. Main specialized library in applied economics (foreign mar-
kets), main documentation service in applied and theoretical
economics

7. Departments or activities: General literature documentation;
Branch documentation; Literature information and research;
Administration; Reprography and computer input preparation

8. Major fields: business and economics
Specific fields: trade, industry, marketing, management
sciences, development problems, economic theory, economic
geography

9. Foreign books, periodicals and "gray" literature are processed

10. The Centre has a library

11. Holdings: books (incl. 2000 directories)   90 000 vols. in total
periodicals and abstract journals 1 800 vols. in total
COM-microfiche (UDC based) subject, conventional cards authors'
catalogues, bibliographical data base for additional cata-

logue-type searching, and list of directories are used

12. The library is open to the public

13. Information services:
    Publications - abstract journals and bibliographies
    SDI
    Bibliographical and literature searches
    Lending and reference services
    Provision of photocopies and/or microforms

14. Automated information system for storage and retrieval.
    Bibliographical data base covering the complete general do-
    cumentation since 1974
    Currently this file is available via LOCKHEED/DIALOG
    Hardware: IBM/360 host computer, IBM terminal
    Software: STAIRS

15. Computer-output on microfilm (COM), reprography machines,
    microfilm machines, offset, etc.

16. Membership in ETPO (European Trade Promotion Organization)
    Relations with informal groups of users of EVD services and
    materials

17. Information services free of charge

125 1. DOCUMENTATION AND LIBRARY DEPARTMENT AT THE MINISTRY OF CUL-
        TURAL AFFAIRS, RECREATION AND SOCIAL WELFARE

        MINISTERIE VAN CULTUUR, RECREATIE EN MAATSCHAPPELIJK WERK/
        AFD. DOCUMENTATIE EN BIBLIOTHEEK

        CRM/Doc

     3. P.O.B. Postbus 5406-Steenvoordelaan 370-2280
        HK RIJSWIJK The Hague
        cable address: Curema
        tel. 070-949393/949233
        telex: 31680

     4. 1952

     5. Director: Schakel,Antonius
        The staff numbers 20 professionals and 3 non-professionals

     6. Focal point in the field of policies on cultural affairs,
        recreation and social welfare

     7. Departments or activities: Documentation; Library

     8. Major fields: cultural affairs, nature conservation, recrea-
        tion, social welfare, general social assistance, war victims
        assistance
        Specific fields: comparative studies on sociology, pedago-
        gics, social history, copyright, administration management,
        official publications of UN, UNESCO, Council of European Com-

munity regarding the above fields

9. National and foreign books, periodicals, "gray" literature
   and official publications are processed

11. Holdings: books   35 000 titles
             periodicals   1 000 titles
             abstract journals   25 titles
    Alphabetical and systematical catalogues are used

12. The library is open to the public

13. Information services:
    Publications - abstract journals and others
    SDI
    Bibliographical and literature searches
    Compilation of documentary syntheses
    Lending and reference services
    Division of photocopies and/or microfilms

15. Printing machine, offset, photocopying machine

16. Relations with FOBID and others in the country and FID,
    IFLA abroad

17. Information services free of charge

126   1. DOCUMENTATION OFFICE FOR EAST EUROPEAN LAW
         DOCUMENTATIEBUREAU VOOR OOSTEUROPEES RECHT
         DBOER

      2. Subordinated to the University of Leyden, Law Faculty

      3. Hugo de Grootstraat 32, 2311 XK Leyden
         tel. 071-149641/420

      4. 1953

      5. Director: Feldbrugge,F.
         The staff numbers 5 professionals and 3 part-time non-pro-
         fessionals

      8. Major fields: law of East European countries (Poland, Cze-
         choslovakia, German Democratic Republic, Hungary, Yugosla-
         via, Romania and Bulgaria) and the Soviet Union

      9. Foreign books, periodicals and microfiches are processed

     10. The Office has a library

     11. Holdings: books, periodicals and
                   abstract journals   21 000 vols. in total
                   microcopies   8 500 in total
         Alphabetical authors', title and systematical catalogues
         (based on UDC) are used

12. The library is open to the public

13. Information services:
    Publications - bibliographies and others
    Translation
    Bibliographical and literature searches
    Lending service
    Provision of photocopies

15. Photocopying machine, offset, printing

17. Information services free of charge and against payment

127   1. INFORMATION AND DOCUMENTATION CENTRE FOR GEOGRAPHY OF THE
          NETHERLANDS

          INFORMATIE - EN DOCUMENTATIE - CENTRUM VOOR DE GEOGRAFIE VAN
          NEDERLAND

          IDG

       2. Subordinated to the Ministry of Education

       3. Heidelberglaan 2, Utrecht
          (Geographical Institute of the State University)
          tel. (0)30-531378

       4. 1964

       5. Director: Meijer,Henk
          The staff numbers 1 professional

       8. Major field: geography of the Netherlands (aim: to supply
          information outside the Netherlands)

       9. National books, periodicals, audio-visual materials and
          maps are processed

      10. The Centre has a library

      11. Holdings: books   150 titles
                    periodicals   10 titles

      12. The library is not open to the public

      13. Information services:
          Publications - bibliographies and others
          SDI
          Translation
          Bibliographical, literature and survey data searches
          Compilation of documentary syntheses
          Lending and reference services
          Provision of photocopies and visual material for educational
          publications

      17. Information services free of charge

128   1. INSTITUTE FOR EASTERN EUROPEAN STUDIES
         OOST-EUROPA INSTITUUT
         OEI

      2. Parent institution: University of Amsterdam

      3. Oude Hoogstraat 24, P.O.B. 19101, 1000 GC Amsterdam
         cable address: Oost-Europa Instituut, University Amsterdam
         tel. 020-525 2267

      4. 1948

      5. Director: Bezemer,J.
         The staff numbers 5 professionals and 4 non-professionals

      6. National centre for documentation on the Soviet Union since
         1921, and on Eastern Europe since 1945

      8. Major fields: Soviet Union since 1921 and Eastern Europe
         since 1945, dissident movement in the USSR, workers'self-
         management in Yugoslavia

      9. Foreign books and periodicals on and from the Soviet Union
         and East Europe and "Arhiv Samizdata" are processed

     10. The Institute has a library

     11. Holdings: books   40 000 vols. in total
                   periodicals   400 titles
         Central book and pamphlet catalogues on the Soviet Union and
         Eastern Europe for holdings of largest Dutch libraries, al-
         phabetical and systematical, periodical articles catalogues
         are used

     12. The library is open to the public

     13. Information services:
         Publications
         Bibliographical, literature and survey data searches
         Lending and reference services
         Provision of photocopies

     15. Photocopying machine

     17. Information services free of charge and against payment

129   1. LIBRARY AND DOCUMENTATION SERVICE OF THE MINISTRY OF SOCIAL
         AFFAIRS
         BIBLIOTHEEK EN DOCUMENTATIC DIENST V/H MINISTERIE VAN SOCI-
         ALE ZAKEN
         BIDOC/SOZA

      2. Subordinated to the Ministry of Social Affairs

   3. Anna Paulownastraat 38/36 Gravenhage
      Branch office - Balen van Andelplein 2, Voorburg, The Netherlands
      tel. 070715911;   branch office 694001
      telex: 32226;   branch office 32427

   4. 1933

   5. Director: van Dam,Jan
      The staff numbers 28 professionals and 7 non-professionals

   6. Central library and documentation service in the indicated
      fields

   7. Departments or activities: Library and documentation sector;
      Labour market; Labour conditions; Social insurance; Labour
      safety and health

   8. Major fields: labour conditions and legislation, labour mar-
      ket, labour safety and health, social insurance, wage and in-
      surance policy

   9. National and foreign books, periodicals and national "gray"
      literature are processed

  11. Holdings: books   70 000 titles
               periodicals   1 400 titles
               abstract journals   28 titles
      Systematical UDC catalogue is used

  12. The library is open to the public

  13. Information services:
      Publications - abstract journals, bibliographies
      SDI
      Bibliographical and literature searches
      Compilation of documentary syntheses
      Lending service
      Provision of photocopies

  15. Photocopying machine

  16. Relations with other information units in the country

  17. Information services free of charge and against payment

130 1. NATIONAL COUNCIL FOR SOCIAL WELFARE
        NATIONALE RAAD VOOR MAATSCHAPPELIJK WELZIJN

     3. Eisenhowerlaan 146, 2517 KP-s'-Gravenhage
        Bibliothek en documentatie
        tel. 070-512141

     4. 1908; Library and documentation - 1949

     5. Director: Van der Gaag,Fred
        The staff numbers 5 professionals and 2 non-professionals

   6. Special library

   8. Major fields: social welfare, social policy and action,
casework, community organization, history, social psychology, sociology, etc

   9. National and foreign books, periodicals, "gray" literature,
and annual reports are processed

  10. The Council has a library

  11. Holdings: books and manuscripts   35 000 titles
           periodicals   711 titles
           abstract journals   9 titles
    Printed catalogue is used

  12. The library is open to the public

  13. Information services:
Publications - abstract journals, bibliographies and direc-
tories
SDI
Bibliographical and literature searches
Compilation of documentary syntheses
Lending service
Provision of photocopies

  15. Printing, photocopying machines

  16. Relations with other information units in the country, member of SAGEMA - documentation pool

  17. Information services free of charge and against payment

31   1. NATIONAL UNION FOR CHILD WELFARE

     WERKVERBAND INTEGRATIE JEUGDWELZYNSWERK NETHERLAND

     WIJN

   3. van Vollenhoven laan 659, Utrecht,   Postbus 3101
tel. 030-944141

   5. Director: Peeters,Harry
The staff numbers 10 professionals

   8. Major fields: child welfare, child law, child psychology,
peadagogics, methods of social work, etc.

   9. Foreign books, periodicals and "gray" literature are processed

  10. The Institution has a library

  11. Holdings: books   25 000 vols. in total
         periodicals   250 vols. in total

  12. The library is open to the public

13. Information services:
    Publications - abstract journals, bibliographies and others
    SDI
    Bibliographical and literature searches
    Lending service
    Provision of photocopies

15. Stencil, offset

16. Relations with SWIDOC in the country and the National Children's Bureau -London, German Youth Institute-München, etc.

17. Information services against payment

132   1. SOCIAL SCIENCE INFORMATION AND DOCUMENTATION CENTRE
         SOCIAAL-WETENSCHAPPELIJK INFORMATIE EN DOCUMENTATIECENTRUM
         SWIDOC

      2. Parent institution: Royal Netherlands Academy of Arts and
         Sciences
         Subordinated to the Ministry of Education

      3. Kleine-Gartmanplantsoen 10,   1017 RR Amsterdam
         tel. 020/225061

      4. 1972

      5. Director: Hogeweg-de Haart,Huiberta
         The staff numbers 13 professionals (6 part-time), 6 non-
         professionals (2 part-time) and 4 auxilliaries (part-time)

      6. Unique position in information on current research, documen-
         tation of doctoral theses, library of research reports, re-
         search data archives, public reference centre on social
         science literature

      7. Departments or activities: Data-archives department and
         others

      8. Major fields: sociology, cultural anthropology, political
         science, public administration sciences, psychology, peda-
         gogics and related sciences, social and economic geography,
         urban and regional planning, demography, social medicine
         and social history

      9. National research reports, periodicals, "gray" literature
         and magnetic tapes are processed

     10. The Centre has a library

     11. Holdings: books   8 500 titles
                    periodicals   100 titles - 1 000 vols.
                    brochures   2 300 titles
                    abstract journals   60 titles -   330 vols.
         Card catalogue for books and reports, KWIC-index for jour-

nal articles are used

12. The library is open to the public

13. Information services:
    Publications - bibliographies, directories and others
    Bibliographical, literature and survey data searches
    Lending service
    Provision of photocopies and/or microfilms

14. Automated information service for searching relevant studies
    in data-archives and journal articles
    Hardware: C.D. CYBER Computer
    Software: RIQS-retrieval system

15. Photocopying machine

17. Information services free of charge and against payment

Norway

133 1. CENTRAL BUREAU OF STATISTICS
        STATISTISK SENTRALBYRÅ

     2. Subordinated to the Ministry of Finance and Customs

     3. Dronningensgt. 16 Postboks 8131. Dep.Oslo 1
        cable address: Statistikk
        tel. 41 38 20

     4. 1876

     5. Director: Bjerve,Jakob
        The staff numbers 180 professionals and 555 non-professio-
        nals

     7. Departments or activities: Production; Statistical; Research;
        Administration, etc.

     8. Major field: statistics

     9. National books, periodicals, audio-visual materials and mag-
        netic tapes are processed

    10. The Bureau has a library

    11. Holdings: books and periodicals   141 500 vols. in total
                  abstract journals   8-10 titles
        Alphabetical authors' and subject catalogues are used

    12. The library is open to the public

    13. Information services:
        Publications - bibliographies
        Bibliographical and literature searches
        Lending and reference services
        Provision of photocopies and/or microforms

    14. Statistical Data Processing

Hardware: HONEYWELL L66/60P
Software: COBOL

17. Information services free of charge and against payment

134   1. LIBRARY OF THE NORWEGIAN PARLIAMENT
         STORTINGSBIBLIOTEKET

      2. Parent institution: Norwegian Parliament

      3. Stortinget, Oslo 1
         tel. 02-413810

      4. 1871

      5. Director: Torp,Olaf
         The staff numbers 6 professionals and 3 non-professionals

      6. Special library for parliamentary use mainly

      8. Major fields: social sciences, modern history, political
         sciences, political parties, government
         Specific fields: party programmes (national), parliamentary
         papers of European countries (esp. Scandinavia)

      9. National and foreign books and periodicals, national "gray"
         literature and audio-visual materials are processed

     11. Holdings: books and periodicals 125 000 vols. in total
                   periodicals (current)   675 vols. in total
                   microcopies   400

     12. The library is not open to the public

     13. Information services:
         Publications - abstract journals, bibliographies, directo-
         ries and others
         Bibliographical and literature searches
         Lending service
         Provision of photocopies and/or microforms

     15. Offset

     17. Information services free of charge

135   1. NOBEL INSTITUTE LIBRARY
         NOBELINSTITUTTETS BIBLIOTEK

      2. Parent institution: Nobel Institute

      3. Drammensvn 19, Oslo 2
         tel. 44 20 63

      4. 1904

5. Director: Sverdrup,Jakob
   The staff numbers 3 professionals

6. Major fields: peace and conflict research, international relations, international organizations, history, international
   law, international economics
   Specific fields: Depository library for UN and EC publications

9. Foreign books and periodicals are processed

11. Holdings: books and periodicals   103 060 vols. in total
    Dictionary catalogue is used

12. The library is open to the public

13. Information services:
    Publications - bibliographies
    Bibliographical searches
    Lending service
    Provision of photocopies

16. Participates in the Union Catalogue-University Library

17. Information services free of charge

136   1. NORDIC DOCUMENTATION CENTRE OF MASS COMMUNICATIONS RESEARCH,
          NORWEGIAN BRANCH

          NORDISK DOKUMENTASJONSSENTRAL FOR MASSEKOMMUNIKASJONS
          FORSKNING AVD.NORGE

          NORDICOM

       3. University of Bergen, Department of Sociology and Political
          Sciences, Christies gt. 15-19,   5014 Bergen U
          tel. 05210040/2174

       4. 1972

       5. Director: Saelen,Kirsti
          The staff numbers 1 professional

       6. Regional documentation centre covering the field of mass
          communications in Norway.

       8. Major field: mass communications research

       9. National books, periodicals and "gray" literature are pro-
          cessed

      10. The Centre has no library

      13. Information services:
          Publications - bibliographies and directories
          Translation
          Bibliographical and literature searches
          Compilation of documentary syntheses

Reference services

14. Computerization of bibliographical data
    Hardware: Papertape AC200, IBM 370/158
    Software: COBOL/MVS/VS2

15. Offset

16. Relations with the respective NORDICOM in Denmark, Finland
    and Sweden

17. Information services free of charge

137   1. NORWEGIAN BIBLIOGRAPHY OF THE SOCIAL SCIENCES

       NORSK SAMFUNNSVITENSKAPELING BIBLIOGRAFI

       NOSAB

    2. Subordinated to the Norwegian Research Council for the
       Sciences and the Humanities and the Royal University Libra-
       ry, Oslo

    3. Postbox 1098, Blindern, Oslo 3
       tel. (02)-46-69-00/8320
       telex: 1-6048 ubn

    4. 1978

    5. Director: Taylor,John
       The staff numbers 1 professional and 1 non-professional

    6. NOSAB is planned to be part of the national bibliography
       and data base system

    8. Major fields: political sciences, economics, geography,
       planning, conservation, sociology, pedagogics, psychology,
       public administration, marketing, etc.
       Specific fields: publications of Parliament, official com-
       mittees, public and private institutions, research estab-
       lishments, political and labour organizations, banks, uni-
       versities, research and planning documents, theses, etc.

    9. National books, periodicals and "gray" literature are por-
       cessed

   10. The Institution has no library

   11. Data (computerized) material for NOSAB publications

   13. Information services:
       Publications - abstract journals, bibliographies, directo-
       ries and others
       SDI
       Bibliographical, literature and survey data searches
       Provision of photocopies

   14. Compilation of bibliographies

Hardware: DEC-10 computer
Software: Norwegian version of MARC programmes-NORMARC

15. Offset

17. Information services free of charge and against payment

138   1. NORWEGIAN CENTRE FOR INFORMATICS

NORSK SENTER FOR INFORMATIKK

NSI

2. Parent institution: Royal Norwegian Council for Scientific
and Industrial Research

3. Forskningsveien 1, Oslo 3,
cable address: Ensi
tel. 02-69 58 80
telex: 11536 ciir n

4. 1944

5. Director: Krog,Hans
The staff numbers 15 professionals and 25 non-professionals

6. Information policy and operational responsibilities covering
information and consultative services

7. Departments or activities: Information retrieval and evaluation searches on international and local data bases; Library
services; Information systems development; Programme pack-
ages, etc.

8. Major fields: technical information, economy, social sciences

9. Foreign books, periodicals, "gray" literature, microfiches
and reports are processed

10. The Centre has a library

11. Holdings: books   25 000 vols. in total
             periodicals   1 200 vols. in total
             abstract journals   100 vols. in total
NSI's system POLYDOC co-ordinate indexing is used

12. The library is open to the public

13. Information services:
Publications - abstract journals and others
SDI
Bibliographical, literature and survey data searches
Compilation of documentary syntheses
Lending service
Provision of photocopies and/or microforms

14. The automated information systems cover the social, manage-

ment, economy fields
Hardware: UNIVAC 1110, NORD-10/S, Interactive terminals
Software: COBOL, SIMULA, POLYDOC system

15. Filmsetter, offset, photocopying machine

16. Relations with national and special libraries in the country
and with some information centres abroad

17. Information services against payment

139 1. NORWEGIAN INSTITUTE FOR URBAN AND REGIONAL RESEARCH. LIBRA-
RY

NORSK INSTITUTT FOR BY- OG REGIONFORSKNING. BIBLIOTEKET

NIRB Library

3. Nycoveien 1, Oslo 4
tel. 02-15 53 10

4. 1970

5. Director: Helgesen,Anne
The staff numbers 2 professionals and 1 non-professional

8. Major fields: urban and regional planning and research

9. National books and "gray" literature are processed

11. Holdings: books   12 000 vols. in total
periodicals   170 vols. in total
abstract journals   12 vols. in total

12. The library is open to the public

13. Information services:
Publications - bibliographies
Bibliographical and literature searches
Lending service
Provision of photocopies and/or microforms

14. Automated information system in the field of urban and regional research in Norway
Software: POLYDOC system

16. Relations with the Norwegian Centre for Informatics

17. Information services against payment

140 1. NORWEGIAN SCHOOL OF ECONOMICS AND BUSINESS ADMINISTRATION.
LIBRARY

NORGES HANDELSHØYSKOLE - BIBLIOTEKET

NHHB

2. Parent institution: Norwegian School of Economics and Business Administration

3. Helleveien 30, 5000 Bergen
tel. 05-25 65 00
telex: via 42690 ubbn

4. 1936

5. Director: Rogne,Odd
The staff numbers 8 professionals and 11 non-professionals

6. Responsible for economics and business administration information in the country

8. Major fields: economics, business administration

9. National and foreign books, periodicals and "gray" literature are processed

11. Holdings: books   100 000 vols. in total
            periodicals   3 200 titles⎫
            abstract journals   25 titles⎭ 60 000 vols. in total
            microcopies   300
            manuscripts   200
Alphabetical and systematical (UDC) catalogues are used

12. The library is open to the public

13. Information services:
Publications - abstract journals, bibliographies, directo-
ries and others
Bibliographical, literature and survey data searches
Lending service
Provision of photocopies and/or microforms

14. Automated information system for small firms documentation
Hardware: UNIVAC 1100
Software: COBOL

15. Offset

16. Participates in European Business School(librarians)and in
Scandinavian School of Economics - the librarian group

17. Information services free of charge

141 1. NORWEGIAN SOCIAL SCIENCE DATA SERVICES
NORSK SAMFUNNSVITENSKAPELIG DATATJENESTE
NSD

2. Parent institution: Norwegian Research Council for Science
and Humanities

3. Christiesgate 15-19, N-5014 Bergen - Universitetet
tel. 05-21 00 40/2117

4. 1971

5. Director: Henrichsen,Bjørn (executive)
   The staff numbers 9 professionals and 2 non-professionals

7. Departments or activities: Main office of University of Bergen; Branch office of university of Oslo, Trondheim, Tromsø

8. Major fields: organization of data banks for general use in all academic cities, data bases for social sciences research

9. Foreign and national magnetic tapes are processed (mostly data from Norwegian statistical production)

10. The Services have no library

13. Information services:
    Publications - directories and others

14. Automated information system for data sources in different data banks
    Hardware: UNIVAC 1110, UNIVAC 1108, DEC 10

15. Offset

16. Member of CESSDA and IFDO

17. Information services free of charge

142   1. UNIVERSITY LIBRARY. SECTION B. TRONDHEIM
         UNIVERSITETSBIBLIOTEKET AVD. B. TRONDHEIM
         UBT/B

      2. Parent institution: University of Trondheim

      3. Erling Skakkes gt. 47 c, 7000 Trondheim
         tel. 92220
         telex: 55384 bibl n

      5. Director: Vedi,Sten
         The staff numbers 52 professionals and 10 non-professionals

      7. Departments or activities: Acquisition; Lending and public services; Administration; Technical services; Special collections; Subject specialists

      8. Major fields: all subjects except technology

      9. National and foreign books, periodicals, audio-visual materials, magnetic tapes and national "gray" literature are processed

     11. Holdings: books   approx 650 000 vols.
                   periodicals   9 217 titles
                   manuscripts   4 674

12. The library is open to the public

13. Information services:
Bibliographical searches
Lending service
Provision of photocopies and/or microforms

14. Acquisition and cataloguing file of new literature
Hardware: UNIVAC 1108, 14 terminals: SPERRYUNIVAC UNISCOPE
200, 10 TANOBERG DATA terminal series 2100
Software: FORTRAN IV

15. Copying machine, offset

17. Information services free of charge

143 1. UNIVERSITY OF TRONDHEIM, NORWEGIAN INSTITUTE OF TECHNOLOGY,
LIBRARY

UNIVERSITET I TRONDHEIM, NORGES TEKNISKE HØGSKOLE, BIBLIO-
TEKET

NTHB

2. Parent institution: Norwegian Institute of Technology

3. N-7034 Trondheim - NIH
cable address: NTHB
tel. 47-75-95110
telex: 55186 nthhb n

4. 1910

5. Director: Thalberg,Knut
The staff numbers 35 professionals and 20 non-professionals

6. Central Technological Library of Norway and services of
the Norwegian industry and the general public

7. Departments or activities: Acquisition; Cataloguing and
classification; Interlibrary loans; Periodicals; Trade literature; Documentation; 5 Faculty libraries

8. Major fields: exact sciences technology, arts, social sciences, etc.

9. National and foreign books, periodicals, "gray" literature,
audio-visual materials and foreign magnetic tapes are processed

11. Holdings: books   658 000 vols.
periodicals   9 000 titles
abstract journals   700 titles
microcopies   85 000
standards   161 000
patents   1 599 000
trade literature   85 000 items
UDC and dictionary catalogues are used

12. The library is open to the public

13. Information services:
    Publications - abstract journals and bibliographies
    SDI
    Bibliographical, literature and survey data searches
    Lending and reference services

14. SDI and retrospective searches from the data base GEOARCHIVE
    processed at the library for Scandinavia; on-line search ser-
    vices: SDC/ORBIT, LOCKHEED/DIALOG, IRS/QUEST, MEDLINE,
    BYGGDOK, CHEM, etc.
    Hardware: UNIVAC 1100, 1108 (for GEOARCHIVE), Terminals:
    TEXAS INSTRUMENTS SILENT, INCOTERM, UNISCOPE
    Software: FORTRAN (for GEOARCHIVE)

15. Photocopying machine, microfiche-duplication, photocopying
    from film offset press

16. Relations in the country with the National Office for Re-
    search and Special Libraries; with regional organizations:
    IATUL, EUSIDIC, Scandia-plancommittee, etc.

17. Information services against payment and free of charge

Poland

144   1. ARCHIVES OF THE POLISH ACADEMY OF SCIENCES
ARCHIWUM POLSKIEJ AKADEMII NAUK

2. Parent institution: Polish Academy of Sciences

3. ul. Nowy Świat 72 (Pałac Staszica)
00-330 Warszawa
tel. 26-52-31, 26-81-30

4. 1954

5. Director: Kolankowski,Zygmunt
The staff numbers 26 professionals and non-professionals

6. A unit of the national social sciences information system

7. Departments or activities: Library; Research study

8. Major fields: history of science and technology in Poland
Specific fields: archives of the Polish Academy of Sciences,
research institutes and learned societies, posthumous manuscripts of Polish scientists

9. National and foreign books, periodicals and "gray" literature are processed

10. The Archives have a library

11. Holdings: books   10 400 vols.
          periodicals   5 600 vols.
Alphabetical catalogue, inventories of archieval units,
correspondents' file are used

12. The library is open to the public

13. Information services:
Publications - bibliographies and others
Bibliographical and survey data searches

Compilation of documentary syntheses
Lending and reference services

17. Information services free of charge

145 1. CENTRE FOR STUDIES ON NON-EUROPEAN COUNTRIES
        ZAKŁAD KRAJÓW POZAEVROPEJSKICH PAN

     2. Parent institution: Polish Academy of Sciences

     3. ul. Nowy Świat 72, 00-330 Warszawa
        tel. 26-50-71, 26-52-31

     4. 1962

     5. Director: Szymański,Edward
        The staff numbers 17 professionals and 15 non-professionals

     6. The information service is a unit in the national social
        sciences information system

     8. Major fields: social and cultural problems of the Third
        World

     9. National and foreign books and periodicals are processed

    10. The Centre has two libraries

    11. Holdings: books   8 358 vols.⎫ African library
                  periodicals   674 vols.⎭
                  books   23 511 vols.⎫ Oriental library
                  periodicals 4 628 vols.⎭
        Alphabetical, subject and geographical catalogues are used

    12. The library is not open to the public

    13. Information services:
        Various publications
        Reference services

    16. Relations with the Scientific Information Centre of PAS

    17. Information services free of charge

146 1. INSTITUTE OF ARTS AT THE POLISH ACADEMY OF SCIENCES
        INSTYTUT SZTUKI POLSKIEJ AKADEMII NAUK

     2. Parent institution: Polish Academy of Sciences

     3. ul. Długa 26/28, 00-950 Warszawa
        cable address: Ispan
        tel. 31-31-49, 31-32-71

     4. 1949

5. Director: Mossakowski,Stanisław
   The staff numbers 170 professionals and non-professionals

7. Departments or activities: Stock-taking of arts monuments in
   Poland; Dictionary of Polish artists; Documentation of Polish folklore; Documentation of Polish theatre; Bibliography; Archives of photographic documentation and measuring;
   Library

8. Major fields: fine arts, theatre, music, films, folklore

9. National and foreign books, periodicals, "gray" literature,
   and magnetic tapes are processed

10. The Institute has a library

11. Holdings: books   approx. 80 000 vols.
             periodicals   approx. 20 000 vols.
             microfilms   approx. 2 000
             manuscripts   approx. 1 200
    Alphabetical and subject catalogues are used

12. The library is open to the public

13. Information services:
    Publications - bibliographies and others
    Bibliographical searches
    Compilation of documentary syntheses
    Lending and reference services

15. Cameras, photocopying machine

17. Information services free of charge

147 1. INSTITUTE FOR HISTORY OF THE MATERIAL CULTURE. POLISH ACA-
        DEMY OF SCIENCES

        INSTYTUT HISTORII KULTURY MATERIALNEJ POLSKIEJ AKADEMII
        NAUK

        IHKM PAN

     2. Parent institution: Polish Academy of Sciences

     3. ul. Świerczewskiego 105, 00-140 Warszawa
        tel. 20-28-81

     4. 1953

     5. Director: Hensel,Witold
        The staff numbers 320 professionals and non-professionals

     6. The documentation and information section is a unit of the
        national social sciences information system

     7. Departments or activities: Documentation and information
        section; Library; Archives; Libraries at the sections in
        separate regions of Poland

8. Major fields: prehistoric archaeology, early mediaeval and industrial archaeology, classical archaeology, history of material culture, ethnography

9. National and foreign books, periodicals, "gray" literature, audio-visual materials and magnetic tapes are processed

10. The Institute has a library

11. Holdings: books   43 527 vols.
             periodicals   926 titles - 30 028 vols.
             microfilms   688
             manuscripts   2 325
    Alphabetical and subject catalogues are used

12. The library is open to the public

13. Information services:
    Publications - abstract journals, bibliographies and others
    SDI
    Lending and reference services

15. Photocopying machine

16. Relations with the Scientific Information Centre of PAS

17. Information services free of charge

148   1. INSTITUTE OF HISTORY AT THE POLISH ACADEMY OF SCIENCES
         INSTYTUT HISTORII POLSKIEJ AKADEMII NAUK

      2. Parent institution: Polish Academy of Sciences

      3. Rynek Starego Miastas 29/31, 00-242 Warszawa
         tel. 31-02-61/64, 31-36-42

      4. 1953

      5. Director: Madajczyk,Czesław
         The staff numbers 6 professionals

      6. The information service is a unit of the national social sciences information system

      7. Departments or activities: Library; Polish bibliography 19th and 20th c.; Documentation section in Cracow

      8. Major fields: history of Poland, universal history, archaeology

      9. National and foreign books and periodicals are processed

     10. The Institute has a library

     11. Holdings: books   32 044 vols.
                   periodicals   11 853 vols.

```
                        microfilms              586
                        manuscripts             407
              Alphabetical and subject catalogues are used
```

12. The library is not open to the public

13. Information services:
    Publications - bibliographies and others
    Bibliographical searches
    Reference services

16. Relations with the Scientific Information Centre of PAS

17. Information services free of charge

149   1. INSTITUTE OF HISTORY OF SCIENCE, EDUCATION AND TECHNOLOGY
          AT THE POLISH ACADEMY OF SCIENCES
          INSTYTUT HISTORII NAUKI, OŚWIATY I TECHNIKI POLSKIEJ AKADE-
          MII NAUK
          IHNOiT PAN

       2. Parent institution: Polish Academy of Sciences

       3. ul. Nowy Świat 72 (Pałac Staszica), 00-330 Warszawa
          tel. 26-87-54

       4. Present organization - 1977

       5. Director: Miaso,Józef
          The staff numbers 6 professionals

       7. Departments or activities: Libraries in Warsaw, Cracow and
          Wrocław

       8. Major fields: history of culture, science, education and
          technology, history of the different scientific disciplines

       9. Foreign books and periodicals are processed

      10. The Institute has a library

      11. Holdings: books   14 353 vols. ⎫
                    periodicals   2 723 vols. ⎬ in Warsaw
                    microfilms   637   ⎪
                    photocopies   1 020   ⎭
          Alphabetical and subject catalogues are used

      12. The library is open to the public

      13. Information services:
          Publications - bibliographies and others
          Bibliographical searches
          Reference services

      15. Photocopying machine

17. Information services free of charge

150   1. INSTITUTE OF LITERARY RESEARCH AT THE POLISH ACADEMY OF
         SCIENCES
         INSTYTUT BADAŃ LITERACKICH POLSKIEJ AKADEMII NAUK
         IBL PAN

      2. Parent institution: Polish Academy of Sciences

      3. ul. Nowy Świat 72 (Pałac Staszica),   00-330 Warszawa
         tel. 26-99-45,   26-52-31

      5. Director: Klimowicz,Mieczysław
         The staff numbers 242 professionals and non-professionals

      6. The scientific information section and library are units of
         the national social sciences information system

      7. Departments or activities: Scientific information section;
         Library; etc.

      8. Major fields: theory of literature, history of Polish lite-
         rature, sociology of literature

      9. National and foreign books, periodicals, and "gray" litera-
         ture are processed

     10. The Institute has a library

     11. Holdings: books   139 830 vols.
                    periodicals   25 062 vols.
                    microfilms   2 429
                    photocopies   763
                    old prints   4 590 vols.
         Alphabetical and subject catalogues are used

     12. The library is not open to the public

     13. Information services:
         Publications - abstract journals, bibliographies and others
         Bibliographical, literature and survey data searches
         Reference services

     15. Photocopying machine

     16. Relations with the Scientific Information Centre of PAS

     17. Information services free of charge

151   1. INSTITUTE OF PHILOSOPHY AND SOCIOLOGY AT THE POLISH ACADEMY
         OF SCIENCES
         INSTYTUT FILOZOFII I SOCJOLOGII POLSKIEJ AKADEMII NAUK
         IFiS PAN

2. Parent institution: Polish Academy of Sciences

3. ul. Nowy Świat 72 (Pałac Staczica), 00-330 Warszawa
   tel. 26-71-81, 26-76-42, 26-99-46

4. 1956

5. Director: Jaroszewski,Tadeusz
   The staff numbers 13 professionals

6. The documentation and scientific information department is
   a unit of the national social sciences information system

7. Departments or activities: Documentation and scientific information; Library; etc.

8. Major fields: philosophy, sociology
   Specific fields: history of Polish philosophy, dialectical
   materialism, logic, theory of socialist society, social
   changes, social structure, social prognostication, etc.

9. National and foreign books and periodicals are processed

10. The Institute has a library

11. Holdings: books   55 569 vols.
             periodicals   1 178 titles
             manuscripts, microfilms and icons   4 798
    Alphabetical, subject and other catalogues are used

12. The library is open to the public

13. Information services:
    Publications - bibliographies and others
    Bibliographical searches
    Compilation of documentary syntheses
    Lending and reference services

16. Relations with the Scientific Information Centre of PAS

17. Information services free of charge

152   1. INSTITUTE OF RURAL AND AGRICULTURAL DEVELOPMENT, POLISH ACA-
         DEMY OF SCIENCES

         INSTYTUT ROZWOJU WSI I ROLNICTWA POLSKIEJ AKADEMII NAUK

         IRWiR PAN

      2. Parent institution: Polish Academy of Sciences

      3. ul. Nowy Świat 72 (Pałac Staszica), 00-330 Warszawa
         tel. 26-94-36

      4. 1971

      5. Director: Gałaj,Dyzma
         The staff numbers 46 professionals

6. The library is a unit of the national social sciences information system

8. Major fields: rural and agricultural development

9. Foreign books and periodicals are processed

10. The Institute has a library

11. Holdings: books   3 500 vols.
              periodicals   593 vols.
    Alphabetical and subject catalogues are used

12. The library is open to the public

13. Information services:
    Publications - bibliographies and others
    Bibliographical searches
    Reference services

15. Photocopying machine

16. Relations with the Scientific Information Centre of PAS

17. Information services free of charge

153   1. INSTITUTE OF THE STATE AND LAW
         INSTYTUT PAŃSTWA I PRAWA POLSKIEJ AKADEMII NAUK

      2. Parent institution: Polish Academy of Sciences

      3. ul. Nowy Świat 72,   00-330 Warszawa
         tel. 26-52-31,   26-50-71

      4. 1956

      5. Director: Łopatka,Adam
         The staff numbers 9 professionals

      6. A unit of the national social sciences information system

      7. Departments or activities: Scientific information and docu-
         mentation section; Library

      8. Major fields: theory of the state and law
         Specific fields: constitutional law, administrative law,
         international law, civil law, penal law, criminology, agri-
         culture law, labour law, family law, law of the national
         economy

      9. Foreign books and periodicals are processed

      10. The Institute has a library

      11. Holdings: books   29 050 vols.
                    periodicals   8 616 vols.

microfilms   66
Alphabetical and periodical catalogues are used

12. The library is open to the public

13. Information services:
Publications - abstract journals, bibliographies and others
Translation
Bibliographical and survey data searches
Lending and reference services

15. Photocopying machine, microfilms

16. Relations with the Scientific Information Centre of PAS

17. Information services free of charge

154   1. INSTITUTE FOR WESTERN AFFAIRS

INSTYTUT ZACHODNI

IZ

2. Subordinated to the Polish Academy of Sciences

3. Stary Rynek 78/79, 61-772 Poznań
tel. 518-33-34,   556-61

4. 1945

5. Director: Czubiński,Antoni
The staff numbers 16 professionals

8. Major fields: history, sociology, economy, politics and law,
contemporary German culture

9. National and foreign books and periodicals are processed

10. The Institute has a library

11. Holdings: books   45 959 vols.
             periodicals   13 658 vols.
             manuscripts   121
Alphabetical and subject catalogues are used

12. The library is not open to the public

13. Information services:
Publications - bibliographies and others
Bibliographical searches
Reference services

15. Copying frame

155   1. JAGIELLONIAN LIBRARY

       BIBLIOTEKA JAGIELLONSKA. UNIVERSYTET JAGIELLONSKI

       BJ

    2. Parent institution: Jagiellonian University
       Subordinated to the central administration of the Ministry
       of Science, Higher Education and Technology

    3. Aleja Mickiewicza 22, 30-059 Kraków
       tel. 335-00, 335-05, 363-77
       telex: 0325682 bj pl

    4. 1364

    5. Director: Grzeszczuk,Stanislaw
       The staff numbers 233 professionals

    6. Central library of social sciences (humanities), member of
       the KRAKUS environmental computer system for scientific in-
       formation, member of National Library Holdings

    7. Departments or activities: Acquisition; Special collections;
       Readers' service

    8. Specific fields: Polonica prints and manuscripts, social
       sciences, history, culture of the Middle Ages and the Re-
       naissance, history of science, theory of literature, com-
       prehensive linguistics, library science, Central and South-
       European countries

    9. National and foreign books, periodicals, magnetic tapes,
       manuscripts (mainly Polonica), graphics and iconography,
       cartography, music documents, microfilms, photocopies are
       processed

   11. Holdings: books   1 103 211 vols.
                 periodicals-current and
                 abstract journals   367 719 vols. in total
                 microcopies   4 988
                 manuscripts   17 427
                 old prints before 1800
                 (books-periodicals)   96 828
       Card (alphabetical, systematical, subject, central of Ja-
       giell.Univ.Institutes libraries) and computer output (cen-
       tral of foreign periodicals in libraries-members of KRAKUS)
       catalogues are used

   12. The library is open to the public

   13. Information services:
       Publications - directories and others
       Bibliographical and literature searches
       Lending and reference services
       Provision of photocopies and microforms

   14. Automated information system covers: the KRAKUS environmen-
       tal scientific information system, central catalogues of
       foreign periodicals, central catalogue of foreign publica-

tions (monographs)
Hardware: Computer ODRA 1305
Software: COBOL, own based on adaptation of UNI-MARC

15. Photocopying machine

17. Information services against payment

156   1. JEWISH HISTORICAL INSTITUTE IN POLAND
         ŻYDOWSKI INSTYTUT HISTORYCZNY W POLSCE

      2. Subordinated in scientific matters to the Polish Academy of
         Sciences

      3. Al.Świerczewskiego 79, 00-090 Warszawa
         tel. 27-18-43, 27-15-30

      4. 1947

      5. Director: Horn,Maurycy

      7. Departments or activities: Library; Archives; Museum

      8. Major fields: history of the Jews (especially of the Jews in
         Poland), martyrology of the Jews during World War II, museum
         of Jewish art and martyrology

      9. National and foreign books, periodicals and "gray" litera-
         ture are processed

     10. The Institute has a library

     11. Holdings: books   39 000 vols.
                    periodicals   4 000 vols.
                    manuscripts   820
         Alphabetical catalogue is used

     12. The library is open to the public

     13. Information services:
         Publications - bibliographies and others
         Bibliographical and literature searches
         Reference services

     17. Information services free of charge

157   1. LIBRARY OF THE CATHOLIC ACADEMY OF THEOLOGY, WARSAW
         BIBLIOTEKA AKADEMII TEOLOGII KATOLICKIEJ
         ATK

      2. Parent institution: Catholic Academy of Theology
         Subordinated to the Ministry of Science, Higher Education
         and Technology

3. ul.Dewajtis Nr.3,   01-653 Warszawa
   tel. 34-72-91

4. 1954

5. Director: Baran,Czesław
   The staff numbers 10 professionals and 2 non-professionals

8. Major fields: theology, philosophy, canon-civil law, patro-
   logy, biblical studies, archaeology, ecclesiastical arts,
   history, linguistics (Latin, Greek, Hebrew, English, German, French, Russian)
   Specific fields: catholic theology, church law, catholic
   philosophy

9. National and foreign books, periodicals, audio-visual materials and magnetic tapes are processed

11. Holdings: books   134 000 vols.
              periodicals   900 vols.
              abstract journals   21 000 vols.
              microcopies   500
              manuscripts   1 100
    Alphabetical - subject headings catalogues are used

12. The library is open to the public

13. Information services:
    Publications - abstract journals, bibliographies, directo-
    ries and others
    SDI
    Bibliographical, literature and survey data searches
    Lending service
    Provision of photocopies and/or microforms

17. Information services free of charge

158 1. LIBRARY OF THE CENTRAL SCHOOL OF PLANNING AND STATISTICS -
        CENTRAL ECONOMIC LIBRARY

        BIBLIOTEKA SZKOŁY GŁÓWNEJ PLANOWANIA I STATYSTYKI - CENTRAL-
        NA BIBLIOTEKA EKONOMICZNA

     2. Parent institution: Central School of Planning and Statis-
        tics

     3. ul. Rakowiecka 22b,   02-521 Warszawa
        tel. 49-50-13,   49-50-98

     4. 1906

     5. Director: Uniejewska,Hanna
        The staff numbers 38 professionals and 40 non-professionals

     6. Central library of economic sciences

     7. Departments or activities: Acquisition; Catalogues; Perio-

dicals; Readers'service; Scientific information and documentation; Management of institutes' and chairs' libraries

8. Major field : social sciences
   Specific fields: economics, political economy, economic policy

9. National and foreign books, periodicals, "gray" literature, national audio-visual materials and magnetic tapes are processed

11. Holdings: books   397 000 vols.
             periodicals and abstract journals 140 000 vols.
             microcopies, manuscripts, reports,
             audio-visual materials   39 000 units
    Subject catalogue adapted from the Library of Congress classification is used

12. The library is open to the public

13. Information services:
    Publications - bibliographies, directories and others
    SDI
    Translation
    Bibliographical and literature searches
    Lending service
    Provision of photocopies and/or microforms

14. Automated information system in experimental stage
    Hardware: ODRA 1305,
    Software: ALGOL

15. Photocopying machine

16. Relations with the Scientific Information Centre of PAS, MISON, ECSSID, ICSSD

17. Information services free of charge

159 1. LIBRARY OF THE NATIONAL INSTITUTE OF OSSOLINSKI'S
        POLSKA AKADEMIA NAUK, ZAKŁAD NARODOWY IM.OSSOLINSKICH. BIBLIOTEKA

     2. Parent institution: Polish Academy of Sciences

     3. ul. Szewska 37, 50-139 Wrocław
        cable address: Bibloos
        tel. 44-44-71/76   373-70
        telex: 0342787 boss pl

     4. 1827

     5. Director: Albin,Janusz
        The staff numbers 108 professionals and non-professionals

     6. A unit of the national social sciences information system

7. Departments or activities: Information and documentation
section

8. Major field: humanities
Specific fields: Polish history, literature, culture, foreign Polonica, history of foreign countries

9. National and foreign books, periodicals, "gray" literature
and microfilms are processed

11. Holdings: books   565 430 vols.
periodicals   94 365 vols.
microfilms   5 843
manuscripts   16 604
old books   76 086
cartography   14 136
graphics   125 208
numismatics   124 297
Alphabetical, subject and topographical catalogues are used

12. The library is open to the public

13. Publications - bibliographies and others
Bibliographical and survey data searches
Reference services
Provision of photocopies and/or microforms

15. Reprographic machine, Pentacta, copying frame, photocopying
machine

16. Relations with the Scientific Information Centre of PAS

17. Information services free of charge

160   1. LIBRARY OF THE POLISH ACADEMY OF SCIENCES, GDANSK
BIBLIOTEKA GDAŃSKA POLSKIEJ AKADEMII NAUK

2. Parent institution: Polish Academy of Sciences

3. ul. Wałowa 15,   80-858 Gdańsk
tel. 31-22-51

4. 1596

5. Director: Kotarski,Edmund
The staff numbers 73 professionals and non-professionals

6. A unit of the national scientific information system in social sciences

7. Departments or activities: Information and documentation
section

8. Major fields: humanities, social sciences
Specific fields: Pomeranian and Gdansk affairs

9. National and foreign books, periodicals and "gray" literature are processed

11. Holdings: books   419 759 vols.
             periodicals   48 335 vols.
             microfilms   2 736
             manuscripts   4 269
    Alphabetical, subject and other catalogues are used

12. The library is open to the public

13. Information services:
    Publications - bibliographies and others
    Bibliographical and survey data searches
    Lending and reference services

16. Relations with the Scientific Information Centre of PAS

17. Information services free of charge

161 1. LIBRARY OF THE POLISH ACADEMY OF SCIENCES, KORNIK
            BIBLIOTEKA KÓRNICKA PAN

         2. Parent institution: Polish Academy of Sciences

         3. 63-120 Kórnik k/Poznania
            tel. 155,200

         4. 1817

         5. Director: Kosman,Marceli
            The staff numbers 26 professionals and non-professionals

         6. A unit of the national social sciences information system

         7. Departments or activities: Facilities; Readers' service

         8. Major fields: social sciences, history, literature
            Specific fields: special collections of manuscripts, incu-
            nabula and iconography

         9. National and foreign books, periodicals, and "gray" litera-
            ture are processed

        11. Holdings: books   152 592 vols.
                     periodicals   57 692 vols.
                     microfilms   4 756
                     manuscripts   13 834
            Alphabetical, subject and other catalogues are used

        12. The library is open to the public

        13. Information services:
            Publications
            Bibliographical and survey data searches
            Reference services

15. Copying frame

16. Relations with the Scientific Information Centre of PAS

17. Information services free of charge

162 1. LIBRARY OF THE POLISH ACADEMY OF SCIENCES, WARSAW
        BIBLIOTEKA POLSKIEJ AKADEMII NAUK U WARSZAWIE

     2. Parent institution: Polish Academy of Sciences

     3. Pałac Kultury i Nauki p.VI, 00-901 Warszawa
        tel. 20-33-02
        telex: 815360 bpan pl

     4. 1908

     5. Director: Łos,Leon
        The staff numbers 49 professionals and non-professionals

     6. A unit of the national social sciences information system

     7. Departments or activities: Acquisition and cataloguing of
        books; Periodicals; Scientific information and classifica-
        tion of collections; Circulation and storage; Library net-
        work of the Polish Academy of Sciences; Methodology of ca-
        taloguing; Library modernization and automation; Research
        for the dictionary of Polish scientific societies; Secreta-
        riat

     8. Major fields: science of science, history of science and
        technology, prognostication, praxiology, library science,
        scientific information

     9. Foreign books and periodicals are processed

    11. Holdings: books   100 410 vols.
                   periodicals   6 906 titles - 76 007 vols.
                   current periodicals 1 048 titles
                   microfilms   743
                   documents of
                   scientific life   3 822
                   theses   1 979
                   others   135
        Alphabetical, systematical, subject and central catalogues
        are used

    12. The library is open to the public

    13. Information services:
        Publications - abstract journals, bibliographies and others
        Bibliographical, literature and survey data searches
        Compilation of documentary syntheses
        Lending and reference services
        Provision of photocopies

15. Electrostatic copying frame, etc.

16. Relations with other libraries in the country and with com-
    mittees and institutes of PAS with library specialization,
    cooperation with institutions and organizations preparing the
    national scientific and technical information system - SINTO

17. Information services free of charge

163 1. LIBRARY OF THE POZNAN SOCIETY OF FRIENDS OF ARTS AND SCIENCE
        BIBLIOTEKA POZNAŃSKIEGO TOWARZYSTWA PRZYJACIÓŁ NAUK

     2. Parent institution: Poznan Society of Friends of Arts and
        Sciences
        Subordinated to the Polish Academy of Sciences

     3. ul. Mielzyńskiego 27/29, 61-725 Poznań
        tel. 574-41

     4. 1857

     5. Director: Olejniczak,Bernard
        The staff numbers 22 professionals and 5 non-professionals

     8. Major fields: history, history of literature
        Specific fields: 19th c. periodicals of Wielkopolska, lite-
        rature concerning Wielkopolska, Serbo-Lusatian literature,
        Czechoslovakian literature

     9. Foreign books and periodicals are processed

    11. Holdings: books   155 065 vols.
                  periodicals   4 079 titles - 68 915 vols.
                  microfilms   613
                  manuscripts   1 003
        Alphabetical and subject catalogues are used

    12. The library is not open to the public

    13. Information services:
        Publications - bibliographies and others
        Bibliographical searches
        Lending and reference services

164 1. LIBRARY OF THE UNIVERSITY OF WARSAW
        BIBLIOTEKA UNIWERSYTECKA W WARSZAWIE
        BUW

     2. Parent institution: University of Warsaw
        Subordinated to the Ministry of Science, Higher Education
        and Technology

     3. Krakowskie Przedmieście 26/28,32, 00-927 Warszawa

tel. 26-41-55, 26-96-19

4. 1817

5. Director: Baculewski,Jan
   The staff of the main library and 60 institute libraries
   numbers 289 professionals and 126 non-professionals

6. Central library of the national social sciences information
   system

7. Departments or activities: Technical services; Public services; Special collections (old books, M.S.S., maps, prints
   and drawings, music); Institute libraries

8. Major fields: humanities and social sciences
   Specific fields: special collections: old Polish books of
   18th c., Polish and foreign prints and drawings (15th-18th
   c.), architectural designs (17th-18th c.), Polish and foreign modern graphics, old cartographic materials, archives
   of Polish 20th c. composers, Rossica until 1915

9. National and foreign books, periodicals and audio-visual
   materials are processed

11. Holdings: main library and 60 institute
libraries	3 553 738 vols. in total
books	2 409 765 vols.
periodicals	723 138 vols.
microcopies	52 252
manuscripts	28 221
other old books, maps, draw- ings, prints, music	340 362 units

    Alphabetical and alphabetical subject catalogues are used

12. The library is open to the public

13. Information services:
    Publications - bibliographies, directories and others
    Bibliographical, literature and survey data searches
    Lending service
    Provision of photocopies

14. A library automated system is in preparation

15. Photocopying machine

16. Relations with the Scientific Information Centre of PAS and
    CINTE; with IFLA

17. Information services free of charge

165 1. MAIN LIBRARY OF THE ADAM MICKIEWICZ UNIVERSITY IN POZNAN
        BIBLIOTEKA GŁOWNA UNIWERSYTETU IM.ADAMA MICKIEWICZA

     2. Parent institution: Adam Mickiewicz University of Poznan

Subordinated to the Ministry of Science, Higher Education and Technology

3. ul. Ratajczaka 38/40, 61-816 Poznań
   tel. 579-16

4. 1919

5. Director: Kubiak,Stanisław
   The staff of the main library numbers 222 professionals and 34 non-professionals and of the subordinated libraries 77 professionals

6. The library is specialized in German affairs

7. Departments or activities: Main library with 12 departments and 36 faculty and institute libraries

8. Major fields: all fields of science, particularly social, philological and historical sciences, German scientific literature, history, society and culture

9. National and foreign books, periodicals, "gray" literature, audio-visual materials, magnetic tapes, incunabula, old books, maps and atlases, music scores and manuscripts are processed

11. Holdings of the main library:
    books   1 155 750 vols.
    periodicals   506 463 vols.
    microcopies   3 483
    manuscripts   3 398
    Holdings of the faculty and institute libraries:
    books   754 303 vols.
    periodicals   169 332 vols.
    Alphabetical, subject, union for the institute libraries and special for manuscripts, maps, music, old books and theses catalogues are used

12. The library is open to the public

13. Information services:
    Publications - bibliographies, directories and others
    Bibliographical, literature and survey data searches
    Compilation of documentary syntheses
    Lending and reference services
    Provision of photocopies

15. Photocopying machine

17. Information services free of charge

166   1. NATIONAL LIBRARY
         BIBLIOTEKA NARODOWA
         BN

2. Subordinated to the Ministry of Culture and Arts

3. ul. Hankiewicza 1, 00-973 Warszawa
   tel. 22-46-21
   telex: 813702 bn pl

4. 1928

5. Director: Stankiewicz,Witold
   The staff numbers 415 professionals and 220 non-professionals

6. Central reference library of general coverage publications,
   central scientific reference library, library science and
   archives library within SINTO

7. Departments or activities: Acquisition and processing of new
   publications; Special collections; Bibliographical institute; Data processing centre

8. Major fields: all sciences, foreign Polonica, reference and
   library science
   Specific fields: social sciences and humanities. Legal depository of copies of all Polish publications since 1927 and
   phonorecording since 1961

9. National and foreign books, periodicals, "gray" literature,
   old printed materials, audio-visual materials, magnetic
   tapes and phonorecordings are processed

11. Holdings: books   1 221 341 titles
             periodicals and
             abstract journals   492 309 vols.
             microcopies   104 274
             manuscripts   11 464
    Alphabetical, subject and union catalogues are used

12. The library is open to the public

13. Information services:
    Publications - abstract journals, bibliographies, directo-
    ries and others
    Bibliographical, literature and survey data searches
    Compilation of documentary syntheses
    Lending service
    Provision of photocopies and/or microforms

14. Automated information system on current national bibliogra-
    phy and on the union catalogue of foreign books in Polish
    libraries
    Hardware: Minicomputer RC-3600, IBM-370, LINOTRON 505 TC
    Software: Data entry system, PL/1, ASSEMBLER, COBOL, RODAN
    (Polish system)

15. Printing press, photocopying machine, duplicating machines,
    offset, photocameras

16. Relations with the Scientific Information Centre of PAS,
    with many foreign institutions and various international or-

ganizations, MISON

17. Information services free of charge

167   1. POLISH INSTITUTE OF INTERNATIONAL AFFAIRS. DEPARTMENT FOR
          SCIENTIFIC INFORMATION AND LIBRARY
          POLSKI INSTYTUT SPRAW MIDZYNARODOWYCH. ZAKŁAD INFORMACJI
          NAUKOWEJ I BIBLIOTEKA
          PISM

       3. ul. Warecka la,   00-950 Warszawa,   P.O.Box 1000
          tel. 26-30-21

       4. 1947

       5. Director: Cyrzyk,Leszek
          The staff numbers 22 professionals

       8. Major fields: politics, economy, international law
          Specific fields: international relations

       9. National and foreign books, periodicals and "gray" litera-
          ture are processed

      11. Holdings: books   67 500 vols. in total
                    periodicals   28 800 vols. in total
                    microcopies   3 400 in total

      12. The library is open to the public

      13. Information services:
          Bibliographical searches
          Lending service

      15. Catalogue cards minigraph, microfilm reader-printer

      17. Information services free of charge

168   1. RESEARCH CENTRE OF MEDITERRANEAN ARCHEOLOGY AT THE POLISH
          ACADEMY OF SCIENCES
          ZAKŁAD ARCHEOLOGII SRÓDZIEMNOMORSKIEJ POLSKIEJ AKADEMII NAUK

       2. Parent institution: Polish Academy of Sciences

       3. Pałac Kultury i Nauki p.XIX, pok. 1909, 00-901 Warszawa
          tel. 20-02-11/20-64

       4. 1956

       5. Director: Michałowski,Kazimierz
          The staff numbers 16 professionals and non-professionals

       8. Major fields: archeology and culture of Mediterranean coun-

tries

9. Foreign books and periodicals are processed

10. The Centre has a library

11. Holdings: books   3 912 vols.
             periodicals   1 706 vols.
             microfilms   125
    Alphabetical and subject catalogues are used

12. The library is not open to the public

13. Information services:
    Publications - bibliographies and others
    Bibliographical searches
    Compilation of documentary syntheses
    Reference services

17. Information services free of charge

169 1. SCIENTIFIC INFORMATION CENTRE AT THE HIGHER SCHOOL OF SOCIAL
            SCIENCES
            OŚRODEK INFORMACJI NAUKOWEJ WYŻSZEJ SZKOŁY NAUK SPOŁECZNYCH
            OIN WSNS

         2. Parent institution: Central Committee of PUWP

         3. ul. Bagatela 2, 00-585 Warszawa
            tel. 28-43-91

         4. 1969

         5. Director: Zaworski,Eligiusz
            The staff numbers 14 professionals and 4 non-professionals

         6. A unit of the national social sciences information system

         8. Major fields: political sciences, philosophy, sociology

         9. National and foreign books and periodicals are processed

        10. The Centre has no library

        13. Information services:
            Publications - bibliographies and directories
            SDI
            Bibliographical and survey data searches

        17. Information services free of charge

170 1. SCIENTIFIC INFORMATION CENTRE, POLISH ACADEMY OF SCIENCES
            OŚRODEK INFORMACJI NAUKOWEJ POLSKIEJ AKADEMII NAUK

EGSSI - F

OIN PAN

2. Parent institution: Polish Academy of Sciences

3. ul. Nowy Świat 72 (Pałac Staszica), 00-330 Warszawa
   tel. 26-84-10
   telex: 815414 pl

4. 1953

5. Director: Ługowski,Bronisław
   The staff numbers 76 professionals and 57 non-professionals

6. Main information centre of the Polish Academy of Sciences.
   Lending centre for social sciences within the national social sciences information system

7. Departments or activities: Organization of scientific information; Information techniques; Methodology; Automation
   processes; Agricultural information; Information publications; Science of science; Library; Scientific information
   laboratories in Cracow and Wrocław; Scientific information
   centre - branch in Poznan

8. Major fields: social sciences, scientific information,
   science of science

9. Foreign books and periodicals are processed

10. The Centre has a library

11. Holdings: books   12 000 vols.
             periodicals   462 titles - 5 584 vols.
    Alphabetical and subject catalogues are used

12. The library is open to the public

13. Information services:
    Publications - abstract journals, bibliographies and others
    Lending and reference services
    Provision of photocopies and/or microforms

14. Prototype of automated retrieval system in the field of
    science of science (AVION)

15. Typography, photocopying machine and photography

16. Relations with the scientific information centres of the
    Academies of Sciences of socialist and other countries.
    Member of MISON

17. Information services free of charge

Romania

171 1. OFFICE OF INFORMATION AND DOCUMENTATION IN SOCIAL AND POLI-
       TICAL SCIENCES

       OFFICIUL DE INFORMARE SI DOCUMENTARE ÎN STIINTELE SOCIALE
       SI POLITICE

       OFDSP

    2. Parent institution: Academy of Social and Political Sciences

    3. Cosmonautilor St. 27-29, Bucuresti 70141, Sector 1
       tel. 150847

    4. 1970

    5. Director: Mircea,Ioanid

    6. Central body

    7. Departments or activities: Ad hoc sections and staff

    8. Major fields: social and political sciences

    9. National and foreign books and periodicals are processed

   10. The Office has a library

   11. Holdings: books   13 300 titles
                 periodicals   1 100 titles
                 abstract journals   170 titles

   12. The library is not open to the public

   13. Information services:
       Publications - abstract journals and others

Spain

172 1. CENTRE OF THIRD WORLD INFORMATION AND DOCUMENTATION IN BAR-
        CELONA
        CENTRE D'INFORMACION I DOCUMENTACION A BARCELONA DEL TERCER
        MUNDO
        CIDOB-TM

     3. c/Lauria, 125-1$^{\underline{o}}$ 1$^{\underline{a}}$, Barcelona 37
        tel. 93-215 89 49

     4. 1971

     5. Director: Ligüerre-Gil,Vicens
        The staff numbers 2 professionals and 2 non-professionals

     7. Departments or activities: Analyses of documents; Ad hoc
        studies of international events (conferences, symposia);
        Relations with universities

     8. Major fields: dynamics of the development of Third World
        countries and related matters

     9. Foreign books and periodicals are processed

    10. The Centre has a library

    11. Holdings: books   5 485 vols. in total
                  periodicals   229 titles
        Decimal-Thesaurus is used

    12. The library is open to the public

    13. Information services:
        Publications - abstract journals, bibliographies, directo-
        ries and others
        SDI
        Translation
        Bibliographical, literature and survey data searches
        Compilation of documentary syntheses

Lending service
Provision of photocopies and/or microforms

15. Photocopying machine

17. Information services against payment

173 1. CONSORTIUM FOR INFORMATION AND DOCUMENTATION OF CATALONIA

CONSORCIO DE INFORMACION Y DOCUMENTACION DE CATALUNYA

CIDC

2. Subordinated to the local and regional administration: The
   Council of Barcelona, the Metropolitan Corporation of Barcelona, the Municipality of Barcelona and the Chamber of
   Commerce and Industry of Barcelona, Gerona, Lerida and Tar-
   ragona

3. c/Urgell, 187 - Barcelona (36)
   tel. 93-321.8000
   telex: 54310 cidc e

4. 1969

5. Director: Carreno-Piera,Luis
   The staff numbers 30 professionals and 20 non-professionals

6. A non-official institution collaborating with national institutions

7. Departments or activities: Data collection; Documentation;
   Analysis and systems; Information dissemination

8. Major fields: statistical and economic information on Spain
   and Catalonia
   Specific fields: social sciences files of ESA, SDC and LOCK-
   HEED data bases

9. National books, periodicals, "gray" literature, audio-visual
   materials and magnetic tapes are processed

10. The Consortium has a library

11. Holdings: books   10 000 vols.
             periodicals   4 000 titles
             abstract journals   30 titles
             microfiches and cassettes 250 000
    Traditional catalogues and KWOC indices are used

12. The library is open to the public

13. Information services:
    Publications - bibliographies
    SDI
    Bibliographical, literature and survey data searches
    Reference services
    Provision of photocopies and/or microforms

14. Numerical data bank, bibliographical systems, external sys-
    tems - producing and/or processing statistical information
    on Catalonia, indexing documentation on the economy of Cata-
    lonia and searches through terminals, (a network of econo-
    mic documentation on Spain is in preparation)
    Hardware: IBM 370/158. Computer communication leased-line
    terminal (2.400 b.p.s.) and one DATA DYNAMICS DIAL-UP ter-
    minal
    Software: PL/1 with own and external packages, IRS/QUEST,
    SDC/ORBIT and LOCKHEED/DIALOG

15. Photocopying machine

17. Information services against payment

174 1. FUND FOR ECONOMIC AND SOCIAL RESEARCH OF THE SPANISH SAV-
        INGS BANKS CONFEDERATION
        FONDO PARA LA INVESTIGACIÓN ECONÓMICA Y SOCIAL DE LA CONFE-
        DERACIÓN ESPAÑOLA DE CAJAS DE AHORROS
        FIES

     2. Parent institution: Spanish Savings Banks Confederation

     3. Padre Domián, 48 - Madrid (16)
        tel. 91-458.61.58

     4. 1967

     5. Director: Fuentes-Quintana,Enrigue
        The staff numbers 10 professionals and 20 non-professionals

     7. Departments or activities: Administration; Research; Editing

     8. Major fields: economics, sociology, law
        Specific fields: savings banks, fiscal law, finances

     9. National and foreign books, periodicals and audio-visual ma-
        terials are processed

    10. The Institution has a library

    11. Holdings: books   10 000 titles - 12 000 vols.
                  periodicals   900 titles - 45 000 vols.
                  abstract journals   15 titles -   80 vols.
        UDC is used

    12. The library is open to the public

    13. Information services:
        Publications - abstract journals, bibliographies and direc-
        tories
        SDI
        Translation
        Lending and reference services
        Provision of photocopies and microforms

    16. Relations with FID

17. Information services free of charge

175   1. INSTITUTE OF INFORMATION AND DOCUMENTATION IN SCIENCE AND
         TECHNOLOGY
         INSTITUTO DE INFORMACION Y DOCUMENTACION EN CIENCIA Y TECH-
         NOLOGIA
         ICYT

      2. Subordinated to the central administration of the Ministry
         of Education and Science

      3. Joaquin Costa, 22 - Madrid (6)
         tel. 91-261 48 08

      5. Director: Alvarez-Ososrio,José R.

      6. An institution of the National Information and Documentation
         Centre

      8. Specific field: management

      9. National and foreign periodicals and foreign magnetic tapes
         are processed

     10. The Institute has a library

     12. The library is open to the public

     13. Information services:
         Publications - abstract journals

     14. Automated information system for abstracting and indexing
         management documentation in cooperation with European Eco-
         nomic Documentation and Information Pool

     16. Relations with the European Economic Documentation and In-
         formation Pool (EMDOC)

     17. Information services against payment

176   1. INSTITUTE OF INFORMATION AND DOCUMENTATION IN SOCIAL SCIEN-
         CES AND HUMANITIES
         INSTITUTO DE INFORMACION Y DOCUMENTACION EN SCIENCIAS SO-
         CIALES Y HUMANIDADES
         ISOC

      2. Subordinated to the Ministry of Education and Science

      3. Vitrubio, 4 Planta 6^a, Madrid (6)
         tel. 91-262 77 55

      4. 1975

5. Director: de la Villa Sanz,Maria
   The staff numbers 9 professionals and 9 non-professionals

6. An institution of the National Information and Documentation
   Centre (acting as a national focal point)

7. Departments or activities: Administrative services; Analysis
   of documentation; Information retrieval and dissemination;
   Reprography library

8. Major fields: humanities and social sciences
   Specific fields: economics, sociology, psychology, education, political science, law, history and auxiliary sciences, art and archeology, geography, linguistics and literature, philosophy and religion

9. National and foreign books, periodicals and magnetic tapes
   are processed

10. The Institute has a library

11. Holdings: books   1 500 vols. in total
             periodicals   1 300 titles - 50 000 vols.
             abstract journals   200 titles - 20 000 vols.
    Subject indices in geographical or linguistic areas are used

12. The library is not open to the public

13. Information services:
    Publications - bibliographies
    SDI
    Bibliographical, literature and survey data searches
    Lending service
    Provision of photocopies and/or microforms

14. Automated information system for retrospective searches and
    SDI through SDC and LOCKHEED services
    Hardware: UNIVAC 1108 and DATA DYNAMICS DIAL-UP terminal
    Software: SDC/ORBIT and LOCKHEED/DIALOG

16. Relations with the Information and Documentation Centre of
    Economics (CIDE) and the Consortium for Information and Do-
    cumentation on Catalonia (CIDC) in the country

17. Information services against payment

177   1. NATIONAL INFORMATION AND DOCUMENTATION CENTRE OF THE SOCIAL
         SERVICE OF OCCUPATIONAL HYGIENE AND SAFETY

         CENTRO NATIONAL DE INFORMACION Y DOCUMENTACION DEL SERVICIO
         SOCIAL DE HIGIENE Y SEGURIDAD DEL TRABAJO

         CNID, SSHISET

      2. Parent institution: Social Service of Occupational Hygiene
         and Safety
         Subordinated to the Ministry of Social Health

3. c/Dulcet, s/n-Barcelona (34)
   tel. 93-2044500/218

4. 1973

5. Director: Turuguet,D.
   The staff numbers 8 professionals and 8 non-professionals

6. The only service concerned with occupational safety and
   health, coordinated with the other information and documentation services in the country

7. Departments or activities: Library; Photocopies; Microfilms;
   Document analyses; Information searches; Publications

8. Major fields: occupational safety and health
   Specific fields: industrial hygiene, safety and prevention
   training, occupational medicine, occupational and health legislation, industrial and occupational psychology, etc.

9. National and foreign books, periodicals and "gray" literature are processed

10. The Centre has a library

11. Holdings: books   8 227 titles - 8 987 vols.in total
              periodicals   215 titles - 1 075 vols.
              abstract journals 15 titles -   60 vols.in total
    Subject, authors', title and UDC catalogues are used

12. The library is open to the public

13. Information services:
    Publications - abstract journals, bibliographies and others
    SDI
    Translation
    Bibliographical, literature and survey data searches
    Compilation of documentary syntheses
    Reference services
    Provision of photocopies and/or microforms

14. Automated information system on occupational safety and
    health literature
    Software: MISTRAL-2

15. Photocopying machine, offset

16. Relations with the Consortium for Information and Documen-
    tation on Catalonia and the Institute of Information and
    Documentation in Social Sciences in the country and the in-
    ternational organizations CIS, OIT, NIOSH

17. Information services free of charge and against payment

Sweden

178 1. LIBRARY OF PARLIAMENT
        RIKSDAGSBIBLIOTEKET

     2. Parent institution: Parliament
        Subordinated to the Administrative Office of the Parliament

     3. S-10012 Stockholm 46
        tel. 08-14 2020
        telex: 10184

     4. 1851

     5. Director: Grönberg,Lennart
        The staff numbers 12 professionals and 15 non-professionals

     6. Special library for legal and political science literature.
        Central Archives of the Parliament

     7. Departments or activities: Lending; Acquisition of books and
        periodicals; Cataloguing and catalogue production; Catalo-
        guing and editing of the annual bibliography of Swedish of-
        ficial publications; Registration and cataloguing of docu-
        ments and publications of international organizations

     8. Major fields: jurisprudence and political science, social
        sciences, constitutional and administrative law, public in-
        ternational law, public general acts and statutes, parlia-
        mentary papers (Swedish and foreign)
        Specific fields: publications of international organiza-
        tions. Depository library for the UN, specialized agencies,
        OECD and other international organizations

     9. National and foreign books, periodicals and "gray" litera-
        ture are processed

    11. Holdings: books   500 000 vols. in total
                   periodicals   2 500 titles
        Alphabetical, classified card and classified printed cata-

logues are used

12. The library is open to the public

13. Information services:
Publications - bibliographies and others
Bibliographical and literature searches
Lending service
Provision of photocopies

14. LIBRIS - The Swedish library information system, covering
books and periodicals in Swedish university and research
libraries
Swedish judicial information system
Hardware: INCOTERM terminal, programmable display unit with
separate keyboards, dual discette unit and printer. ALFASCOP
display unit with printer

15. Photocopying machine, reader-printer

16. Relations with other research libraries in the country and
parliamentary libraries abroad, with the United Nations and
specialized agencies, Council of Europe, Nordic Council,
OECD, and others

17. Information services free of charge

179   1. LUND UNIVERSITY LIBRARY

       LUNDS UNIVERSITETSBIBLIOTEK

    2. Parent institution: University of Lund

    3. Box 1010, S-221 03 Lund 1
       tel. 046-124620
       telex: 322208, 33248

    4. 1671

    5. Director: Tell,Björn
       The staff numbers 40 professionals and 110 non-professionals

    6. Second National Library

    7. Departments or activities: Administration; Acquisition; Ca-
taloguing; References and loans; Faculty service; Rare
books; Technical services; Undergraduate library; Science
library; Law library; Business and economics library; Legal
deposit

    8. Major fields: all fields of science

    9. National and foreign books and periodicals and national
"gray" literature are processed

   11. Holdings: 2.5 million vols. in total
Authors' and classified card catalogues are used

12. The library is open to the public

13. Information services:
    Publications - abstract journals, bibliographies and direc-
    tories
    SDI
    Bibliographical and literature searches
    Lending service
    Provision of photocopies and/or microforms

14. Computerized interactive on-line searches (ESA, LOCKHEED,
    SDC, etc.) LIBRIS
    Hardware: INCOTERM SPD 10/20, CYBER 10, TEXAS INSTRUMENTS
    SILENT 600
    Software: ASSEMBLER

16. Relations with ERIC at the Royal Institute of Technology,
    Stockholm; participates in individual organizations abroad -
    LOCKHEED and SDC, and in regional and international organi-
    zation SCANNET

17. Information services free of charge and against payment

180   1. MEDICAL INFORMATION CENTRE, KAROLINSKA INSTITUTE
         MEDICINSKA INFORMATIONSCENTRALEN, KAROLINSKA INSTITUTET
         MIC

      2. Subordinated to the Karolinska Institute

      3. P.O.Box 60201, S-104 01 Stockholm
         cable address: Karolinst
         tel. + 46 8-23 22 70
         telex: 171 78 karolin s

      4. 1963

      5. Director: Falkenberg,Göran
         The staff numbers 20 professionals and 6 non-professionals

      6. National and Nordic information centre for life sciences.
         Contractual partner for data bases from the National Libra-
         ry of Medicine, Bethesda, Maryland, USA

      7. Departments or activities: MEDLARS on-line vendor; Informa-
         tion retrieval (retrospective and SDI-services); Education;
         Indexing for MEDLARS; Programming and computing; Administra-
         tion and marketing
         Special projects: MI-10 (evaluation of teratology data) on
         data base TEDAB, NOSPLINE (Locator file for Nordic libra-
         ries), EXTEMPLO (electronic journal on SCANNET)

      8. Major fields: social sciences, psychology, environmental
         sciences, etc.

      9. National and foreign literature on magnetic tapes is pro-
         cessed

10. The Centre is a division of the Karolinska Institute Library and Information Centre (KIBIC)

13. Information services:
Publications - bibliographies
SDI and retrospective searches
Compilation of documentary syntheses

14. Hardware: IBM 370/165, DEC-10, NORD-10, 10 TTY-compatible terminals
Software: PL/1, ASSEMBLER, SIMULA, ELHILL III, EPOS/VIRA

15. Photocomposition for publications produced

16. Relations with the Information and Documentation Centre, Royal Institute of Technology Library, Stockholm; the Swedish Society for Technical Documentation and several Nordic research organizations; with organizations abroad - NLM, APA, CAS, BIOSIS, LOCKHEED, SDC, IRS-QUEST, and the European and international organizations - EUSIDIC, ASIDIC, EUSIREF

17. Information services against payment

181 1. NATIONAL LIBRARY FOR PSYCHOLOGY AND EDUCATION

STATENS PSYKOLOGISK-PEDAGOGISKA BIBLIOTEK

SPPB

2. Parent institution: Ministry of Education

3. Box 23099, S-104 35 Stockholm
tel. 08-32 48 70

4. 1885

5. Director: Ekman,Elin
The staff numbers 9 professionals and 5 non-professionals

6. National special library for psychology and education

7. Departments or activities: Library organization administration; Purchases; Loans, etc. Documentation sections for editing of abstract publications and for computerized information searches

8. Major fields: education and psychology in general, etc.
Specific fields: complete file of ERIC microfiches

9. National periodicals are processed

11. Holdings: books ⎫
periodicals ⎬ 195 000 vols.
abstract journals ⎭
manuscripts   3 450
microcopies   215 000
periodicals and abstract journals   800 titles
Subject and alphabetical indices are used

12. The library is open to the public

13. Information services:
    Publications - abstract journals
    SDI
    Compilation of documentary syntheses
    Reference services

14. Magnetic tapes (available in Stockholm) connected to inter-
    national search systems are used
    Hardware: Teletype terminal

15. Photocopying machine, microfiche copier, stencil, micro-
    fiche reader-printers

16. Participates in a project for Scandinavian educational and
    psychological information

17. Information services free of charge

182 1. ROYAL INSTITUTE OF TECHNOLOGY. LIBRARY, INFORMATION AND DO-
        CUMENTATION CENTRE

        KUNGLIGA TEKNISKA HÖGSKOLANS BIBLIOTEK, INFORMATIONS- OCH
        DOKUMENTATIONS- CENTRALEN

        IDC-KTHB

     2. Parent institution: Royal Institute of Technology

     3. S-100 44 Stockholm
        cable address: Technology
        tel. + 46 8 787 89 50
        telex: 103 89 kthb s

     4. 1967

     5. Director: Hjerppe,Roland
        The staff numbers 18 professionals and 7 non-professionals

     6. National centre for science and technology and for IRS-sys-
        tem QUEST

     7. Departments or activities: SDI-service from about 20 data
        bases on an in-house system (EPOS/VIRA); QUEST-concentra-
        tor for Sweden and Finland; Education of students; Program-
        ming and computing
        Special projects: implementation of data bases and user
        adaptation of 3RIP (Swedish interactive searching and edit-
        ing system); cooperation with the Portuguese organization
        CDCT in introducing modern methods for information transfer
        in Portugal; updating and handling of EUSIDIC Data base
        Guide

     8. Major fields: social sciences, education, etc.

     9. National and foreign periodicals, books and reports on mag-
        netic tapes are processed

    10. The Centre is a department within the library

13. Information services:
    Publications
    SDI
    Bibliographical searches

14. Hardware: IBM 370/165, DEC 10, PDP 11 (two), 6 TTY-compati-
    ble terminals and 1 dedicated terminal (QUEST)
    Software: EPOS/VIRA, 3 RIP, PL/1, ASSEMBLER, SIMULA

16. Relations with MIC, SPPB, Studsvik Energi Teknik, Swedish
    University of Agriculture, Forestry and Veterinary Medicine,
    Ultuna (Sweden), CNRS (France), CDCT (Portugal), European
    Space Agency IRS (Italy), LOCKHEED, SDC, New York Times In-
    formation Bank, BLAISE (Great Britain), and with regional
    and international organizations - EUSIDIC and connected
    working groups in referral and policy, ASIDIC, ASIS

17. Information services against payment

183   1. ROYAL LIBRARY

       KUNGLIGA BIBLIOTEKET

       KB

      3. Box 5039, S-102 41 Stockholm 5
         tel. 08-24 10 40
         telex: 196 40 kbs s

      4. 16th c.

      5. Director: Tynell,Lars
         The staff numbers 167 professionals and 58 non-professionals

      6. National Library

      8. Major fields: humanities and social sciences
         Specific fields: all Swedish publications

      9. National and foreign books and periodicals are processed

     11. Holdings: 60 000 shelf metres

     12. The library is open to the public

     13. Information services:
         Publications - abstract journals, bibliographies and others
         Lending and reference services
         Provision of photocopies

     14. Cataloguing, localization and catalogue production
         Hardware: SAAB D223 and SAAB D5
         Software: COBOL - Library, Information system (LIBRIS-II)

     15. Electrostatic copying and stenciling

184   1. STOCKHOLM SCHOOL OF ECONOMICS LIBRARY
          HANDELSHÖGSKOLANS BIBLIOTEK

       2. Parent institution: Stockholm School of Economics

       3. Box 6501, S-113 83 Stockholm
          tel. 08-736 0120

       5. Director: Janson,Birgitta
          The staff numbers 13 professionals and 10 non-professionals

       6. Inofficial central library for economics and management

       7. Departments or activities: Acquisition; Cataloguing; Loans
          and documentation

       8. Major fields: economics, management, law, economic geogra-
          phy, transportation economics
          Specific fields: company information, history of industrial
          enterprises, multinational companies

       9. National and foreign books, periodicals and "gray" litera-
          ture are processed

      11. Holdings: books   170 000 vols.
                    periodicals   2 400 titles
                    abstract journals   15 titles
          Alphabetical, classified UDC catalogue, periodical indices
          and EMDOC are used

      12. The library is open to the public

      13. Information services:
          Publications - abstract journals and bibliographies
          Bibliographical and literature searches
          Lending service
          Provision of photocopies

      14. Lists ECON, SCANP, in cooperation with the Helsinki School
          of Economics, periodicals lists

      15. Photocopying machine, offset and stencils

      16. Relations with other units in social sciences information
          and documentation in the country

      17. Information services free of charge and against payment

185   1. UNIVERSITY LIBRARY UMEÅ
          UMEÅ UNIVERSITETSBIBLIOTEK

       2. Subordinated to the Umeå University

       3. Box 718, S-901 10 Umeå
          tel. 090-165000

telex: 540 60 ubumea s

4. 1964

5. Director: Snellman,Karin
   The staff numbers 13 professionals and 72 non-professionals

7. Departments or activities: Acquisition; Cataloguing; Lending

8. Major fields: natural and social sciences and, to a lesser
   extent, humanities, etc.

9. Foreign books, periodicals, "gray" literature and national
   newspapers are processed

11. Holdings: books   approx. 380 000 vols.
              periodicals   7 500 titles
              abstract journals approx.   20 titles
    Own card catalogue and a standard collection of national and
    international bibliographies in nearly all fields are used

12. The library is open to the public

13. Information services:
    Lending service

14. Automated information system used is MEDLINE
    Hardware: TEXAS INSTRUMENTS SILENT 733 terminal

15. Reader-printer printing from microfilms, photocopying ma-
    chine

17. Information services free of charge

186 1. UPPSALA UNIVERSITY LIBRARY

     UPPSALA UNIVERSITETSBIBLIOTEK

     UUB

     2. Parent institution: Uppsala University

     3. Box 510,75120 S - Uppsala
        tel. 018-139440
        telex: 76076 ubupps-s

     4. 1620

     5. Director: Totties,Thomas
        The staff numbers 44 professionals and 125 non-professionals

     7. Departments or activities: Swedish books; Foreign books;
        Manuscripts; Cataloguing; Reading rooms and circulation;
        Institute library service; Administration

     8. Major fields: all subjects except technology
        Specific field: depository library for Swedish literature

9. Foreign books and periodicals, national "gray" literature
   and newspapers on microfilms are processed

11. Holdings: books   more than 2 000 000 vols.
             periodicals and
             abstract journals approx. 8 000 foreign and all
                                 Swedish periodicals
    Authors', systematical and special catalogues are used

12. The library is open to the public

13. Information services:
    Publications - bibliographies and others
    SDI (MEDLARS and other data bases LOCKHEED, SDC, ESA, etc.)
    Bibliographical, literature and survey data searches
    Lending and reference services
    Provision of photocopies

14. MEDICINE terminal (bio-medical), LIBRIS terminal
    Hardware: INCOTERM terminals, TEXAS INSTRUMENTS SILENT 700
    Software: LIBRIS, ELHILL, EPOS-VIRA

15. Printing and duplicating machines

16. Relations with MIC and IDC-KTAHB in the country and with
    UNESCO, IFLA and FIO abroad

17. Information services free of charge and against payment

Switzerland

187 1. LIBRARY OF THE ST.GALLEN GRADUATE SCHOOL OF ECONOMICS, BUSI-
NESS AND PUBLIC ADMINISTRATION

     BIBLIOTHEK DER HOCHSCHULE ST.GALLEN FÜR WIRTSCHAFTS- UND SO-
ZIALWISSENSCHAFTEN

     Library of H.S.G.

  2. Subordinated to the central administration of the St.Gallen
Graduate School

  3. Dufourstr. 50, CH-9000 St.Gallen
tel. 071-23 31 49

  4. 1889

  5. Director: Bischoff,Rosmarie
The staff numbers 4 professionals and 6 non-professionals

  6. University library

  8. Major fields: economics, business, public administration

  9. National and foreign books and periodicals are processed

 11. Holdings: books   124 150 vols. in total
         periodicals   700 vols. in total
Authors' and systematical catalogues are used

 12. The library is not open to the public

 13. Information services:
Publications - abstract journals and bibliographies
Bibliographical and literature searches
Reference services

 15. Photocopying machine

 17. Information services free of charge

188   1. RESEARCH CENTRE FOR SWISS POLITICS

FORSCHUNGSZENTRUM FÜR SCHWEIZERISCHE POLITIK

2. Subordinated to the central administration of the University of Bern

3. Neubrückstrasse 10,   3012 Bern
tel. 031 65 8331

4. 1965

5. Director: Gruner,Erich
The staff numbers 8 professionals and 3 non-professionals

8. Major field: Swiss politics
Specific fields: institutions, parties, labour movement, etc.

9. Foreign books and periodicals, national "gray" literature, and documentation on Swiss politics are processed

10. The Centre has a library

11. Holdings: books   7 000 titles
             periodicals   110 titles
Alphabetical catalogue is used

12. The library is open to the public

13. Information services
Publications
Lending service

189   1. SWISS ECONOMIC ARCHIVES

SCHWEIZERISCHES WIRTSCHAFTSARCHIV - ARCHIVES ÉCONOMIQUES SUISSES

SWA resp. AES

2. Subordinated to the Public Library of the University of Basel

3. Kollegienhaus der Universität, Petersgraben, CH-4051 Basel
P.O.Box, CH-4003 Basel
tel. 061 254499

4. 1910

5. Director: Mentha,Claude
The staff numbers 2 professionals and 8 non-professionals

6. The most important specialized library and documentation centre in economic and social policies of the country

7. Departments or activities: Specialized library; Documentation centre; Historical; Press cuttings; Lending; Cataloguing; Information; Secretariat

8. Major fields: economic policy of Switzerland and its general
   aspects, economies of different countries, financial and social policies of Switzerland, documentation of firms and economic associations in the country, major firms and organizations in foreign countries
   Specific fields: documentation on personalia in business,
   scientific and political life of the country, business archives of old firms, merchant and banking houses of Basel
   and its region, other manuscripts, papers and documents concerning the economic life during 18th and 19th c.

9. National books, periodicals, "gray" literature and manuscripts are processed

10. The Archives have a library

11. Holdings: books and periodicals   365 000 vols. in total
              periodicals   1 000 titles
              dossiers with manuscripts   500 in total
              press cuttings   1 000 000 in total
    Alphabetical and systematical catalogues are used

12. The library is open to the public

13. Information services:
    Bibliographical and literature searches
    Lending service
    Provision of photocopies

15. Photocopying machine

16. Participates in the Union catalogue of the Swiss National
    Library in Bern

17. Information services free of charge

190   1. SWISS SOCIAL ARCHIVES
         SCHWEIZERICHES SOZIALARCHIV

      3. 8001 Zurich, Neumarkt 28
         tel. 01-32.76.44

      4. 1906

      5. Director: Tucek,Miroslav
         The staff numbers 10 professionals

      7. Departments or activities: Books; Periodicals; Press-cut-
         tings; Small documents

      8. Major fields: society, sociology, civilization, law, admi-
         nistration, politics, socialism, cooperative society, wel-
         fare, social policy, labour, unions, political economy

      9. National books, periodicals, "gray" literature and foreign
         press-cuttings are processed

11. Holdings: books   80 000 vols.
             periodicals   4 300 titles
             "gray" literature   750 000
             press-cuttings   750 000

13. Information services:
    Publications - abstract journals, directories and others
    SDI
    Bibliographical, literature and survey data searches
    Lending service
    Provision of photocopies and/or microforms

16. Relations with other information units in the country

17. Information services free of charge

Union of the Soviet Socialist Republics

191   1. ALL-UNION SCIENTIFIC AND TECHNICAL INFORMATION CENTRE
         VSESOJUZNYI NAUCNO-TEHNICESKII INFORMACIONNYI CENTR
         VNTIC

      2. Subordinated to the State Committee for Science and Techno-
         logy

      3. Moscow 125493, ul.Smoljanaya 14
         tel. 4568200

      4. 1967

      5. Director: Sytchev,Vjatcheslav
         The staff in social sciences numbers 11 professionals

      6. All-union centre

      7. Departments or activities: Input line; Indexing; Microfilm-
         ing; Compilation of scientific holdings; Automated data pro-
         cessing and publishing polygraphy

      8. Major fields: all fields of science
         Specific fields: social sciences, registration, accounting
         and information of research and development projects and
         theses

      9. Soviet "gray" literature is processed

     10. The Centre has a library

     11. Holdings: manuscripts 62 320 in total in social sciences
         Subject, numerical, alphabetical and reference catalogues
         are used

     12. The library is open to the public

     13. Information services:

Various publications
Literature searches

14. Automated preparation of publications
Hardware: Prototypesetting machine DIGISET, EC 1040 computer

15. Printing machines

16. Relations with the International Scientific and Technical
Information Centre of the CMEA member-countries, partici-
pates in the State Scientific and Technical Information
System

17. Information services free of charge and against payment

192   1. ALL-UNION STATE LIBRARY OF FOREIGN LITERATURE

VSESOUZNAJA GOSUDARSTVENNAJA BIBLIOTEKA INOSTRANNOJ LITERA-
TURI

VGBIL

2. Subordinated to the USSR Ministry of Culture

3. Moscow 109189, ul.Uljanovskaja 1
cable address: Moscow 240 Stacii
tel. 297 28 39
telex: Stacii 7234 SU

4. 1922

5. Director: Gvishiani,Ludmila
The staff numbers over 500 professionals and 100 non-professionals

6. All-union library, interlibrary loan centre on literature in
foreign languages

7. Departments or activities: Funds registration; Cataloguing;
Book storage; Reference bibliographic; Subscriptions; Read-
ing-rooms; Audiovisual means; International book exchange;
International library relations; Lecture-exhibition; Theory
and practice of collections acquisition; Asia and Africa;
Library science; Scientific and bibliographical; Scientific
and analytical on foreign belles-lettres and drama problems;
Rare books; Book hygiene and restoration; Automation and me-
chanization of library and bibliographical processes

8. Major fields: foreign library science, bibliography of fic-
tion, drama and art, methods of foreign language teaching,
latest foreign literature in social sciences
Specific fields: methodical guidance of foreign literature
departments within the system of the Ministry of Culture

9. Soviet and foreign books, periodicals, "gray" literature,
audio-visual materials and magnetic tapes are processed

11. Holdings: books   1 579 319 vols. in total
             periodicals   2 626 996 vols. in total
    Alphabetical and systematical catalogues are used

12. The library is open to the public

13. Information services:
    Publications - bibliographies, directories and others
    Russian editorial office of the journal of "UNESCO Bulletin
    for Libraries"
    SDI
    Translation
    Bibliographical, literature and survey data searches
    Compilation of documentary syntheses
    Lending and reference services
    Provision of photocopies and/or microforms

15. Printing and duplication machines

16. Relations with the Information Centre on Culture and Arts
    of the Lenin State Library

17. Information services free of charge and against payment

193 1. CENTRE OF SCIENTIFIC INFORMATION ON SOCIAL SCIENCES OF THE
        ACADEMY OF SCIENCES OF THE AZERBAIJAN SSR

        CENTR NAUCNOJ INFORMACII PO OBSTESTVENNIM NAUKAM AKADEMII
        NAUK AZERBAJDZANSKOJ SSR

        CNION AN ASSR

     2. Parent institution: Academy of Sciences of the Azerbaijan
        SSR

     3. 370143 Baku - 143, prosp.Narimanova 31
        Akademic campus
        tel. 37-80-28

     4. 1971

     5. Director: Zargarov,Abdul
        The staff numbers 25 professionals and 24 non-professionals

     6. Republican information centre

     7. Departments or activities: Abstract information; Bibliogra-
        phical information; Publications and translations; Reference
        information collection

     8. Major fields: social sciences, foreign literature related to
        Azerbaijan studies, foreign literature on social sciences,
        related to Middle East countries

     9. National and foreign books and periodicals are processed

    11. Holdings: books   1 751 titles - 3 053 vols.

                              periodicals   97 titles - 3 110 vols. in total
                              abstract journals 30 titles -   450 vols. in total
             Uses the Central Scientific Library of the Republic's Acade-
             my of Sciences

      12. The library is open to the public

      13. Information services:
          Publications - abstract journals, bibliographies, directo-
          ries and others
          SDI
          Translation
          Bibliographical, literature and survey data searches
          Compilation of documentary syntheses
          Lending and reference services

      15. Uses the Printing house of the Academy of Sciences of the
          Azerbaijan SSR

      16. Relations with INION AS USSR and republican scientific in-
          formation centres on social sciences

194   1. CENTRE OF SCIENTIFIC INFORMATION ON SOCIAL SCIENCES OF THE
         ACADEMY OF SCIENCES OF THE LITHUANIAN SSR

         CENTR NAUCNOJ INFORMACII PO OBSTESTVENNIM NAUKAM AKADEMII
         NAUK LITOVSKOJ SSR

      2. Parent institution: Academy of Sciences of the Lithuanian
         SSR

      3. 232034 Vilnus, ul.Michurina 1/46
         tel. 73-24-43

      4. 1971

      5. Director: Balsys,Antanas
         The staff numbers 15 professionals and 1 non-professional

      6. Republican information centre

      7. Departments or activities: Soviet Lithuanian studies and
         foreign Lithuanian studies

      8. Major field: social sciences

      9. National books, periodicals and "gray" literature are pro-
         cessed

      10. The Centre has no library

      11. Uses the Central Scientific Library of the Republic's Aca-
          demy of Sciences

      13. Information services:
          Publications - bibliographies and directories
          Translation

Bibliographical, literature and survey data searches
Compilation of documentary syntheses
Provision of photocopies and/or microforms

15. Printing machines

16. Relations with INION AS USSR and republican scientific information centres on social sciences

17. Information services free of charge

195   1. DEPARTMENT OF SCIENTIFIC INFORMATION ON SOCIAL SCIENCES OF
THE ACADEMY OF SCIENCES OF THE BYELORUSSIAN SSR

OTDEL NAUCNOJ INFORMACII PO OBSTESTVENNIM NAUKAM AKADEMII
NAUK BYELORUSSKOI SSR

ONION AN BSSR

2. Parent institution: Academy of Sciences of the Byelorussian
SSR

3. 220072 Minsk-72, Akademicheskaya 25
cable address: Minsk Nauka, ONION AN BSSR
tel. 39-45-43

4. 1970

5. Director: Ampilov,Vladimir
The staff numbers 17 professionals and 6 non-professionals

6. Republican information centre

7. Departments or activities: National literature; Foreign literature

8. Major field: social sciences

9. National books and periodicals are processed

11. Holdings: books   1 260 vols. in total
             periodicals   4 760 vols. in total
             abstract journals   225 vols. in total
Main reference card file is used
Uses the Central Scientific library of the Republic's Aca-
demy of Sciences

12. The library is open to the public

13. Information services:
Publications - abstract journals and bibliographies
SDI
Translation
Bibliographical searches
Compilation of documentary syntheses
Lending service

196 1. DEPARTMENT OF SCIENTIFIC INFORMATION ON SOCIAL SCIENCES OF
THE ACADEMY OF SCIENCES OF THE KAZAKH SSR

OTDEL NAUCNOJ INFORMACII PO OBSTESTVENNIM NAUKAM AKADEMII
NAUK KAZAKHSKOI SSR

ONION AN KSSR

2. Parent institution: Academy of Sciences of the Kazakh SSR

3. 480021 Alma-Ata, 21, ul.Shevtchenko 28
tel. 68-22-31

4. 1977

5. Director: Achmedova,Nurkhan
The staff numbers 21 professionals

6. Republican information centre

7. Departments or activities: Soviet literature; Foreign literature; Reference-information collection

8. Major field: social sciences
Specific field: scientific information on Kazakh studies

9. National and foreign books, periodicals, theses and "gray"
literature are processed

10. The Department has a library

11. Holdings: books   332 titles - 470 vols. in total
             periodicals   15 titles - 150 vols. in total
             abstract journals   6 titles - 13 vols. in total
Various catalogues and indices are used
Uses the Central Scientific Library of the Republic's Acade-
my of Sciences

12. The library is open to the public

13. Information services:
Publications - bibliographies and others
Translation
Bibliographical searches
Compilation of documentary syntheses
Lending service

15. Printing machines

16. Relations with INION AS USSR and with the republican scientific information centres on social sciences

17. Information services free of charge

197 1. INFORMATION CENTRE ON CULTURE AND ARTS AT THE LENIN STATE
LIBRARY

INFORMACIONNIJ CENTR PO PROBLEMAM KULTURI I ISKUSTVA GOSU-

DARSTVENNOJ BIBLIOTEKI IM.LENINA

Informculture

2. Subordinated to the central administration of the Lenin State Library

3. 101000 Moscow, prospect Kalinina 3
tel. 202-83-12, 222-86-59
telex: 7167 wg bibl SU

4. 1972

5. Bagrova,Irina
The staff numbers 90 professionals and 50 non-professionals

6. A central information unit on culture and arts

7. Departments or activities: General problems of culture; Library science; Bibliographical studies; Museum studies; Functional sections

8. Major fields: culture, music, arts and library studies

9. Soviet and foreign books, periodicals and national "gray" literature are processed

12. Holdings: manuscripts   8 187 in total
Uses all the catalogues of the Lenin State Library

13. Information services:
Publications - bibliographical and others
SDI
Bibliographical, literature and survey data searches
Compilation of documentary syntheses
Lending and reference services
Provision of photocopies and/or microforms

14. Automated information system in the field of culture and arts is in preparation

15. The Centre uses the facilities of the Lenin State Library

16. Relations with INION AS USSR, branch information centres, foreign information centres and the Vienna Centre

17. Information services free of charge

198 1. INFORMATION CENTRE ON SOCIAL SCIENCES OF THE ACADEMY OF SCIENCES OF THE ESTONIAN SSR

CENTR NAUCNOJ INFORMACII PO OBSTESTVENNIM NAUKAM AKADEMII NAUK ESTONSKOJ SSR

CNION AN ESSR

2. Parent institution: Academy of Sciences of the Estonian SSR

3. 200 101 Tallin, bld.Estonia 7
   tel. 449-370, 605-159

4. 1976

5. Director: Kahk,Uhan
   The staff numbers 8 professionals and 12 non-professionals

6. Republican information centre

7. Departments or activities: Operational and printing information; Bibliographical information; Laboratory of information techniques

8. Major field: social sciences
   Specific fields: Estonian and Finno-Ugric studies

9. National and foreign books, periodicals and national "gray" literature are processed

11. Holdings: books   56 586 vols. in total
             periodicals   322 055 vols. in total
             manuscripts   95 750 in total
    Uses the Central Scientific Library of the Republic's Academy of Sciences

12. The library is open to the public

13. Information services:
    Publications - bibliographies and others
    SDI
    Translation
    Bibliographical and literature searches
    Compilation of documentary syntheses
    Lending service
    Provision of photocopies/or microforms

14. Automated information system is in preparation
    Hardware: CONSUL-253, OPTIMA-527
    Software: PL/1, FORTRAN

15. Reprographic machine and operational polygraphy

16. Relations with INION AS USSR and republican scientific information centres on social sciences

17. Information services free of charge

199 1. INFORMATION DEPARTMENT OF THE NATIONAL SCIENTIFIC RESEARCH INSTITUTE FOR HIGHER EDUCATION

OTDEL NAUCNOJ INFORMACII NAUCNOISSLEDOVATELSKOGO INSTITUTA PROBLEM VISSEJ SKOLI

ONI NIIVS

2. Subordinated to the Ministry of Higher and Specialized Secondary Education

3. 105318 Moscow, Uzmailovskoye Shos. 4
   tel. 369-20-23

4. 1973

5. Director: Zamuruev,Edward
   The staff numbers 23 professionals and 30 non-professionals

6. Central branch scientific and technical information unit in
   the field of higher and specialized secondary education

7. Departments or activities: Information accumulation, processing, storage, retrieval, preparation of information materials for publication; Request-lending information services

8. Major fields: higher and specialized secondary education
   Specific fields: university and specialized secondary school
   education and communist upbringing, management, economy and
   forecasting of higher education development, organization
   of university research work, higher and specialized secondary education abroad

9. Soviet and foreign books, periodicals, "gray" literature
   and national audio-visual materials are processed

10. The Department has a library

11. Holdings: books   25 345 vols in total
             periodicals   660 titles - 14 733 vols. in total
             abstract journals 81 titles - 1 270 vols. in total
             microcopies   27 in total
             manuscripts   6 470 in total

12. The library is open to the public

13. Information services:
    Publications - bibliographies, directories and others
    SDI
    Translation
    Bibliographical, literature and survey data searches
    Compilation of documentary syntheses
    Lending and reference services
    Provision of xerocopies

14. Automated information system - SDI on higher education
    Hardware: EC-1020

15. Printing and duplicating machines

16. Relations with INION AS USSR and the All-Union Scientific
    and Technical Information Centre in the country and with
    CEPES, UNESCO abroad

17. Information services free of charge and against payment

200   1. K.D.USHINSKI STATE SCIENTIFIC PEDAGOGICAL LIBRARY OF THE
         ACADEMY OF PEDAGOGICAL SCIENCES OF THE USSR

         GOSUDARSTVENNAJA NAUCNO-PEDAGOGICESKAJA BIBLIOTEKA AKADEMII
         PEDAGOGICESKIH NAUK SSSR IM.K.D.USINSKOGO

         GNPB

      2. Subordinated to the central administration of the USSR Aca-
         demy of Pedagogical Sciences

      3. Moscow 109017, 3 Bolshoi Tolmachevsky pereulok
         tel. 231-05-85

      4. 1925

      5. Director: Serebrov,Nikolai
         The staff numbers 131 professionals and 34 non-professionals

      6. A branch state library

      7. Departments or activities: usual library ones

      8. Major field: pedagogics

      9. Soviet and foreign books and periodicals are processed

     11. Holdings: books   1 168 741 vols. in total
                   periodicals   419 316 vols. in total
         Alphabetical and systematical catalogues are used

     12. The library is open to the public

     13. Information services:
         Publications - bibliographies
         Bibliographical searches
         Lending and reference services

     15. Duplicating machines

     16. Relations with branch information centres on social sciences,
         INION AS USSR, Information Centre of Culture and Arts, In-
         formation Department of the National Research Institute for
         Higher Education, Scientific Information Department of the
         All-Union Vocational Research Institute; with the scientific
         information centres and pedagogical libraries in the socia-
         list countries

     17. Information services free of charge

201   1. LENIN STATE LIBRARY

         GOSUDARSTVENNAJA ORDENA LENINA BIBLIOTEKA IMENI LENINA

         GBL

      2. Subordinated to the Ministry of Culture

      3. Moscow 101000, 3 Prospect Kalinina

tel. 202-40-56
telex: 4167 Wg bibl. SU

4. 1862

5. Director: Sicorsky,Nikolaj
   The staff numbers 2502 professionals and 782 non-professionals

6. National universal library, leading information-bibliographical organization in scientific auxiliary and recommendation bibliography, coordination centre on interlibrary lending problems, leading research organization in library and
   bibliography science and book history, all-union scientific-
   methodological centre for the libraries in the country

7. Departments or activities: National acquisition and inner-
   union book exchange; Foreign acquisition and international
   book exchange; Cataloguing; Book storage; Hygiene and restoration; Microphoto-copying; Lending service; International
   library contacts; Library science; Scientific-methodologi-
   cal; Scientific-organizational; Technological; Computing;
   Educational; Periodicals, theses, cartography, music, publications and records, manuscripts and rare books; Information-bibliographical; Recommendation library; Information
   centre on culture and arts

8. Major fields: all fields of science
   Specific fields: culture and arts, library and bibliography
   sciences and book history, state storage of press articles
   of the USSR peoples, foreign literature and manuscripts

9. Soviet and foreign books, periodicals, "gray" literature,
   audio-visual materials and magnetic tapes, cards, notes,
   isography and microforms are processed

10. Holdings: books   11 894 690 vols. in total
              periodicals   11 248 940 vols. in total
              microcopies   695 208 in total
              manuscripts   331 556 in total
    Alphabetical, systematical and subject catalogues and union
    catalogues of the holdings of the larger Soviet libraries
    are used

12. The library is open to the public

13. Information services:
    Publications - bibliographies, directories and others
    SDI
    Bibliographical, literature and survey data searches
    Compilation of documentary syntheses
    Lenidng service
    Provision of photocopies and/or microforms

14. Integrated automated system on library, bibliographical and
    information processes is in preparation and partly used in
    a test regime
    Hardware: computers, orgautomates, storage on magnetic tapes
    Software: PL/1, ALGOL, FORTRAN

15. Microfilming, duplicating, printing and other machines

16. Relations with the All-Union Book Chamber, VINITI AS USSR,
    State Public Scientific and Technical Library, INION AS
    USSR, participates indirectly in ISTIC of CMEA member-coun-
    tries

17. Information and library services free of charge and against
    payment

202 1. LIBRARY OF THE ACADEMY OF SCIENCES OF THE USSR

     BIBLIOTEKA AKADEMII NAUK SSSR

     BAN SSSR

     3. 199164 Leningrad, V-164,   Birzhevaja Linija, 1
        tel. 218-35-92

     4. 1714

     5. Director: Lyutova,Kcenija
        The staff numbers 645 professionals and 142 non-professionals

     6. All-union universal scientific library

     7. Departments or activities: National and foreign literature
        acquisition; Cataloguing; Classification; Main collection
        storage; Readers' services; Reference-bibliographical; In-
        formation; Scientific-bibliographical; Scientific-methodi-
        cal; Literature on the languages of Asian and African coun-
        tries; Cartographic materials; Manuscripts and rare books;
        Book history; Scientific-organizational; Mechanization and
        automation of library processes; Book hygiene; Network of
        libraries of the Leningrad institutes

     8. Major fields: all fields of science
        Specific fields: library and bibliography science, organi-
        zation and storage of archive copies and bibliographical
        accounting of USSR AS publications, organization and sto-
        rage of scientific works awarded with prizes of the USSR AS

     9. Soviet and foreign books, periodicals, "gray" literature
        and microfilms are processed

    11. Holdings: books   569 839 vols. in total
                  periodicals   6 590 168 vols. in total
                  microcopies   125 596 in total
                  manuscripts   16 359 in total
        Alphabetical, systematical, subject catalogues, reference-
        bibliographical card file are used

    12. The library is open to the public

    13. Information services:
        Publications - bibliographies, directories and others
        Bibliographical literature and survey data searches

Lending service
Provision of photocopies and/or microforms

15. Printing, duplicating and photocomposing machines

16. Relations with other information units and libraries in the country

17. Information services free of charge and against payment

203 1. M.E.SALTIKOV-SHCHEDRIN STATE PUBLIC LIBRARY

GOSUDARSTVENNAJA ORDENA TRUDOVOGO KRASNOGO ZNAMENI PUBLIC-
NAJA BIBLIOTEKA IMENI M.E.SALTIKOVA-STEDRINA

GPB

2. Subordinated to the Ministry of Culture

3. 191069 Leningrad, ul.Sadovaya 18
cable address: Leningrad Mysl
tel. 215-28-56

4. 1814

5. Director: Shilov,Leonid
The staff numbers 1130 professionals and 320 non-professionals

6. All-union universal library; Branch centre of interlibrary
lending, main scientific research body and national coordination centre in library science, bibliography and bibliology; Methodological centre of libraries in the system of
the Ministry of Culture

7. Departments or activities: Acquisition; Processing and cataloguing; Collections and services; General reading; Lending; Information-bibliographical; Literature of USSR peoples'
languages; Literature in Asian and African national languages; Newspapers; Prints; Music and sound recordings; Cartography; Manuscripts and rare books; Conservation and restoration; Microphotoxerox; Scientific research; Bibliography
and bibliology; Scientific methodological

8. Major fields: all fields of science
Specific fields: library science, bibliography, bibliology,
state holdings of printed publications of USSR peoples, foreign literature and others, all-union depository, coordination of holdings of foreign literature and reference information activities with larger libraries in Leningrad and
in the country

9. Soviet and foreign books, periodicals, audio-visual materials, musical, cartographic, graphic-arts works and national "gray" literature are processed

11. Holdings: books   9 878 000 vols. in total

> periodicals   6 202 700 vols. in total
> microcopies   59 500 in total
> manuscripts   5 591 400 in total

Alphabetical and systematical catalogues, subject card files are used

12. The library is open to the public

13. Information services:
Publications - bibliographies and others
SDI
Translation
Bibliographical and survey data searches
Lending service
Provision of photocopies and/or microforms

15. Printing, duplication and microfilming equipment

16. Relations with other information units and libraries in the country; participates in the preparation and publication of union catalogues of collections of larger USSR libraries

17. Information services free of charge and against payment

204 1. SCIENTIFIC INFORMATION CENTRE ON SOCIAL SCIENCES OF THE ACA-
DEMY OF SCIENCES OF THE ARMENIAN SSR

SEKTOR NAUCNOJ INFORMACII PO OBSTESTVENNIM NAUKAM AKADEMII NAUK ARMJANSKOJ SSR

CNION AN ASSR

2. Parent institution: Academy of Sciences of the Armenian SSR

3. 375019 Jerevan, ul.Barekamutyan, 24-D
tel. 58-72-02

4. 1970

5. Director: Barsegyan,Hikar
The staff numbers 21 professionals and 23 non-professionals

6. Republican scientific information centre

7. Departments or activities: Information on economics; Philo-
sophy and law; Historical sciences; Philological sciences;
Publications; Manuscripts deposition; Scientific library;
Rotaprint section

8. Major field: social sciences
Specific fields: scientific information on Armenian studies

9. National and foreign books, periodicals and national "gray" literature are processed

11. Holdings: books   72 200 titles - 161 600 vols.
              periodicals   270 titles - 35 800 vols.

           abstract journals   50 titles - 3 800 vols.
           manuscripts   3 300

12. The library is open to the public

13. Information services:
    Publications - bibliographies, directories and others
    Translation
    Bibliographical searches
    Compilation of documentary syntheses
    Lending and reference services
    Provision of photocopies and/or microforms

15. Printing and duplicating machines

16. Relations with INION AS USSR and the republican scientific
    information centres

17. Information services free of charge

205 1. SCIENTIFIC INFORMATION DEPARTMENT OF THE SOCIAL SCIENCES
        DIVISION AT THE ACADEMY OF SCIENCES OF THE UKRAINIAN SSR

        OTDEL NAUCNOJ INFORMACII SEKCII OBSTESTVENNIH NAUK AKADEMII
        NAUK UKRAINSKOJ SSR

     2. Parent institution: Academy of Sciences of the Ukrainian SSR

     3. 252001, Kiev GSP.1, ul.Kirova 4
        tel. 229-76-52

     4. 1977

     5. Director: Valko,Ivan
        The staff numbers 8 professionals and 3 non-professionals

     6. Republican coordination centre of scientific information

     7. Departments or activities: History; Economics; Philosophy;
        Law; Literary criticism; Linguistics; Art reviews

     8. Major field : social sciences
        Specific fields: studies on scientific concepts of society's
        social and economic development, theoretical generalization
        of information problems

     9. National books and periodicals are processed

    10. The Department has no library

    11. Uses the Central Scientific Library of the Republic's Aca-
        demy of Sciences

    13. Information services:
        Publications
        Bibliographical and literature services

    16. Relations with INION AS USSR and the republican scientific
        information centres on social sciences

206   1. SECTION OF SCIENTIFIC INFORMATION ON SOCIAL SCIENCES AT THE
       ACADEMY OF SCIENCES OF THE GEORGIAN SSR

       SEKTOR NAUCNOJ INFORMACII PO OBSTESTVENNIM NAUKAM AKADEMII
       NAUK GRUZINSKOJ SSR

      2. Parent institution: Academy of Sciences of the Georgian SSR

      3. 380004 Tbilisi 4, ul.Dzerdjinskogo 8
       tel. 99-99-95, 99-78-61

      4. 1970

      5. Director: Kikvadze,Nadar
       The staff numbers 63 professionals and 22 non-professionals

      6. Republican scientific information unit

      7. Departments or activities: Philology; Economics; Abstract-
       ing of national and foreign materials; Bibliographies in
       economics and philosophy; References; Publications

      8. Major field: social sciences

      9. National and foreign books, periodicals and national "gray"
       literature are processed

    10. The institution has a library

    11. Holdings: books   55 000 titles - 128 249 vols. in total
             periodicals   350 titles - 17 200 vols. in total
             abstract journals 200 titles -   1 296 vols. in total
             microcopies   102
             manuscripts   127

    12. The library is open to the public

    13. Information services:
       Publications - bibliographies, directories and others
       SDI
       Translation
       Bibliographical and literature services
       Compilation of documentary syntheses
       Lending and reference services
       Provision of photocopies and/or microforms

    15. Printing, duplicating and microfilming machines

    16. Relations with INION AS USSR and the republican centres on
       scientific information

    17. Information services free of charge

207 1. SOCIAL SCIENCES INFORMATION INSTITUTE AT THE ACADEMY OF
        SCIENCES OF THE USSR

        INSTITUT NAUCNOJ INFORMACII PO OBSTESTVENNIM NAUKAM AKADEMII
        NAUK SSSR

        INION AN SSSR

     2. Parent institution: Academy of Sciences of the USSR

     3. 117418 Moscow, ul.Krasikova 28/45
        tel. 128-89-30

     4. 1968

     5. Director: Vinogradov,Vladimir
        The staff numbers 1130 professionals and 230 non-professionals

     6. Main coordinating body of the social sciences scientific in-
        formation subsystem of the State Scientific and Technical
        Information System

     7. Departments or activities: Branch scientific and informa-
        tion (abstract and bibliographical); Acquisition; Scienti-
        fic collections; Library services; Description of informa-
        tion materials; Reference-bibliographical services; Publi-
        cations and translations; Linguistic provision of informa-
        tion systems; Research and elaboration of information sys-
        tems; Administration

     8. Major field: social sciences
        Specific fields: research on information problems in social
        sciences. Coordination of work in the field of scientific
        information on social sciences

     9. Soviet and foreign books and periodicals, microfilms and
        mimcographic UNO documents are processed

    10. The Institute has a library

    11. Holdings: total number of units 10 360 700
        Alphabetical and subject catalogues, systematical card files
        are used

    12. The library is not open to the public

    13. Information services:
        Publications - abstract journals, bibliographies, directo-
        ries and others
        SDI
        Translation
        Bibliographical, literature and survey data searches
        Compilation of documentary syntheses
        Lending service
        Provision of photocopies and/or microforms

    14. Automated information system in the field of social sciences
        Publication of information materials, SDI, retrospective in-
        formation and others. AIS-MISON in preparation
        Hardware: Computers and photocomposing machines M-4030,
        DIGISET 40T2, HEWLETT-PACKARD 3000 series II; Computer com-
        munication leased-line with SIC-BAS (Sofia)

Software: ASSEMBLER, PL/1, SPL

15. Printing, duplicating and microfilming machines

16. Relations with the national, branch, republican and other
    information units in social sciences in the country and ab-
    road and with the international organizations: FID, IFLA,
    the International Economic History Association, the Inter-
    national Committee for Social Sciences Information and Do-
    cumentation, the Vienna Centre, the International Economic
    Association, UNESCO projects. Member and main body of MISON

17. Information services free of charge and against payment

208   1. STATE PUBLIC HISTORICAL LIBRARY OF THE RUSSIAN SOVIET FEDE-
         RAL SOCIALIST REPUBLIC

         GOSUDARSTVENNAJA PUBLICNAJA ISTORICESKAJA BIBLIOTEKA RSFSR

         GPIB

      2. Subordinated to the Ministry of Culture

      3. 101839 Moscow, Starosadskij pereulok 9
         tel. 228-05-22
         telex: 112062

      4. 1938

      5. Director: Kurantseva,Klavdija
         The staff numbers 276 professionals and 85 non-professionals

      6. Republican library

      7. Departments or activities: Acquisition; Storage; Literature
         processing; Services; Methodical bibliographical; Reference;
         Research; Rare books

      8. Major field: historical sciences
         Specific fields: library science, theory of scientific and
         recommendation bibliography

      9. Soviet and foreign books, periodicals and "gray" literature
         are processed

     11. Holdings: books   294 927 vols. in total
                   newspapers and journals 1 138 640 vols. in total
                   microcopies   12 903 in total
                   manuscripts   265

     12. The library is open to the public

     13. Information services:
         Publications - bibliographies and directories
         SDI
         Bibliographical and survey data searches
         Lending and reference services

Provision of photocopies and/or microforms

16. Relations with other libraries in the country; participates in union catalogues

17. Information services free of charge and against payment

Yugoslavia

209 1. FOREIGN TRADE RESEARCH INSTITUTE. LIBRARY
        INSTITUT ZA SPOLJNU TRGOVINU, BIBLIOTEKA

     2. Parent institution: Foreign Trade Research Institute

     3. Moše Pijade 8/III, 11000 Beograd
        cable address: Trgoinstitut
        tel. 339-041

     4. 1955

     5. The staff numbers 2 professionals

     8. Major fields: foreign trade, economics, statistics

     11. Holdings: books   19 632 vols. in total
                   periodicals   20 000 vols. in total
         Alphabetical indices are used

     12. The library is not open to the public

     13. Information services:
         Lending service
         Provision of photocopies

     15. Photocopying machine

210 1. INSTITUTE OF COMPARATIVE LAW. LIBRARY
        BIBLIOTEKA INSTITUTA ZA UPOREDNO PRAVO

     3. Beograd, Terazije 41
        tel. 338-198

     4. 1956

5. Director: Jovanović,Vladimir (of the Institute)
   The staff numbers 5 professionals

8. Major field: international comparative law

9. National and foreign books and periodicals are processed

11. Holdings: books   18 172 titles - 3 100 vols.
              periodicals   565 titles - 5 588 vols.

12. The library is open to the public

13. Information services:
    Translation
    Bibliographical, literature and survey data searches
    Compilation of documentary syntheses
    Lending service

17. Information services free of charge

211   1. INSTITUTE OF SOCIOLOGICAL, POLITICAL AND JURIDICAL RESEARCH-
         SKOPJE

         INSTITUT ZA SOCIOLOŠKI I POLITIČKO-PRAVNI ISTRAŽUVANJA -
         SKOPJE

      2. Parent institution: "Cyril and Methodius" University, Skopje

      3. "Partizanski otredi" bb, 91000 Skopje
         tel. 091-258-222; 258-935

      5. Director: Taškovski,Dragan
         The staff numbers 25 professionals and 12 non-professionals

      6. The library is a basic unit

      8. Major fields: sociology, political life, local self-manage-
         ment, history of social ideas, etc.
         Specific fields: rural sociology, system of communal self-
         management, juvenile delinquency

      9. Foreign books and periodicals and research documents are
         processed

     10. The Institute has a library

     11. Holdings: books   3 785 vols. in total
                   periodicals   127 titles - 1 460 vols. in total

     12. The library is open to the public

     13. Information services:
         Publications - abstract journals, bibliographies and others
         Bibliographical, literature and survey data searches
         Lending service

     15. Photocopying machine

16. Cooperation with University and National Library - Skopje

17. Information services free of charge

212   1. LIBRARY OF THE ECONOMICS FACULTY. UNIVERSITY OF SARAJEVO
         BIBLIOTEKA EKONOMISKOG FACULTETA U SARAJEVU

      2. Subordinated to the central administration

      3. Oslobodenja 1,   71 000 Sarajevo
         tel. 35-200

      4. 1952

      5. Director: Volf,Vera
         The staff numbers 4 professionals and 1 non-professional

      6. The library is part of the information system of the Socia-
         list Republic of Bosnia and Herzegovina

      8. Major field: economics

      9. National and foreign books, periodicals and "gray" litera-
         ture are processed

     11. Holdings: books   41 510 titles - 62 710 vols. in total
                   periodicals and
                   abstract journals 1 485 titles - 76 986 vols. in total
         Alphabetical, UDC, topographical and countries' catalogues
         are used

     12. The library is not open to the public

     13. Information services:
         Publications - abstract journals, bibliographies, directo-
         ries and others
         SDI
         Bibliographical, literature and survey data searches
         Compilation of documentary syntheses
         Lending and reference services

     17. Information services free of charge

213   1. LIBRARY OF THE LAW FACULTY OF THE UNIVERSITY OF SARAJEVO
         BIBLIOTEKA PROVNOG FAKULTETA UNIVERSITETA U SARAJEVO

      2. Parent institution: University of Sarajevo

      3. 71 000 Sarajevo,   Obala 7
         tel. 071-34-044

      4. 1947

5. Director: Grebo,Zdravko
   The staff numbers 1 professional and 3 non-professionals

8. Major field: social sciences
   Specific field: law

9. National and foreign books, periodicals and "gray" literature are processed

11. Holdings: books   65 670 titles - 66 662 vols.
             periodicals   2 044 titles - 12 264 vols.
    Alphabetical catalogue is used

12. The library is not open to the public

13. Information services:
    Publications
    Bibliographical, 'literature and survey data searches
    Compilation of documentary syntheses
    Lending service

15. Photocopying machine

16. Relations with other information units in the country and
    regional and international organizations

17. Information services against payment

214   1. NATIONAL AND UNIVERSITY LIBRARY OF BOSNIA AND HERZEGOVINA

         NARODNA I UNIVERSITETSKA BIBLIOTEKA BOSNE I HERZEGOVINE

      3. 71 000 Sarajevo, Obala 42
         tel. 071-22-825
         telex: nubb 41477

      4. 1945

      5. Director: Ivković,Gragiša
         The staff numbers 58 professionals and 35 non-professionals

      6. Main national institution of the information system in the
         Socialist Republic of Bosnia and Herzegovina

      7. Departments or activities: Acquisition of documentation;
         Cataloguing; Information and reference activities, National
         bibliography

      8. Major field: social sciences
         Specific fields: sociology, statistics, politics, economy,
         law, social protection, traffic, ethnology, commerce, educa-
         tion

      9. National and foreign books and periodicals, national "gray"
         literature and audio-visual materials, and secondary publi-
         cations are processed

11. Holdings: books   110 900 titles - 116 000 vols.
           periodicals   3 440 titles -   30 500 vols.
           abstract journals   60 titles -   1 800 vols.
           microcopies   510
           manuscripts   3 200
Alphabetical and UDC catalogues for books and periodicals as well as a national catalogue are used

12. The library is open to the public

13. Information services:
Publications - bibliographies and others
SDI
Bibliographical, literature and survey data searches
Compilation of documentary syntheses
Lending and reference services
Provision of photocopies and/or microforms

15. Photocopying machine

17. Information services free of charge

215   1. SERVICE FOR SCIENTIFIC INFORMATION AND DOCUMENTATION. INSTI-
TUTE OF INTERNATIONAL POLITICS AND ECONOMICS, BELGRADE

OOUR ZA NAUČNU INFORMACIJU I DOKUMENTACIJU INSTITUTA ZA ME-
DJUNARODNU POLITIKU, BEOGRAD

2. Subordinated to the central administration

3. 11001 Beograd, Pošt fah 750
tel. 321-433

4. 1947

5. Director: Pantić,Vladan
The staff numbers 18 professionals and 8 non-professionals

6. The Service is one of the main centres for scientific information in the field of political sciences

7. Departments or activities: Library and documentation

8. Major fields: international relations and law, international
economy, regional development, international organizations,
international workers' and liberation movements

9. National and foreign books, periodicals and "gray" literature are processed

10. The Service has a library

11. Holdings: books   250 000 vols.
           periodicals   1 016 titles
           abstract journals   34 titles
Two authors', subject and title of periodicals and articles,
as well as of UN and other publications catalogues are used

12. The library is open to the public

13. Information services:
    Publications - bibliographies and others
    Translation
    Bibliographical, literature and survey data searches
    Compilation of documentary syntheses
    Lending and reference services
    Provision of photocopies

15. Photocopying machine, stencil, offset

16. Relations: (exchange of literature/sources) with 278 foreign
    institutions

17. Information services free of charge and against payment

Alphabetical List of Institutions

1 ADMINISTRATIVE LIBRARY OF THE FEDERAL MINISTRY OF EDUCATION AND ARTS AND THE FEDERAL MINISTRY OF SCIENCE AND RESEARCH /AMSTBIB-LIOTHEK DES BUNDESMINISTERIUMS FÜR UNTERRICHT UND KUNST UND d.BM. f.WISSENSCHAFT UND FORSCHUNG/ (AUSTRIA) No 1

2 ALL-UNION SCIENTIFIC AND TECHNICAL INFORMATION CENTRE /VSESOJUZ-NYI NAUCNO-TEHNICESKII INFORMACIONNYI CENTR/ (USSR) No 191

3 ALL-UNION STATE LIBRARY OF FOREIGN LITERATURE /VSESOJUZNAJA GO-SUDARSTVENNAJA BIBLIOTEKA INOSTRANNOJ LITERATURI/ (USSR) No 192

4 ARCHIVES OF THE POLISH ACADEMY OF SCIENCES /ARCHIWUM POLSKIEJ AKADEMII NAUK/ (POLAND) No 144

5 ATHENS CENTRE OF SETTLEMENT SYSTEMS. LIBRARY /ATHENAIKO KENTRO OIKISTIKES. BIBLIOTHEKI/ (GREECE) No 98

6 AUSTRIAN INSTITUTE OF EAST AND SOUTH-EAST EUROPEAN STUDIES. LIB-RARY AND DOCUMENTATION DEPARTMENT /ÖSTERREICHISCHES OST- UND SÜDOSTEUROPA INSTITUT ABT.BIBLIOTHEK UND DOKUMENTATION/ (AUS-TRIA) No 2

7 AUSTRIAN NATIONAL LIBRARY /ÖSTERREICHISCHE NATIONALBIBLIOTHEK/ (AUSTRIA) No 3

8 CENTRAL ARCHIVES FOR EMPIRICAL SOCIAL RESEARCH, UNIVERSITY OF COLOGNE /ZENTRALARCHIV FÜR EMPRIRISCHE SOZIALFORSCHUNG DER UNI-VERSITÄT ZU KÖLN/ (GERMANY, FEDERAL REPUBLIC OF) No 88

9 CENTRAL BUREAU OF STATISTICS /STATISTISK SENTRALBYRÅ/ (NORWAY) No 133

10 CENTRAL INSTITUTE FOR ANCIENT HISTORY AND ARCHEOLOGY, DEPARTMENT OF INFORMATION AND LIBRARY /ZENTRALINSTITUT FÜR ALTE GESCHICHTE UND ARCHÄOLOGIE, ABTEILUNG INFORMATION-BIBLIOTHEK/ (GERMAN DE-MOCRATIC REPUBLIC) No 76

11 CENTRAL INSTITUTE OF HISTORY, DEPARTMENT OF INFORMATION AND DOCU-MENTATION /ZENTRALINSTITUT FÜR GESCHICHTE, ABTEILUNG INFORMA-TION-DOKUMENTATION/ (GERMAN DEMOCRATIC REPUBLIC) No 77

12   CENTRAL INSTITUTE FOR INFORMATION IN THE HISTORY OF THE WORKING-
      CLASS MOVEMENT AND RESEARCH ON MARX AND ENGELS /ZENTRALSTELLE
      FUR INFORMATION UND DOKUMENTATION DER GESCHICHTE DER ARBEITER-
      BEWEGUNG UND MARX-ENGELS-FORSCHUNG/ (GERMAN DEMOCRATIC REPUBLIC)
      No 78

13   CENTRAL INSTITUTE OF JUVENILE RESEARCH, DEPARTMENT OF INFORMA-
      TION AND DOCUMENTATION /ZENTRALSTELLE FÜR JUGENDFORSCHUNG, AB-
      TEILUNG INFORMATION UND DOKUMENTATION/ (GERMAN DEMOCRATIC RE-
      PUBLIC) No 79

14   CENTRAL LIBRARY AT THE BULGARIAN ACADEMY OF SCIENCES /CENTRALNA
      BIBLIOTEKA PRI BĂLGARSKA AKADEMIJA NA NAUKITE/ (BULGARIA) No 24

15   CENTRAL LIBRARY OF THE K.MARX UNIVERSITY OF ECONOMIC SCIENCES
      /MARX KAROLY KÖZGAZDASAGTUDOMANYI EGYETEM KÖZPONTI KÖNYVTARA/
      (HUNGARY) No 103

16   CENTRAL LIBRARY AND MUSEUM OF EDUCATION /ORSZÁGOS PEDAGÓGIAI
      KÖNYVTÁR ÉS MUZEUM/ (HUNGARY) No 104

17   CENTRAL LIBRARY OF THE SLOVAK ACADEMY OF SCIENCES /ÚSTREDNÁ
      KNIŽNINA SLOVENSKEJ AKADÉMIE VIED/ (CZECHOSLOVAKIA) No 35

18   CENTRAL LIBRARY OF THE STATE UNIVERSITY OF GHENT /CENTRALE BIB-
      LIOTHEEK VAN DE RIJKSUNIVERSITEIT - GENT/ (BELGIUM) No 16

19   CENTRAL UNION FOR SOCIAL SECURITY /SOSIAALITURVAN KESKUSLIITTO
      (FINLAND) No 46

20   CENTRE FOR INFORMATION AND DOCUMENTATION IN LIBRARIANSHIP /ZEN-
      TRALSTELLE FÜR INFORMATION UND DOKUMENTATION BIBLIOTHEKSWESEN/
      (GERMAN DEMOCRATIC REPUBLIC) No 80

21   CENTRE OF PEDAGOGIC DOCKMENTATION AND INFORMATION /CENTĂR ZA
      PEDAGOGIČESKA DOKUMENTACIJA I INFORMACIJA/ (BULGARIA) No 25

22   CENTRE OF RESEARCH AND DOCUMENTATION ON CONTEMPORARY CHINA
      /CENTRE DE RECHERCHES ET DE DOCUMENTATION SUR LA CHINE CONTEM-
      PORAINE/ (FRANCE) No 61

23   CENTRE FOR SCIENTIFIC INFORMATION IN PHYSICAL CULTURE AND SPORTS
      /ZENTRUM FUR WISSENSCHAFTSINFORMATION KÖRPERKULTUR UND SPORT/
      (GERMAN DEMOCRATIC REPUBLIC) No 81

24   CENTRE OF SCIENTIFIC INFORMATION ON SOCIAL SCIENCES OF THE ACA-
      DEMY OF SCIENCES OF THE AZERBAIJAN SSR /CENTR NAUCNOJ INFORMA-
      CII PO OBSTESTVENNIM NAUKAM AKADEMII NAUK AZERBAJDZANSKOJ SSR/
      (USSR) No 193

25   CENTRE OF SCIENTIFIC INFORMATION ON SOCIAL SCIENCES OF THE ACA-
      DEMY OF SCIENCES OF THE LITHUANIAN SSR /CENTR NAUCNOJ INFORMA-
      CII PO OBSTESTVENNIM NAUKAM AKADEMII NAUK LITOVSKOJ SSR/ (USSR)
      No 194

26   CENTRE FOR SCIENTIFIC AND TECHNICAL DOCUMENTATION /CENTRE DE
      DOCUMENTATION SCIENTIFIQUE ET TECHNIQUE (FRANCE) No 62

27   CENTRE FOR SOCIAL SCIENCE INFORMATION AND DOCUMENTATION AT THE
      ACADEMY OF SCIENCES OF THE GDR /ZENTRALE LEITUNG FÜR GESELL-
      SCHAFTSWISSENSCHAFTLICHE INFORMATION UND DOKUMENTATION BEI DER
      AdW DER DDR/ (GERMAN DEMOCRATIC REPUBLIC) No 82

28   CENTRE FOR SOCIOLOGICAL INFORMATION AND DOCUMENTATION /ZENTRAL-
      STELLE FUR SOZIOLOGISCHE INFORMATION UND DOKUMENTATION/ (GERMAN
      DEMOCRATIC REPUBLIC) No 83

29 CENTRE FOR STUDIES ON NON-EUROPEAN COUNTRIES /ZAKŁAD KRAJÓW PO-
ZAEVROPEJSKICH PAN/ (POLAND) No 145

30 CENTRE OF THIRD WORLD INFORMATION AND DOCUMENTATION IN BARCELONA
/CENTRE D'INFORMACION I DOCUMENTACION A BARCELONA DEL TERCER
MUNDO/ (SPAIN) No 172

31 CENTRE FOR USSR AND EAST EUROPEAN STUDIES /CENTRE D'ETUDES SUR
L'URSS ET L'EUROPE ORIENTALE/ (FRANCE) No 63

32 CHAMBER OF COMMERCE, DEPARTMENT OF SCIENCE AND EDUCATIONAL POLI-
CY /BUNDESKAMMER DER GEWERBLICHEN WIRTSCHAFT, WISSENSCHAFTLICHE
UND BILDUNGSPOLITISCHE ABTEILUNG/ (AUSTRIA) No 4

33 COMMUNICATION CENTRE FOR FUTUROLOGY AND PEACE RESEARCH OF HANNO-
VER /KOMMUNIKATIONSZENTRUM FÜR ZUKUNFTS- AND FRIEDENSFORSCHUNG
IN HANNOVER/ (GERMANY, FEDERAL REPUBLIC OF) No 89

34 CONSORTIUM FOR INFORMATION AND DOCUMENTATION OF CATALONIA /CON-
SORCIO DE INFORMACION Y DOCUMENTACION DE CATALUNYA/ (SPAIN)
No 173

35 CYRIL AND METHODIUS NATIONAL LIBRARY /NARODNA BIBLIOTEKA "KIRIL
I METODIJ"/ (BULGARIA) No 26

36 DANISH DATA ARCHIVES /DANSK DATA ARKIV/ (DENMARK) No 39

37 DENMARKS STATISTICS /DANMARKS STATISTIK/ (DENMARK) No 40

38 DEPARTMENT OF FRENCH DOCUMENTATION /DIRECTION DE LA DOCUMENTA-
TION FRANÇAISE/ (FRANCE) No 64

39 DEPARTMENT OF JOURNALISM, KARL MARX UNIVERSITY, LEIPZIG /SEK-
TION JOURNALISTIK DER KARL-MARX-UNIVERSITÄT LEIPZIG/ (GERMAN
DEMOCRATIC REPUBLIC) No 84

40 DEPARTMENT FOR PHILOSOPHICAL INFORMATION AND DOCUMENTATION
/ZENTRALSTELLE FÜR PHILOSOPHISCHE INFORMATION UND DOKUMENTATION/
(GERMAN DEMOCRATIC REPUBLIC) No 85

41 DEPARTMENT OF SCIENTIFIC INFORMATION AND DOCUMENTATION AT THE
INSTITUTE OF SOCIOLOGY - BULGARIAN ACADEMY OF SCIENCES /OTDEL
ŽA NAUČNA INFORMACIJA I DOKUMENTACIJA PRI INSTITUTA PO SOCIOLO-
GIJA. BĂLGARSKA AKADEMIJA NA NAUKITE/ (BULGARIA) No 27

42 DEPARTMENT OF SCIENTIFIC INFORMATION ON SOCIAL SCIENCES OF THE
ACADEMY OF SCIENCES OF THE BYELORUSSIAN SSR /OTDEL NAUCNOJ IN-
FORMACII PO OBSTESTVENNIM NAUKAM AKADEMII NAUK BYELORUSSKOI SSR/
(USSR) No 195

43 DEPARTMENT OF SCIENTIFIC INFORMATION ON SOCIAL SCIENCES OF THE
ACADEMY OF SCIENCES OF THE KAZAKH SSR /OTDEL NAUCNOJ INFORMACII
PO OBSTESTVENNIM NAUKAM AKADEMII NAUK KAZAKHSKOI SSR/ (USSR)
No 196

44 DOCUMENTATION CENTRE. COOPERATION AND AUTOMATION DEPARTMENT /DI-
VISION DE LA COOPERATION ET DE L'AUTOMATISATION, CENTRE DE DOCU-
MENTATION/ (FRANCE) No 65

45 DOCUMENTATION CENTRE OF THE ECONOMIC INFORMATION SERVICE /CEN-
TRALE DOCUMENTATIE VAN DE ECONOMISCHE VOORLICHTINGSDIENST/
(NETHERLANDS) No 124

46 DOCUMENTATION CENTRE OF THE GERMAN FOUNDATION FOR INTERNATIONAL
DEVELOPMENT /DEUTSCHE STIFTUNG FÜR INTERNATIONALE ENTWICKLUNG.
ZENTRALE DOKUMENTATION/ (GERMANY, FEDERAL REPUBLIC OF) No 90

47 DOCUMENTATION CENTRE ON INTERNATIONAL ORGANIZATIONS AND EUROPEAN
    COMMUNITIES /CENTRO DI DOCUMENTAZIONE SULLE ORGANIZZAZIONI IN-
    TERNAZIONALI E LE COMUNITA'EUROPEE/ (ITALY) No 119

48 DOCUMENTATION CENTRE. INSTITUTE OF POLITICAL SCIENCES - UNIVERSI-
    TY OF SOCIAL SCIENCES, GRENOBLE II /CENTRE DE DOCUMENTATION -
    INSTITUT D'ETUDES POLITIQUES - UNIVERSITÉ DES SCIENCES SOCIALES
    DE GRENOBLE II/ (FRANCE) No 66

49 DOCUMENTATION CENTRE FOR SOCIAL SCIENCES AND HUMANITIES /CENTRE
    DE DOCUMENTATION SCIENCES HUMAINES/ (FRANCE) No 67

50 DOCUMENTATION CENTRE FOR URBAN STUDIES /KOMMUNALWISSENSCHAFT-
    LICHES DOKUMENTATIONSZENTRUM/ (AUSTRIA) No 5

51 DOCUMENTATION AND LIBRARY DEPARTMENT AT THE MINISTRY OF CULTURAL
    AFFAIRS, RECREATION AND SOCIAL WELFARE /MINISTERIE VAN CULTUUR,
    RECREATIE EN MAATSCHAPPELIJK WERK/AFD. DOCUMENTATIE EN BIBLIO-
    THEEK/ (NETHERLANDS) No 125

52 DOCUMENTATION ON "NORD-PICARDIE" MANAGEMENT /DOCUMENTATION A
    MENAGEMENT NORD-PICARDIE/ (FRANCE) No 68

53 DOCUMENTATION OFFICE FOR EAST EUROPEAN LAW /DOCUMENTATIEBUREAU
    VOOR OOSTEUROPEES RECHT/ (NETHERLANDS) No 126

54 DOCUMENTATION OFFICE OF HIGHER EDUCATION AND SCIENCE POLICY
    /HOCHSCHULDOKUMENTATION. DOKUMENTATIONSBÜRO FÜR HOCHSCHULWESEN
    UND WISSENSCHAFTSPOLITIK/ (AUSTRIA) No 6

55 DOCUMENTATION AND RESEARCH CENTRE FOR MAINLAND AND INSULAR SOUTH-
    EAST ASIA /CENTRE DE DOCUMENTATION ET DE RECHERCHES SUR L'ASIE
    DU SUD-EST ET LE MONDE INSULINDIEN/ (FRANCE) No 69

56 DOCUMENTATION SERVICES OF THE NATIONAL FOUNDATION OF POLITICAL
    SCIENCES /SERVICES DE DOCUMENTATION DE LA FOUNDATION NATIONALE
    DES SCIENCES POLITIQUES/ (FRANCE) No 70

57 ECONOMIC INFORMATION UNIT, HUNGARIAN ACADEMY OF SCIENCES /MTA
    KÖZGAZDASÁGI INFORMÁCIÓS CSOPORT/ (HUNGARY) No 105

58 FEDERAL ENVIRONMENTAL AGENCY /UMWELTBUNDESAMT, FACHBEREICH I,
    GRUPPE INFORMATION UND DOKUMENTATION/ (BERLIN, WEST) No 19

59 FEDERAL RESEARCH INSTITUTE FOR REGIONAL GEOGRAPHY AND REGIONAL
    PLANNING. ABSTRACT LITERATURE INFORMATION /BUNDESFORSCHUNGSANS-
    TALT FÜR LANDESKUNDE UND RAUMORDUNG. REFERAT LITERATURINFORMA-
    TION/ (GERMANY, FEDERAL REPUBLIC OF) No 91

60 FINNISH INSTITUTE OF INTERNATIONAL AFFAIRS /ULKOPOLIITTINEN
    INSTITUUTTI _ UTRIKESPOLITISKA INSTITUTET/ (FINLAND) No 47

61 FOREIGN TRADE RESEARCH INSTITUTE. LIBRARY /INSTITUT ZA SPOLJNU
    TRGOVINU, BIBLIOTEKA/ (YUGOSLAVIA) No 209

62 FREE UNIVERSITY OF BERLIN. CLEARING HOUSE FOR POLITICAL INFORMA-
    TION AND DOCUMENTATION /FREIE UNIVERSITÄT BERLIN. LEITSTELLE
    POLITISCHE DOKUMENTATION/ (BERLIN, WEST) No 20

63 FUND FOR ECONOMICS AND SOCIAL RESEARCH OF THE SPANISH SAVINGS
    BANKS CONFEDERATION /FONDO PARA LA INVESTIGACIÓN ECONÓMICA Y
    SOCIAL DE LA CONFEDERACIÓN ESPAÑOLA DE CAJAS DE AHORROS/ (SPAIN)
    No 174

64 GEOGRAPHICAL INFORMATION AND DOCUMENTATION LABORATORY /C N R S
    - LABORATOIRE D'INFORMATION ET DE DOCUMENTATION EN GEOGRAPHIE/
    (FRANCE) No 71

65 GERMAN CENTRAL INSTITUTION FOR SOCIAL PROBLEMS /DEUTSCHES ZEN-
TRALINSTITUT FÜR SOZIALE FRAGEN/ (BERLIN, WEST) No 21

66 GERMAN SOCIETY FOR PEACE AND CONFLICT RESEARCH /DEUTSCHE GESELL-
SCHAFT FÜR FRIEDENS- UND KONFLIKTFORSCHUNG e.V./ (GERMANY, FEDE-
RAL REPUBLIC OF) No 92

67 GIANGIACOMO FELTRINELLI FOUNDATION /FONDAZIONE GIANGIACOMO FEL-
TRINELLI/ (ITALY) No 120

68 HELSINKI SCHOOL OF ECONOMICS LIBRARY /HELSINGIN KAUPPAKORKEA-
KOULUN KIRJASTO/ (FINLAND) No 48

69 HIGHER EDUCATION INFORMATION SYSTEM - LIBRARY AND DOCUMENTATION
SERVICE /HOCHSCHUL - INFORMATION - SYSTEM - BIBLIOTHEK UND DO-
KUMENTATION/ (GERMANY, FEDERAL REPUBLIC OF) No 93

70 HUNGARIAN CENTRAL TECHNICAL LIBRARY AND DOCUMENTATION CENTRE
/ORSZÁGOS MŰSZAKI KÖNYVTAR ÉS DOKUMENTÁCIÓS KÖZPONT/ (HUNGARY)
No 106

71 INFORMATION CENTRE ON CULTURE AND ARTS AT THE LENIN STATE LIBRARY
/INFORMACIONNIJ CENTR PO PROBLEMAM KULTURI I ISKUSTVA GOSUDARST-
VENNOJ BIBLIOTEKI IM.LENINA/ (USSR) No 197

72 INFORMATION CENTRE OF THE INSTITUTE FOR INTERNATIONAL RELATIONS
AND SOCIALIST INTEGRATION. BULGARIAN ACADEMY OF SCIENCES /INFOR-
MACIONEN CENTAR NA INSTITUTA ZA MEŽDUNARODNI OTNOŠENIJA I SOCIA-
LISTIČESKA INTEGRACIJA. BĂLGARSKA AKADEMIJA NA NAUKITE/ (BULGA-
RIA) No 28

73 INFORMATION CENTRE ON SOCIAL SCIENCES OF THE ACADEMY OF SCIENCES
OF THE ESTONIAN SSR /CENTR NAUCNOJ INFORMACII PO OBSTESTVENNIM
NAUKAM AKADEMII NAUK ESTONSKOJ SSR/ (USSR) No 198

74 INFORMATION DEPARTMENT OF THE NATIONAL SCIENTIFIC RESEARCH IN-
STITUTE FOR HIGHER EDUCATION /OTDEL NAUCNOJ INFORMACII NAUCNO-
ISSLEDOVATELSKOGO INSTITUTA PROBLEM VISSEJ SKOLI/ (USSR) No 199

75 INFORMATION AND DOCUMENTATION CENTRE FOR GEOGRAPHY OF THE NE-
THERLANDS /INFORMATIE - EN DOCUMENTATIE - CENTRUM VOOR DE GEO-
GRAFIE VAN NEDERLAND/ (NETHERLANDS) No 127

76 INSTITUTE OF ARTS AT THE POLISH ACADEMY OF SCIENCES /INSTYTUT
SZTUKI POLSKIEJ AKADEMII NAUK/ (POLAND) No 146

77 INSTITUTE OF COMPARATIVE LAW. LIBRARY /BIBLIOTEKA INSTITUTA ZA
UPOREDNO PRAVO/ (YUGOSLAVIA) No 210

78 INSTITUTE FOR EASTERN EUROPEAN STUDIES /OOST-EUROPA INSTITUUT/
(NETHERLANDS) No 128

79 INSTITUTE OF ECONOMICS AT THE HUNGARIAN ACADEMY OF SCIENCES,
LIBRARY AND DOCUMENTATION /MTA KÖZGAZDASÁGTUDOMÁNYI INTÉZETE,
KÖNYVTAR ÉS DOKUMENTÁCIÓ/ (HUNGARY) No 107

80 INSTITUTE FOR EDUCATIONAL RESEARCH /KASVATUSTIETEIDEN TUTKIMUS-
LAITOS/ (FINLAND) No 49

81 INSTITUTE OF EMPLOYMENT RESEARCH /INSTITUT FÜR ARBEITSMARKT UND
BERUFSFORSCHUNG DER BUNDESANSTALT FÜR ARBEIT/ (GERMANY, FEDERAL
REPUBLIC OF) No 94

82 INSTITUTE FOR FOREIGN CULTURAL RELATIONS, LIBRARY AND DOCUMENTA-
TION DEPARTMENT /INSTITUT FÜR AUSLANDSBEZIEHUNGEN BIBLIOTHEK
UND DOKUMENTATION/ (GERMANY, FEDERAL REPUBLIC OF) No 95

83   INSTITUTE FOR FUTURE STUDIES   /INSTITUT FÜR ZUKUNFTSFORSCHUNG.
     GmbH/   (BERLIN, WEST)   No 22

84   INSTITUTE FOR HISTORY OF THE MATERIAL CULTURE. POLISH ACADEMY OF
     SCIENCES   /INSTYTUT HISTORII KULTURY MATERIALNEJ POLSKIEJ AKADE-
     MII NAUK/   (POLAND)   No 147

85   INSTITUTE OF HISTORY AT THE POLISH ACADEMY OF SCIENCES   /INSTY-
     TUT HISTORII POLSKIEJ AKADEMII NAUK/   (POLAND)   No 148

86   INSTITUTE OF HISTORY OF SCIENCE, EDUCATION AND TECHNOLOGY AT THE
     POLISH ACADEMY OF SCIENCES   /INSTYTUT HISTORII NAUKI, OŚWIATY I
     TECHNIKI POLSKIEJ AKADEMII NAUK/   (POLAND)   No 149

87   INSTITUTE OF INFORMATION AND DOCUMENTATION IN SCIENCE AND TECH-
     NOLOGY   /INSTITUTO DE INFORMACION Y DOCUMENTACION EN CIENCIA Y
     TECHNOLOGIA/   (SPAIN)   No 175

88   INSTITUTE OF INFORMATION AND DOCUMENTATION IN SOCIAL SCIENCES
     AND HUMANITIES   /INSTITUTO DE INFORMACION Y DOCUMENTACION EN
     SCIENCIAS SOCIALES Y HUMANIDADES/   (SPAIN)   No 176

89   INSTITUTE OF LITERARY RESEARCH AT THE POLISH ACADEMY OF SCIENCES
     /INSTYTUT BADAŃ LITERACKICH POLSKIEJ AKADEMII NAUK/   (POLAND)
     No 150

90   INSTITUTE OF PHILOSOPHY AND SOCIOLOGY AT THE POLISH ACADEMY OF
     SCIENCES   /INSTYTUT FILOZOFII I SOCJOLOGII POLSKIEJ AKADEMII
     NAUK/   (POLAND)   No 151

91   INSTITUTE OF POLITICAL SCIENCE, UNIVERSITY OF AARHUS   /INSTITUT
     FOR STATSKUNDSKAB, ÅARHUS UNIVERSITY/   (DENMARK)   No 41

92   INSTITUTE OF RURAL AND AGRICULTURAL DEVELOPMENT, POLISH ACADEMY
     OF SCIENCES   /INSTYTUT ROZWOJU WSI I ROLNICTWA POLSKIEJ AKADEMII
     NAUK/   (POLAND)   No 152

93   INSTITUTE OF SOCIOLOGICAL, POLITICAL AND JURIDICAL RESEARCH -
     SKOPJE   /INSTITUT ZA SOCIOLOŠKI I POLITIČKO-PRAVNI ISTRAŽUVANJA
     - SKOPJE/   (YUGOSLAVIA)   No 211

94   INSTITUTE OF SOCIOLOGY   /ISTITUTO DI SOCIOLOGIA/   (ITALY) No 121

95   INSTITUTE OF THE STATE AND LAW   /INSTYTUT PAŃSTWA I PRAWA POLS-
     KIEJ AKADEMII NAUK/   (POLAND)   No 153

96   INSTITUTE OF STUDIES ON RESEARCH AND SCIENTIFIC DOCUMENTATION
     /ISTITUTO DI STUDI SULLA RICERCA E DOCUMENTAZIONE SCIENTIFICA/
     (ITALY)   No 122

97   INSTITUTE FOR THEORY, HISTORY AND ORGANIZATION OF SCIENCE, DE-
     PARTMENT OF INFORMATION, DOCUMENTATION, LIBRARY   /INSTITUT FÜR
     THEORIE, GESCHICHTE UND ORGANIZATION DER WISSENSCHAFT, ABTEILUNG
     INFORMATION, DOKUMENTATION, BIBLIOTHEK/   (GERMAN DEMOCRATIC RE-
     PUBLIC)   No 86

98   INSTITUTE FOR WESTERN AFFAIRS   /INSTYTUT ZACHODNI/ (POLAND)
     No 154

99   INTERNATIONAL INFORMATION CENTRE OF BALKAN STUDIES   /MEŽDUNARO-
     DEN INFORMACIONEN CENTÅR PO BALKANISTIKA/   (BULGARIA)   No 29

100 INTERNATIONAL INFORMATION CENTRE FOR TERMINOLOGY   /INTERNATIO-
     NALES INFORMATIONSZENTRUM FÜR TERMINOLOGIE/   (AUSTRIA)   No 7

101 ITALIAN COUNCIL FOR SOCIAL SCIENCES   /CONSIGLIO ITALIANO PER
     LE SCIENZE SOCIALI/   (ITALY)   No 123

102 JAGIELLONIAN LIBRARY /BIBLIOTEKA JAGIELLONSKA. UNIVERSYTET JA-
     GIELLONSKI/ (POLAND) No 155

103 JEWISH HISTORICAL INSTITUTE IN POLAND /ŻYDOWSKI INSTYTUT HIS-
     TORYCZNY W POLSCE/ (POLAND) No 156

104 JYVASKYLA UNIVERSITY LIBRARY /JYVÄSKYLÄN YLIOPISTON KIRJASTO/
     (FINLAND) No 50

105 K.D.USHINSKI STATE SCIENTIFIC PEDAGOGICAL LIBRARY OF THE ACADE-
     MY OF PEDAGOGICAL SCIENCE OF THE USSR /GOSUDARSTVENNAJA NAUCNO-
     PEDAGOGICESKAJA BIBLIOTEKA AKADEMII PEDAGOGICESKIH NAUK SSSR IM.
     K.D.USINSKOGO/ (USSR) No 200

106 LENIN STATE LIBRARY /GOSUDARSTVENNAJA ORDENA LENINA BIBLIOTEKA
     IMENI LENINA/ (USSR) No 201

107 LIBRARY OF THE AARHUS SCHOOL OF BUSINESS AND ECONOMICS /HAN-
     DELSHØJSKOLENS BIBLIOTEK-ÅARHUS/ (DENMARK) No 42

108 LIBRARY OF ÅBO ACADEMY /ÅBO AKADEMIS BIBLIOTEK/ (FINLAND)
     No 51

109 LIBRARY OF THE ACADEMY OF SCIENCES OF THE USSR /BIBLIOTEKA
     AKADEMII NAUK SSSR/ (USSR) No 202

110 LIBRARY OF THE AUSTRIAN INSTITUTE FOR ECONOMIC RESEARCH /BIB-
     LIOTHEK ÖSTERREICHISCHES INSTITUT FÜR WIRTSCHAFTSFORSCHUNG/
     (AUSTRIA) No 8

111 LIBRARY OF THE CATHOLIC ACADEMY OF THEOLOGY, WARSAW /BIBLIOTE-
     KA AKADEMII TEOLOGII KATOLICKIEJ/ (POLAND) No 157

112 LIBRARY OF THE CENTRAL SCHOOL OF PLANNING AND STATISTICS - CEN-
     TRAL ECONOMIC LIBRARY /BIBLIOTEKA SZKOŁY GŁÓWNEJ PLANOWANIA I
     STATYSTYKI - CENTRALNA BIBLIOTEKA EKONOMICZNA/ (POLAND) No 158

113 LIBRARY OF CONTEMPORARY INTERNATIONAL DOCUMENTS /BIBLIOTHEQUE
     DE DOCUMENTATION INTERNATIONALE CONTEMPORAINE/ (FRANCE) No 72

114 LIBRARY OF THE DEPARTMENT OF INTERNATIONAL DEVELOPMENT COOPERA-
     TION, MINISTRY OF FOREIGN AFFAIRS /ULKOASIAINMINISTERIÖN KE-
     HITYSYHTEISTYÖOSASTON KIRJASTO/BIBLIOTEKET VID UTRIKESMINISTE-
     RIETS AVDELNING FÖR INTERNATIONELLT UTVECKLINGSSAMARBETE/
     (FINLAND) No 52

115 LIBRARY-DOCUMENTATION-ARCHIVES DEPARTMENT - LIBRARY OF THE NA-
     TIONAL INSTITUTE OF STATISTICS AND ECONOMICS /DIVISION BIBLIO-
     THEQUE-DOCUMENTATION-ARCHIVES-BIBLIOTHEQUE DE L'INSTITUT NATIO-
     NAL DE LA STATISTIQUE ET DES ETUDES ECONOMIQUES/ (FRANCE) No 73

116 LIBRARY AND DOCUMENTATION OF THE AUSTRIAN INSTITUTE OF URBAN AND
     REGIONAL PLANNING /BIBLIOTHEK UND DOKUMENTATION DES ÖSTERREI-
     CHISCHEN INSTITUTS FÜR RAUMPLANUNG/ (AUSTRIA) No 9

117 LIBRARY AND DOCUMENTATION OF THE INSTITUTE OF AGRICULTURAL ECO-
     NOMICS /BIBLIOTHEK UND DOKUMENTATIONSSTELLE DES AGRARWIRTSCHAFT-
     LICHEN INSTITUTS DES BUNDESMINISTERIUMS FÜR LAND- UND FORSTWIRT-
     SCHAFT/ (AUSTRIA) No 10

118 LIBRARY AND DOCUMENTATION SERVICE OF THE CENTRAL STATISTICAL
     OFFICE /KÖZPONTI STATISZTIKAI HIVATAL KÖNYVTÁR ÉS DOKUMENTÁ-
     CIÓS SZOLGÁLAT/ (HUNGARY) No 108

119 LIBRARY AND DOCUMENTATION SERVICE OF THE MINISTRY OF SOCIAL AF-
     FAIRS /BIBLIOTHEEK EN DOCUMENTATIC DIENST V/H MINISTERIE VAN
     SOCIALE ZAKEN/ (NETHERLANDS) No 129

120   LIBRARY OF THE ECONOMICS FACULTY. UNIVERSITY OF SARAJEVO   /BIB-
      LIOTEKA EKONOMISKOG FACULTETA U SARAJEVU/   (YUGOSLAVIA) No 212

121   LIBRARY OF THE ECONOMIC, SOCIAL AND POLITICAL SCIENCES   /BIBLIO-
      THÈQUE DE LA FACULTÉ DES SCIENCES ECONOMIQUES, SOCIALES ET PO-
      LITIQUES - UNIVERSITÉ CATHOLIQUE DE LOUVAIN/   (BELGIUM)   No 17

122   LIBRARY OF THE ETHNOGRAPHICAL MUSEUM   /NÉPRAJZI MUZEUM KÖNYVTÁ-
      RA/   (HUNGARY)   No 109

123   LIBRARY OF THE FEDERAL MINISTERIES OF SOCIAL ADMINISTRATION AND
      HEALTH AND ENVIRONMENTAL PROTECTION   /MINISTERIALBIBLIOTHEK DER
      BUNDESMINISTERIEN FÜR SOZIALE VERWALTUNG UND FÜR GESUNDHEIT UND
      UMWELTSCHUTZ/   (AUSTRIA)   No 11

124   LIBRARY OF THE FEDERAL WORKING SOCIETY FOR REHABILITATION
      /BÜCHEREI DER BUNDESARBEITSGEMEINSCHAFT FÜR REHABILITATION/
      (GERMANY, FEDERAL REPUBLIC OF)   No 96

125   LIBRARY OF HUMANITIES AND SOCIAL SCIENCES, FREE UNIVERSITY OF
      BRUSSELS   /BIBLIOTHEEK HUMANE EN SOCIALE WETENSCHAPPEN, VRIJE
      UNIVERSITEIT-BRUSSEL/   (BELGIUM)   No 18

126   LIBRARY OF THE HUNGARIAN ACADEMY OF SCIENCES   /MAGYAR TUDOMÁNYOS
      AKADÉMIA KÖNYVTÁRA/   (HUNGARY)   No 110

127   LIBRARY OF THE HUNGARIAN PARLIAMENT   /ORSZÁGGYÜLÉSI KÖNYVTÁR/
      (HUNGARY)   No 111

128   LIBRARY OF THE INSTITUTE OF INDUSTRIAL ECONOMICS OF THE HUNGA-
      RIAN ACADEMY OF SCIENCES   /MTA IPARGAZDASÁGTANI KUTATÓCSOPORT
      KÖNYVTÁRA/   (HUNGARY)   No 112

129   LIBRARY OF THE INSTITUTE FOR LEGAL AND ADMINISTRATIVE SCIENCES
      /MTA ÁLLAM - ÉS YOGTUDOMÁNYI INTÉZETÉNEK KÖNYVTÁRA/   (HUNGARY)
      No 113

130   LIBRARY OF THE INSTITUTE FOR PSYCHOLOGY AT THE HUNGARIAN ACADE-
      MY OF SCIENCES   /MTA PSZICHOLÓGIAI INTÉZETÉNEK KÖNYVTÁRA/
      (HUNGARY)   No 114

131   LIBRARY OF THE LAW FACULTY OF THE UNIVERSITY OF SARAJEVO   /BIB-
      LIOTEKA PROVNOG FAKULTETA UNIVERSITETA U SARAJEVO/   (YUGOSLAVIA)
      No 213

132   LIBRARY AT THE NATIONAL CENTRE OF SOCIAL RESEARCH   /ETHNIKO
      KENTRO KOINONIKON EREYNON. BIBLIOTHEKI/   (GREECE)   No 99

133   LIBRARY OF THE NATIONAL INSTITUTE OF OSSOLINSKI'S   /POLSKA AKA-
      DEMIA NAUK, ZAKŁAD NARODOWY IM.OSSOLIŃSKICH. BIBLIOTEKA/   (PO-
      LAND)   No 159

134   LIBRARY OF THE NATIONAL MANAGEMENT DEVELOPMENT CENTRE   /ORSZÁGOS
      VEZETŐKÉPZŐ KÖZPONT KÖNYVTÁRA/   (HUNGARY)   No 115

135   LIBRARY OF THE NORWEGIAN PARLIAMENT   /STORTINGSBIBLIOTEKET/
      (NORWAY)   No 134

136   LIBRARY AT THE PANHELLENIC CONFEDERATION OF UNIONS OF AGRICUL-
      TURAL COOPERATIVES   /PANELLENIOS SYNOMOSPONDIA ENOSEON GEORGIKON
      SYNETARISMON, BIBLIOTHEKI/   (GREECE)   No 100

137   LIBRARY OF PARLIAMENT   /EDUSKUNNAN KIRJASTO RIKSDAGSBIBLIOTEKET/
      (FINLAND)   No 53

138   LIBRARY OF PARLIAMENT   /RIKSDAGSBIBLIOTEKET/   (SWEDEN)   No 178

139 LIBRARY OF THE POLISH ACADEMY OF SCIENCES, GDANSK /BIBLIOTEKA
     GDAŃSKA POLSKIEJ AKADEMII NAUK/ (POLAND) No 160

140 LIBRARY OF THE POLISH ACADEMY OF SCIENCES, KORNIK /BIBLIOTEKA
     KÓRNICKA PAN/ (POLAND) No 161

141 LIBRARY OF THE POLISH ACADEMY OF SCIENCES, WARSAW /BIBLIOTEKA
     POLSKIEJ AKADEMII NAUK U WARSZAWIE/ (POLAND) No 162

142 LIBRARY OF THE POZNAN SOCIETY OF FRIENDS OF ARTS AND SCIENCE
     /BIBLIOTEKA POZNAŃSKIEGO TOWARZYSTWA PRZYJACIÓŁ NAUK/ (POLAND)
     No 163

143 LIBRARY OF THE SCHOOL OF SOCIAL WORK - FOUNDATION FOR THE DE-
     VELOPMENT OF SOCIAL WORK /BIBLIOTHEKI ANOTERAS SXOLES KOINO-
     NIKES ERGASIAS - IDRUMA ANAPTUXEOS KOINONIKES ERGASIAS/
     (GREECE) No 101

144 LIBRARY OF SOFIA UNIVERSITY /UNIVERSITETSKA BIBLIOTEKA - SOFIA/
     (BULGARIA) No 30

145 LIBRARY OF THE ST.GALLEN GRADUATE SCHOOL OF ECONOMICS, BUSINESS
     AND PUBLIC ADMINISTRATION /BIBLIOTHEK DER HOCHSCHULE ST.GALLEN
     FÜR WIRTSCHAFTS- UND SOZIALWISSENSCHAFTEN/ (SWITZERLAND) No 187

146 LIBRARY OF THE UNIVERSITY OF WARSAW /BIBLIOTEKA UNIWERSYTECKA
     W WARSZAWIE/ (POLAND) No 164

147 LINGUISTIC INFORMATION AND DOCUMENTATION CENTRE OF THE GDR
     /ZENTRALSTELLE FÜR SPRACHWISSENSCHAFTLICHE INFORMATION UND DO-
     KUMENTATION DER DDR/ (GERMAN DEMOCRATIC REPUBLIC) No 87

148 LUND UNIVERSITY LIBRARY /LUNDS UNIVERSITETSBIBLIOTEK/ (SWEDEN)
     No 179

149 MAIN LIBRARY OF THE ADAM MICKIEWICZ UNIVERSITY IN POZNAN /BIB-
     LIOTEKA GŁOWNA UNIWERSYTETU IM ADAMA MICKIEWICZA/ (POLAND)
     No 165

150 MAIN LIBRARY - SCIENTIFIC INFORMATION CENTRE OF THE CZECHOSLOVAK
     ACADEMY OF SCIENCES /ZAKLADNÍ KNIHOVNA - ÚSTŘEDÍ VĚDECKÝCH IN-
     FORMACÍ CÉSKOSLOVENSKÉ AKADEMIE VĚD/ (CZECHOSLOVAKIA) No 36

151 MAX-PLANCK-INSTITUTE OF EDUCATIONAL RESEARCH /MAX-PLANCK-INSTI-
     TUT FÜR BILDUNGSFORSCHUNG/ (BERLIN, WEST) No 23

152 MEDICAL INFORMATION CENTRE, KAROLINSKA INSTITUTE /MEDICINSKA
     INFORMATIONSCENTRALEN, KAROLINSKA INSTITUTET/ (SWEDEN) No 180

153 M.E.SALTIKOV-SHCHEDRIN STATE PUBLIC LIBRARY /GOSUDARSTVENNAJA
     ORDENA TRUDOVOGO KRASNOGO ZNAMENI PUBLICNAJA BIBLIOTEKA IMENI
     M.E.SATIKOVA-STEDRINA/ (USSR) No 203

154 MUNICIPAL LIBRARY ERVIN SZABO /FÖVÁROSI SZABÓ ERVIN KÖNYVTÁR/
     (HUNGARY) No 116

155 MUSEUM FOR AUSTRIAN SOCIAL AND ECONOMIC AFFAIRS /ÖSTERREICHI-
     SCHES GESELLSCHAFTS- UND WIRTSCHAFTSMUSEUM/ (AUSTRIA) No 12

156 NATIONAL COUNCIL FOR SOCIAL WELFARE /NATIONALE RAAD VOOR
     MAATSCHAPPELIJK WELZIJN/ (NETHERLANDS) No 130

157 NATIONAL INFORMATION AND DOCUMENTATION CENTRE OF THE SOCIAL
     SERVICE OF OCCUPATIONAL HYGIENE AND SAFETY /CENTRO NATIONAL
     DE INFORMACION Y DOCUMENTACION DEL SERVICIO SOCIAL DE HIGHIENE
     Y SEGURIDAD DEL TRABAJO/ (SPAIN) No 177

158 NATIONAL INSTITUTE FOR DEMOGRAPHIC RESEARCH   /INSTITUT NATIONAL
     D'ETUDES DEMOGRAPHIQUES/   (FRANCE) No 74

159 NATIONAL LIBRARY /BIBLIOTEKA NARODOWA/ (POLAND) No 166

160 NATIONAL LIBRARY FOR PSYCHOLOGY AND EDUCATION   /STATENS PSYKO-
     LOGISK-PEDAGOGISKA BIBLIOTEK/   (SWEDEN) No 181

161 NATIONAL SCIENTIFIC AND INFORMATION CENTRE OF CULTURE   /NACIO-
     NALEN NAUČNO-INFORMACIONEN CENTĂR PO KULTURA/ (BULGARIA) No 31

162 NATIONAL STATISTICAL SERVICE OF GREECE - PUBLICATIONS AND INFOR-
     MATION DIVISION - LIBRARY /ETHNIKI STATISTIKI IPIRESIA TIS
     ELLADOS - DIEFTHINSI DIMOSIEFSEON KE PLIROFORION - BIBLIOTHEKI/
     (GREECE) No 102

163 NATIONAL UNION FOR CHILD WELFARE /WERKVERBAND INTEGRATIE
     JEUGDWELZYNSWERK NETHERLAND/ (NETHERLANDS) No 131

164 NATIONAL AND UNIVERSITY LIBRARY OF BOSNIA AND HERZEGOVINA
     /NARODNA I UNIVERSITETSKA BIBLIOTEKA BOSNE I HERZEGOVINE/
     (YUGOSLAVIA) No 214

165 NOBEL INSTITUTE LIBRARY /NOBELINSTITUTTETS BIBLIOTEK/ (NOR-
     WAY) No 135

166 NORDIC DOCUMENTATION CENTRE FOR MASS COMMUNICATION RESEARCH
     /POHJOISMAINEN TIEDOTUSTUTKIMUKSEN PALVELUKESKUS, NORDISK DO-
     KUMENTATIONSCENTRAL FÖR MASSKOMMUNIKATIONS-FORSKNING/ (FINLAND)
     No 54

167 NORDIC DOCUMENTATION CENTRE OF MASS COMMUNICATION RESEARCH,
     NORWEGIAN BRANCH /NORDISK DOKUMENTASJONSSENTRAL FOR MASSEKOMMU-
     NIKASJONSFORSKNING, ADV.NORGE/ (NORWAY) No 136

168 NORWEGIAN BIBLIOGRAPHY OF THE SOCIAL SCIENCES /NORSK SAMFUN-
     NSVITENSKAPELING BIBLIOGRAFI/ (NORWAY) No 137

169 NORWEGIAN CENTRE FOR INFORMATICS /NORSK SENTER FOR INFORMATIKK/
     (NORWAY) No 138

170 NORWEGIAN INSTITUTE FOR URBAN AND REGIONAL RESEARCH. LIBRARY
     /NORSK INSTITUTT FOR BY- OG REGIONFORSKNING. BIBLIOTEKET/
     (NORWAY) No 139

171 NORWEGIAN SCHOOL OF ECONOMICS AND BUSINESS ADMINISTRATION.
     LIBRARY /NORGES HANDELSHØYSKOLE - BIBLIOTEKET/ (NORWAY) No 140

172 NORWEGIAN SOCIAL SCIENCE DATA SERVICES /NORSK SAMFUNNSVITEN-
     SKAPELIG DATATJENESTE/ (NORWAY) No 141

173 ODENSE UNIVERSITY LIBRARY /ODENSE UNIVERSITETSBIBLIOTEK/
     (DENMARK) No 43

174 OFFICE OF INFORMATION AND DOCUMENTATION IN SOCIAL AND POLITICAL
     SCIENCES /OFFICIUL DE INFORMARE SI DOCUMENTARE ÎN STIINTELE
     SOCIALE SI POLITICE/ (ROMANIA) No 171

175 OFFICE FOR SCIENTIFIC ECONOMIC INFORMATION AT THE INSTITUTE OF
     ECONOMICS. BULGARIAN ACADEMY OF SCIENCES /SLUŽBA ZA NAUČNA
     IKONOMIČESKA INFORMACIJA PRI IKONOMIČESKIJA INSTITUT. BĂLGARSKA
     AKADEMIJA NA NAUKITE/ (BULGARIA) No 32

176 OFFICE FOR SCIENTIFIC INFORMATION AND DOCUMENTATION. INSTITUTE
     OF THE STATE AND LAW. BULGARIAN ACADEMY OF SCIENCES /SLUŽBA ZA
     NAUČNA INFORMACIJA I DOKUMENTACIJA. INSTITUT PO NAUKITE ZA DĂR-
     ZAVATA I PRAVOTO. BĂLGARSKA AKADEMIJA NA NAUKITE/ (BULGARIA)
     No 33

177   OULU UNIVERSITY LIBRARY /OULUN YLIOPISTON KIRJASTO / UNIVERSI-
      TETSBIBLIOTEKET IN ULEÅBORG/ (FINLAND) No 55

178   POLISH INSTITUTE OF INTERNATIONAL AFFAIRS. DEPARTMENT FOR
      SCIENTIFIC INFORMATION AND LIBRARY /POLSKI INSTYTUT SPRAW
      MIDZYNARODOWYCH. ZAKŁAD INFORMACJI NAUKOWEJ I BIBLIOTEKA/ (PO-
      LAND) No 167

179   REFERENCE LIBRARY OF THE NATIONAL BANK OF HUNGARY /MAGYAR
      NEMZETI BANK SZAKKÖNYVTÁRA/ (HUNGARY) No 117

180   RESEARCH CENTRE OF MEDITERRANEAN ARCHEOLOGY OF THE POLISH ACA-
      DEMY OF SCIENCES /ZAKŁAD ARCHEOLOGII SRÓDZIEMNOMORSKIEJ POLS-
      KIEJ AKADEMII NAUK/ (POLAND) No 168

181   RESEARCH CENTRE FOR SWISS POLITICS /FORSCHUNGSZENTRUM FÜR
      SCHWEIZERISCHE POLITIK/ (SWITZERLAND) No 188

182   ROYAL INSTITUTE OF TECHNOLOGY. LIBRARY, INFORMATION AND DOCUMEN-
      TATION CENTRE /KUNGLIGA TEKNISKA HÖGSKOLANS BIBLIOTEK, INFORMA-
      TIONS- OCH DOKUMENTATIONS- CENTRALEN/ (SWEDEN) No 182

183   ROYAL LIBRARY /DET KONGELIGE BIBLIOTEK/ (DENMARK) No 44

184   ROYAL LIBRARY /KUNGLIGA BIBLIOTEKET/ (SWEDEN) No 183

185   SCIENCE INFORMATION CENTRE AT THE HIGHER SCHOOL OF SOCIAL
      SCIENCES /OSRODEK INFORMACJI NAUKOWEJ WYŻSZEJ SZKOŁY NAUK
      SPOŁECZNYCH/ (POLAND) No 169

186   SCIENTIFIC INFORMATION CENTRE FOR NATURAL, MATHEMATICAL AND SO-
      CIAL SCIENCES AT THE BULGARIAN ACADEMY OF SCIENCES /CENTĂR ZA
      NAUČNA INFORMACIJA PO ESTESTVENI, MATEMATIČESKI I OBSTESTVENI
      NAUKI PRI BĂLGARSKA AKADEMIJA NA NAUKITE/ (BULGARIA) No 34

187   SCIENTIFIC INFORMATION CENTRE, POLISH ACADEMY OF SCIENCES/OSRO-
      DEK INFORMACJI NAUKOWEJ POLSKIEJ AKADEMII NAUK/ (POLAND)
      No 170

188   SCIENTIFIC INFORMATION CENTRE ON SOCIAL SCIENCES OF THE ACADEMY
      OF SCIENCES OF THE ARMENIAN SSR /SEKTOR NAUCNOJ INFORMACII PO
      OBSTESTVENNIM NAUKAM AKADEMII NAUK ARMJANSKOJ SSR/ (USSR)
      No 204

189   SCIENTIFIC INFORMATION DEPARTMENT OF THE SOCIAL SCIENCES DIVISION
      AT THE ACADEMY OF SCIENCES OF THE UKRAINIAN SSR /OTDEL NAUCNOJ
      INFORMACII SEKCII OBSTESTVENNIH NAUK AKADEMII NAUK UKRAINSKOJ
      SSR/ (USSR) No 205

190   SCIENTIFIC INFORMATION SERVICE. INSTITUTE FOR WORLD ECONOMICS
      AT THE HUNGARIAN ACADEMY OF SCIENCES /MTA VILÁGGAZDASÁGI KUTA-
      TÓINTÉZETE, TUDOMÁNYOS TÁJÉKOZTATÓ SZOLGÁLAT/ (HUNGARY) No 118

191   SECTION OF SCIENTIFIC INFORMATION ON SOCIAL SCIENCES AT THE ACA-
      DEMY OF SCIENCES OF THE GEORGIAN SSR /SEKTOR NAUCNOJ INFORMA-
      CII PO OBSTESTVENNIM NAUKAM AKADEMII NAUK GRUZINSKOJ SSR/
      (USSR) No 206

192   SERVICE FOR SCIENTIFIC INFORMATION AND DOCUMENTATION. INSTITUTE
      OF INTERNATIONAL POLITICS AND ECONOMICS, BELGRADE /OOUR ZA NA-
      UČNU INFORMACIJU I DOKUMENTACIJU INSTITUTA ZA MEDJUNARODNU PO-
      LITIKU, BEOGRAD/ (YUGOSLAVIA) No 215

193   SLOVAK NATIONAL BIBLIOGRAPHY /MATICA SLOVENSKÁ/ (CZECHOSLOVA-
      KIA) No 37

194   SOCIAL INSURANCE INSTITUTION LIBRARY   /KANSANELÄKELAITOKSEN KIRJASTO FOLKPENSIONSANSTALTENS BIBLIOTEK/   (FINLAND) No 56

195   SOCIAL SCIENCES DOCUMENTATION   /SOZIALWISSENSCHAFTLICHE DOKU-MENTATION D.KAMMER F.ARBEITER U.ANGESTELLTE F.WIEN/ (AUSTRIA) No 13

196   SOCIAL SCIENCES INFORMATION CENTRE   /INFORMATIONSZENTRUM SOZIAL-WISSENSCHAFTEN/   (GERMANY, FEDERAL REPUBLIC OF)   No 97

197   SOCIAL SCIENCE INFORMATION AND DOCUMENTATION CENTRE   /SOCIAAL-WETENSCHAPPELIJK INFORMATIE EN DOCUMENTATIECENTRUM/   (NETHER-LANDS)   No 132

198   SOCIAL SCIENCE INFORMATION INSTITUTE AT THE ACADEMY OF SCIENCES OF THE USSR   /INSTITUT NAUCNOJ INFORMACII PO OBSTESTVENNIM NAU-KAM AKADEMII NAUK SSSR/   (USSR)   No 207

199   SOCIAL SCIENCES LIBRARY   /SOZIALWISSENSCHAFT STUDIENBIBLIOTHEK D.KAMMER F.ARBEITER U.ANGESTELLTE F.WIEN/   (AUSTRIA)   No 14

200   SOCIAL SCIENCES LIBRARY OF HELSINKI UNIVERSITY   /HELSINGIN YLIOPISTON VALTIOTIETEELLISEN TIEDEKUNNAN KIRJASTO/ (FINLAND) No 57

201   SOCIOLOGICAL RESEARCH CENTRE. LIBRARY AND DOCUMENTATION SERVICE /CENTRE D'ETUDES SOCIOLOGIQUES. BIBLIOTHÈQUE ET SERVICE DE DO-CUMENTATION/   (FRANCE)   No 75

202   STATE LIBRARY OF THE CZECH SOCIALIST REPUBLIC   /STÁTNÍ KNIHOVNA ČSR/   (CZECHOSLOVAKIA)   No 38

203   STATE PUBLIC HISTORICAL LIBRARY OF THE RUSSIAN SOVIET FEDERAL SOCIALIST REPUBLIC   /GOSUDARSTVENNAJA PUBLICNAJA ISTORICESKAJA BIBLIOTEKA RSFSR/   (USSR)   No 208

204   STATE AND UNIVERSITY LIBRARY   /STATSBIBLIOTEKET/   (DENMARK) No 45

205   STATISTICS LIBRARY   /TILASTOKIRJASTO/STATISTIKBIBLIOTEKET/ (FINLAND)   No 58

206   STOCKHOLM SCHOOL OF ECONOMICS LIBRARY   /HANDELSHÖGSKOLANS BIB-LIOTEK/   (SWEDEN)   No 184

207   SWISS ECONOMIC ARCHIVES   /SCHWEIZERISCHES WIRTSCHAFTSARCHIV - ARCHIVES ÉCONOMIQUES SUISSES/   (SWITZERLAND)   No 189

208   SWISS SOCIAL ARCHIVES   /SCHWEIZERICHES SOZIALARCHIV/ (SWITZER-LAND)   No 190

209   TURKU UNIVERSITY LIBRARY   /TURUN YLIOPISTON KIRJASTO/ (FINLAND) No 59

210   UNIVERSITY LIBRARY. SECTION B.TRONDHEIM   /UNIVERSITETSBIBLIO-TEKET AVD. B. TRONDHEIM/   (NORWAY)   No 142

211   UNIVERSITY LIBRARY UMEÅ   /UMEÅ UNIVERSITETSBIBLIOTEK/   (SWEDEN) No 185

212   UNIVERSITY OF TAMPERE LIBRARY   /TAMPEREEN YLIOPISTON KIRJASTO/ (FINLAND)   No 60

213   UNIVERSITY OF TRONDHEIM, NORWEGIAN INSTITUTE OF TECHNOLOGY. LIBRARY   /UNIVERSITET I TRONDHEIM, NORGES TEKNISKE HØGSKOLE, BIBLIOTEKET/   (NORWAY)   No 143

214   UPPSALA UNIVERSITY LIBRARY   /UPPSALA UNIVERSITETSBIBLIOTEK/
      (SWEDEN)   No 186

215   VIENNA INSTITUTE FOR COMPARATIVE ECONOMICS STUDIES AND DOCUMEN-
      TATION   /WIENER INSTITUT FÜR INTERNATIONALE WIRTSCHAFTSVER-
      GLEICHE, DOKUMENTATION/   (AUSTRIA)   No 15

Subject Index

Administrative law, 153,178
Administrative sciences, 13,14,60,66,68,70,113,125,190
African studies, 95,119
Agricultural economics, 10,100,107
Agricultural law, 153
Agriculture, 100,152
All fields of science, 16,26,36,38,45,63,142,165,166,179,186,191,
    201,202,203
Anglistics, 87
Anthropology, 68,69,98,99,121,132
Arab countries, 119
Archeology, 76,147,148,157,168,176
Arts, 3,29,31,143,176,192,197,201
Asian studies, 95

Balkan countries, 29,63
Bangladesh, 52
Banking, 117,137,174,189
Bibliographic sciences, 37,192,201,202,203
Biography, 37
Business sciences, 17,42,48,124,140,189

Canon-civil law, 157
Capitalist society, 83
Cartography, 71
Child law, 131,211
Child psychology, 131
China, 61
Civil law, 13,14,70,153
Classical studies, 110,157
Comparative psychology, 114
Computer science, 39
Conflict research, 92,135
Constitutional law, 153,178
Coordination of terminology, 7
Copyright, 125
Criminology, 121,153
Cuba, 52

Automated Information Systems

Country and Serial No. of Inform. Institution	Major fields	Activities	Type of hardware	Type of software
1	2	3	4	5
AUSTRIA 4	Economics, legal sciences, social and economic policy	Periodical documentation	IBM/370	PL/1, ASSEMBLER, Own keyword system
7	Terminology of all fields and languages	For the purposes of particular projects only	Cooperation with computer centres of other countries	
BELGIUM 17	Ecomonics, socio-logy, demography, history, mass communications, politics, business	Bibliographical references	IBM/370	PL/1
18	All social sciences	On-line interactive catalogue, public retrieval and cataloguing functions	Minicomputer DIGITAL EQUIPMENT CORPORATION	MUMPS/VUBIS
BERLIN, WEST 19	Environment		SIEMENS	GOLEM, FIDAS, ADABAS

1	2	3	4	5
BULGARIA				
24	Social sciences, etc.	Publication of machine-readable catalogues and lists of periodicals	EC-1040	"BISES" package
26	All fields of science	Processing of periodicals	IBM 370/135	ISIS
27	Sociology	Off-line, on-line searches OBNA-BAS	IBM 370/135	STAIRS
29	Political, economic, cultural history of the Balkan peoples	Off-line, on-line searches OBNA-BAS	IBM 370/135	STAIRS
31	Arts, culture, mass communications, etc.	in preparation	IBM 370/135 ES-1022	DOC-ES, OS-VS1, COBOL, FORTRAN, PL/1
32	Political economy of socialism	Off-line, on-line searches OBNA-BAS	IBM 370/135	STAIRS
33	Legal sciences	Off-line, on-line searches OBNA-BAS	IBM 370/135	STAIRS
34	Social sciences	Off-line, on-line searches OBNA-BAS	IBM 370/135 Terminals IBM and VIDEOTON. Computer communication leased-line terminal with UNION data bases	STAIRS

1	2	3	4	5
CZECHOSLOVAKIA				
35	Social sciences, etc.	Bibliography of new foreign books in the Slovak scientific libraries	TESLA/200	ARDIS
36	Social sciences	Participates in the building up of AIS MISON	IBM/370, EC 1040	
37	Slovak culture and libraries	Current Slovak national bibliography	HEWLETT-PACKARD 2100 S	ASSEMBLER, ALGOL, FORTRAN, ASTI
38	All fields of science	Catalogue of foreign non-periodical literature; Czech national bibliography – in preparation; Computerized cataloguing line for the State library	EC 1040 (ROBOTRON R 40); EC 1040 + DIGISET 40 T1, SIEMENS 7755	For EC 1040 – USS with data formats compatible in all CMEA countries
DENMARK				
39	All social sciences	Retrieval of text information	IBM 3033 MVS	ASSEMBLER, PL/1, APL
44	Social sciences, humanities	Information retrieval using Dialog-system (Polo Alte)	TTY terminal	
45	All fields of science	On-line searches	3 on-line terminals	

1	2	3	4	5
FINLAND				
48	Economics, business, applied psychology, economic geography, sociology, statistics, languages, etc.	Catalogue of periodicals (service of Finnish economic periodicals and Scandinavian periodical articles)	HEWLET-PACKARD 3000	FORTRAN
50	Humanities, social sciences	On-line literature searches	NOKIA NOP 30 terminals	No information input
56	Social insurance, social security	Cataloguing	IBM 370/168	ASSEMBLER, Own system
FRANCE				
62	Multidisciplinary sciences		IBM 370/168 and 135, LINOTRON, SFENA lourd terminal	ASSEMBLER, PL/1, System PASCAL/3
64	Politics	Data base	IRIS-80	MISTRAL
65	Information and library science	Participates in the PASCAL system CNRS		
67	All humanities and social sciences	SDI and on-line searches, FRANCIS	IBM 370/168	PL/1, ASSEMBLER, SPLEEN, MISTRAL, SEGUR, CARAT, Interfaces with ISIS, STAIRS, etc.
68	Economics, law, geography, administrative sciences, sociology, anthropology, statistics, demography		CII HB(IRIS 80)	MISTRAL V4

1	2	3	4	5
70	Social sciences	Catalogue of periodicals	CII-HB (IRIS 55)	AGAPE
71	Human and economic geography, cartography	Bibliography and SDI	IBM	FORTRAN O.S.
75	Sociology	Current and retrospective bibliography, on-line regime	IBM	COBOL, ASSEMBLER, EPOS-VIRA, PL/1, SPLEEN 2, SPLEEN 3
GERMAN DEMOCRATIC REPUBLIC				
85	Philosophy	Bibliography, SDI	ESSR 1040	SOPS AIDOS gen.var.
GERMANY, FEDERAL REPUBLIC OF				
88	All fields of empirical social research	Survey questions study descriptions (Z.A.R.-system)	IBM 370/158, OS VS2/MDS 2400, DELTA, ITT, Teleray CRT's	IBM-ASSEMBLER, PL/1, APL-GD
89	Peace research, futurology	Information retrieval system	CYBER 76-12, 73-16	FORTRAN, SCOPE 2.1
97	Sociology, political sciences, mass communications, psychology, social policy, etc.	On-line searches	SIEMENS 4004/151	GOLEM 2

1	2	3	4	5
HUNGARY				
106	Science and technology, applied economics	SDI	R 20	Own system
110	Social sciences, life sciences	Sciences Citation Index machine readable data base	IBM/370 and 3031 computer	of the ISI-ASCA
111	Political sciences	Card service and KWIC indices	R 20	Own system
115	Management science and development	Document processing	ICL 1905/E	Own system
ITALY				
119	International relations	Data bank of international documents	IBM/370/145 and videodisplay unit	DOS/VS, CICS, STAIRS
122	Science policy, informatics	Automated catalogues	IBM 370/158	COBOL/OS
NETHERLANDS				
124	Economics and business	Storage and retrieval bibliographical data base	IBM/360 host computer, IBM terminal	STAIRS
132	Sociology, political sciences, psychology, pedagogics, demography, etc.	Searching relevant documents in data-archives and journal articles	C.D.CYBER computer	RIQS-retrieval system

1	2	3	4	5
NORWAY				
133	Statistics	Statistical data processing	HONEYWELL L66/60P	COBOL
136	Mass communications research	Bibliographical data	Papertape AC200, IBM 370/158	COBOL/MVS/VS2
137	Political sciences, economics, sociology, pedagogics, etc.	Compilation of bibliographies	DEC-10 computer	Norwegian version of MARC programmes - NORMARC
138	Economics, social sciences, informatics		UNIVAC 1110, NORD-10/S, Interactive terminals	COBOL, SIMULA, POLYDOC system
139	Urban and regional research in Norway			POLYDOC system
140	Economics, business, administration	Small firms documentation	UNIVAC 1100	COBOL
141	Social sciences	Data sources in different data banks	UNIVAC 1100, UNIVAC 1108, DEC 10	
142	All subjects except technology	Acquisition and cataloguing file of new literature	UNIVAC 1108, 14 terminals: SPERRYUNIVAC UNISCOPE 200, 10 TANOBERG DATA terminal series 2100	FORTRAN IV

1	2	3	4	5
143	Arts, social sciences, etc.	SDI and retrospective searches; On-line: SDC/ORBIT, LOCKHEED/DIALOG, IRS/QUEST, MEDLINE, etc.	UNIVAC 1100, 1108 (for Geoarchive), Terminals: TEXAS INSTRUMENTS SILENT, INCOTERM, UNISCOPE	FORTRAN (for Geoarchive)
POLAND				
155	Social sciences, history, history of sciences, literature, etc.	KRAKUS environmental system, central catalogues of foreign periodicals and monographs	ODRA 1305	COBOL, Own, based on adaptation of UNI-MARC
158	Social sciences	In preparation	ODRA 1305	ALGOL
164	Humanities and social sciences	In preparation		
166	All fields of science, library science	Union catalogue of foreign books, current national bibliography	Minicomputer RC-3600, IBM/370, LINOTRON 505 TC	Data entry system, PL/1, ASSEMBLER, COBOL, RODAN (Polish system)
170	Science of science	AVION		
SPAIN				
173	Statistics, economics, social sciences	Numerical data bank, bibliographical systems, external systems - producing and processing statistical information, indexing of documentation, etc.	Computer communication leased-line terminal, DATA DYNAMICS DIAL-UP terminal, IBM 370/158	IRS/QUEST, SDC/ORBIT, PL/1 with own and external packages, LOCKHEED/DIALOG

1	2	3	4	5
175	Management	Abstracting and indexing		SDC/ORBIT LOCKHEED/DIALOG
176	Humanities and social sciences	Retrospective searches, SDI-through SDC and LOCKHEED services	UNIVAC 1108, DATA DYNAMICS DIAL-UP terminal	
SWEDEN				
178	Legal and political sciences, social sciences	Books and periodicals LIBRIS (the Swedish library information system), Swedish judicial information system	ALFASCOP display unit with printer, INCOTERM terminal	
179	All fields of science	Interactive on-line searches (ESA, LOCKHEED, SDC) LIBRIS	INCOTERM SPD 10/20, CYBER 10, TEXAS IN-STRUMENTS SILENT 600	ASSEMBLER
180	Psychology, social sciences, environmental sciences		IBM 370/165, DEC-10, NORD-10, 10 TTY compatible terminals	PL/1, ASSEMBLER, SIMULA, ELHILL III, EPOS/VIRA
181	Education, psychology	Magnetic tapes of international search systems	Teletype terminal	
182	Social sciences, education, etc.	SDI, retrospective searches	IBM 370/165, DEC 10, PDP 11(two), 6 TTY-compatible terminals, 1 dedicated terminal	EPOS/VIRA, 3 RIP, PL/1, ASSEMBLER, SIMULA

1	2	3	4	5
183	Humanities and social sciences	Cataloguing and catalogue production	SAAB D223, SAAB D5	COBOL, LIBRIS - II
184	Economics, management, law, etc.	Periodicals lists, List ECON, SCANP		
185	Social sciences, humanities, etc.	MEDLINE	TEXAS INSTRUMENTS SILENT 733 terminal	
186	All subjects except technology		INCOTERM terminal, TEXAS INSTRUMENTS SILENT 700	LIBRIS, ELHILL, EPOS-VIRA systems
U S S R				
191	All fields of science	Preparation of publications	Phototypesetting machine DIGISET, EC 1040 computer	
197	Culture and arts	In preparation		
198	Social sciences	In preparation	CONSUL - 253, OPTIMA - 527	PL/1, FORTRAN
199	Higher education	SDI	EC-1020	
201	All fields of science	In preparation and partly used in a test regime	Computers, orgauto-mates, storage on magnetic tapes	PL/1, ALGOL, FORTRAN
207	Social sciences	Publication of information materials, SDI, retrospective searches, others	Computers and photo-composing machines: M-4030, DIGISET 40T2, HEWLETT-PACKARD 3000 ser.II. Computer communication leased-line with SIC-BAS (Sofia)	ASSEMBLER, PL/1, SPL

Questionnaire

```
         COUNTRY: ........................................................

1.       FULL NAME OF THE INFORMATION CENTRE (or library):

1.1      In English .............................................................

1.2      In official language(s) of country .........................

1.3      Acronym (if any) ..............................................

2.       OFFICIAL STATUS:

2.1      Independent ....................................................

2.2      Parent institution ...........................................

2.3      Subordinated to:

         - central administration ....................................

         - international organization ..............................

         - international association ................................

3.       FULL ADDRESS: ..............................................
         ...........................................................
         ...........................................................

         Cable address: ...............................................

         Telephone no.: ..............................................

         Telex no.: ....................................................
```

231

4.   DATE OF FOUNDATION ....

5.   STAFF:

5.1   Director: ....
                    (family name, first name)

5.2   Number of staff:

      - professional ....

      - non-professional ....

6.   POSITION IN NATIONAL INFORMATION SYSTEM: ....

      ....

      ....

      ....

7.   FUNCTIONAL STRUCTURE (departments or activities): ....

      ....

      ....

      ....

      ....

8.   SUBJECT COVERAGE:

8.1   Major fields ....

      ....

      ....

      ....

8.2   Specific fields ....

      ....

      ....

      ....

9.   NATURE OF DOCUMENTS PROCESSED AND GEOGRAPHICAL ORIGIN:
      (Please check appropriate box)

      | yes | | no | books | national | | foreign |
      | yes | | no | periodicals | national | | foreign |

yes	no	"gray" literature	national	foreign

yes	no	audio-visual materials	national	foreign

yes	no	magnetic tapes	national	foreign

others: ....

....

10.   DOES THE CENTRE HAVE A LIBRARY?
      (Please check appropriate box)

yes	no

11.   IF YES, KIND OF HOLDINGS
      (Please answer in
      appropriate columns)

	no. of titles	no. of volumes	Total no.
- books	....	....	......
- periodicals	....	....	......
- abstract journals	....	....	......
- microcopies	....	....	......
- manuscripts	....	....	......

Please indicate types of
catalogues and indices used ....

12.   IS THE LIBRARY OPEN TO THE PUBLIC?
      (Please check appropriate box)

yes	no

13.   INFORMATION SERVICES:

13.1 Publications (Please check appropriate box)

	yes	no
Abstract journals		
Bibliographies		
Directories		
Others		

Please supply a list of publications indicating character,
title, language, frequency of publication, form, and subscrip-
tion price.

13.2   Selective dissemination information

....

13.3   Translation ....

13.4   Searches:

       - bibliographical ....

       - literature ....

       - survey data ....

13.5   Compilation of documentary syntheses ....

13.6   Library services:

       - lending ....

       - reference only ....

13.7   Provision of photocopies and/or microforms ....

yes	no

14.   AUTOMATED INFORMATION SYSTEMS:

14.1   Activity and fields covered ....

       ....

14.2   Type of hardware used ....

       ....

14.3   Software ....

       ....

15.   TECHNICAL MEANS USED FOR DUPLICATION AND PUBLISHING ....

       ....

       ....

16.   RELATIONS WITH OTHER INFORMATION UNITS AND/OR PARTICIPATION IN

       SSID SYSTEMS:

16.1   In the country:

16.2   Individual organizations abroad:

16.3   Regional and international organizations:

17.   INFORMATION SERVICES PROVIDED TO USERS:

free of charge	against payment